DATA PROCESSING

WITH

FOURTH GENERATION LANGUAGES

GARY W. HANSEN

BRIGHAM YOUNG UNIVERSITY

Published by

SOUTH-WESTERN PUBLISHING CO.

J62

CINCINNATI   WEST CHICAGO, IL   DALLAS   LIVERMORE, CA

ISBN: 0–538–10620–4

Library of Congress Catalog Card Number: 87–61762

1 2 3 4 5 6 7 8 9 0 D 6 5 4 3 2 1 0 9 8 7

Printed in the United States of America

PREFACE

Current textbooks on database processing for business courses deal principally with the problem of database design. While the importance of adequate coverage of this problem is indisputable, there is clearly an equal need to provide some depth of coverage to the languages available for accessing and manipulating databases. In the long run, the number of practitioners involved in accessing databases is probably greater than the number involved in designing databases.

This text is intended to provide a greater depth of coverage of data languages than is provided in currently available texts. These languages have been called (somewhat colloquially) "fourth generation languages" and are available in a large number of commercial products. My intent has been to extract a few basic principles that tend to be common to the majority of these products as the structural basis for this book. Specifically, the focus of the text is on relational database theory and relational languages, including a variety of commercial implementations of relational languages. Other fourth generation concepts, such as visual programming and integrated programming environments, are also covered in some depth.

The book is intended for business students who have had at least one course in a traditional programming language (COBOL, BASIC, etc.). No other prerequisites are assumed.

The structure of the book allows considerable flexibility in the presentation of topics. Only Chapter 1 (designing fourth generation languages) and Chapter 3 (describing the relational model and the two basic relational languages) should be considered required reading. Since a large number of exercises have been included, Chapter 3 can be covered in as much depth as desired. The other chapters of the book have been written to be as self-contained as possible, and may be covered in any order.

I would like to express my appreciation to Jim Hansen and Gary Carlson, my colleagues at BYU, for their many helpful suggestions. Mark Oenbrink of Teradata Corporation and Thomas Hext of Thomas More College assisted in the technical review of the manuscript. The contributions of Microrim, Inc., and Applied Data Research, Inc., are also gratefully acknowledged. Finally, I wish to thank Susan and our children for their patience; their support is always appreciated.

Gary W. Hansen

CONTENTS

PART FOUR

USER-ORIENTED INTERFACES 247

■

PART ONE

FOURTH GENERATION LANGUAGES

A multitude of diverse activities over the past two decades has led to the development of advanced programming languages commonly designated as "fourth generation languages". In Part One we introduce fourth generation languages, give a definition for these languages, and discuss their impact on data processing practice. Chapter 1 introduces the concepts which these languages embody and explains their relationship to previous generations of languages. Chapter 2 describes the physical environment of fourth generation languages and introduces the concept of prototyping—an important application of these languages in the system development process.

CHAPTER 1

WHAT IS A FOURTH GENERATION LANGUAGE?

■ ■

Fourth generation computer languages (4GLs) are redefining the way computer applications are developed. In this chapter, we shall explore the differences between 4GLs and the languages which preceded them. In addition, we shall present the five principles used to define 4GLs, examine controversial issues surrounding 4GLs, and determine when 4GLs are suitable for various applications.

LIFE IN THE THIRD GENERATION

To illustrate the needs addressed by 4GLs, we present a scenario of problems confronting data processing personnel using third generation languages. This scenario involves three data processing professionals—an entry-level programmer, a maintenance programmer, and a DP manager. The problems faced by each are similar to those problems facing many DP professionals today.

The Data Processing Department at XYZ Corporation

Van Copple, an entry-level programmer for XYZ Corporation, arrives at work every evening at 8. His job is to fix programs which terminate abnormally during the batch cycle. Some nights he has nothing to do. Many nights he has more than he can handle.

When a program aborts, he obtains a memory dump (a listing of the contents of memory in computer readable code), a current source listing of the program, and extensive documentation of the program's functions. He then proceeds with the tedious task of wading through all of this material so that he can identify the problem, develop an appropriate solution, and get the program running again.

Finding his way through some other programmer's abstruse logic at 2 A.M. does not fill Van with enthusiasm. (This is *not* what he had in mind when he applied for an "8 to 5" job.) He makes a living but gets very little real satisfaction from his work. He is "paying his dues", he feels, so that he will eventually merit a job during normal working hours.

Darlene Smithhart is a maintenance programmer, which is what Van thinks he would like to be. Darlene makes changes to production programs so that they will properly handle revised business and legal requirements. Like Van, Darlene must also wade through the logic of existing programs. However, she enjoys several advantages that Van does not:

1. She works during the day.
2. The pressure for an immediate solution is usually not as severe.
3. She has many colleagues. 70% of the programmers at XYZ are maintenance programmers.

Despite these advantages Darlene is bored (and, of course, Van would be, too). The prospects for genuine career advancement within XYZ seem extremely dim. She will probably have to go elsewhere to get more rewarding opportunities.

Ellis Parker is the DP manager at XYZ. He is conscientious and competent, yet he feels he gets very little credit for the contribution that he and his department make to the company. Users have been clamoring for years for far more applications systems than his limited staff can provide. (Remember, 70% of his programmers spend all of their time on maintenance to existing systems.) The department gets no credit for the maintenance work being done, yet shoulders most of the blame for the large backlog of requests for new applications systems.

What worries Ellis most is that computer hardware technology is improving far more rapidly than his department's ability to create new systems. Without more effective methods of system development, increased computer power may sit idle. As a loyal employee and an enthusiastic supporter of the computer revolution, Ellis is anxious to utilize technology to the fullest extent possible to increase the profitability of his company. But it is difficult for him to see how this is possible.

The Need for More Powerful Tools

Let's sum up the problems illustrated above.

1. Most of the DP staff feels they are in a career dead-end. Their work is boring and will probably stay that way.
2. Users are unhappy with the data processing department because very few of their requests for new applications systems are satisfied.
3. The DP department devotes an enormous portion of its human resources to maintenance of existing systems. Thus, it is unable to respond to most of the requests for new systems.

These problems lead to additional problems.

4. An "invisible backlog" is accumulating. This means that many users have stopped making requests for new systems, even though there are many requests they would make if they thought there were any possibility of obtaining service. They are looking for solutions to their DP problems from sources other than their DP departments.

5. The company does not offer a promising career path to young DP professionals. These people lack the opportunity to develop skills in systems analysis and design, because they are stuck in a morass of maintenance programming.

6. There is a high degree of risk associated with those few development projects that are undertaken. Users endeavor to include as much functionality as possible, since they may not have another chance to get what they need. This lengthens the requirements definition phase of these projects, which in turn lengthens the design, programming, and installation phases. When the system is finally installed, it is frequently way over budget and extremely late. Worse yet, business requirements have usually changed, and the system must be modified substantially to be useful.

What is clearly needed is a means of more effectively utilizing existing DP staff. If programmers could spend less time programming, they could spend more time developing analysis and design skills. Consequently, they would be in a position to address the large backlog of applications requests. If programming were simpler, fewer maintenance programmers would be needed. This would again increase the pool of potential analysts and designers, and at the same time provide richer career opportunities for more people. Faster, more efficient programming methods would promote the development of prototype systems. Prototypes are model systems which can be used to determine whether system requirements have been adequately defined, thus decreasing the risk associated with large, long-term projects.

4GLs provide the programming capability needed to effectively utilize DP staff. They are powerful software development tools which significantly reduce the amount of effort required to code and install application systems. They also provide ways for users to solve many of their own information systems problems. Thus, they not only make the current DP staff more effective, but, in a sense, they expand the DP staff by providing direct help to the users.

THE FIRST THREE GENERATIONS

Why do we speak of *fourth* generation languages? What were the first three generations? Figure 1.1 summarizes the characteristics of the first three generations, along with the characteristics of the 4GLs which will be discussed in detail in this chapter.

1st Generation	Numeric instructions Numeric data addresses Immediately executable code Machine oriented
2nd Generation	Mnemonic instructions Symbolic data names Code must be translated (assembled) Machine oriented
3rd Generation	Problem-oriented instructions - Formulas - IF statements - Looping conditions - Keyed data access Symbolic data names
4th Generation	Most 3rd generation facilities Database processing Data dictionary Visual programming Graded-skill user interface Interactive programming environment

FIGURE 1.1   Comparison of the Four Generations of Computer Languages

First Generation Languages

1GLs were machine languages. In these languages, operations and data addresses were designated by binary, octal, or hexadecimal numbers. Programs coded in machine language could be immediately executed. However, they were very difficult to code, read, and debug.

Second Generation Languages

2GLs were assembler languages. These languages used mnemonics or symbolic references both for operations and for data addresses, greatly facilitating the coding and debugging of programs. These programs could no longer be immediately executed as could machine language programs. Instead, they had to be translated into machine language operations and data addresses by an intermediate program called an *assembler*.

Although assembler languages were a decisive step forward, they still had a serious defect: programs had to be coded in terms of the architecture (instruction set, registers, and main memory) of the machine on which they were to run. For example, if we wanted to add values A and B to obtain C, the assembler language coding to do this might be as follows.

```
Load Register 1 with A
Load Register 2 with B
Add Register 1 to Register 2
Store Register 2 in C
```

The phrase "add A and B to obtain C" is clearly much easier to understand (and to code) than the 4 lines of assembler coding shown above. An even more straightforward representation would be C = A + B.

Third Generation Languages

Since the solutions to many problems were expressed in terms like these, a language was clearly needed which would allow program coding to reflect the nature of the problem *being solved*, rather than the architecture of the machine. Although there have been numerous approaches to developing a language suitable for human use, we shall use the term *problem-oriented* as a loose designation for the entire collection of languages which departed from the First and Second Generation *machine-oriented* approach.

As we shall see, the concept that a language should be problem-oriented rather than machine-oriented is of critical importance for both 3GLs and 4GLs (as well as for other areas of system development).

Problem-oriented languages made programming possible for people who did not understand the intricacies of the machine, but who did understand the logic of the problems they were trying to solve. These languages also made possible the creation of "portable" programs which could be run on different machines. Thus, when a more advanced machine was installed, existing software could be installed on the new machine without recoding.

3GLs were the first generalized problem-oriented languages. Examples of 3GLs are COBOL, PL/1, FORTRAN, BASIC, and Pascal. The earliest of these were introduced around 1960 and had a significant impact on the growth of computer usage. Today these languages (especially COBOL) dominate business data processing.

Although 3GLs are dominant in business data processing today, they did not receive a universally enthusiastic reception in their early years. Some reasons for this are listed below.

■ *Main memory expense.* In comparison to 2GLs, 3GLs consumed a very large amount of memory. The 3GL compiler would generate significantly more code than an assembler language programmer would write to do the same thing. Since main memory was extremely expensive in those days, many businesses computers were simply too small to use 3GLs.

■ *CPU expense.* As noted above, 3GL compilers generated large amounts of code. Moreover, this code was not optimized for fast execution. Thus, 3GL programs tended to execute much more slowly than assembler programs. Many organizations felt they could not allow valuable CPU time to be consumed by COBOL programs; thus for many years they continued to code their most important production systems in assembler.

■ *Many established programmers preferred assembler.* They felt that the real challenges in programming were in the assembler language systems.

In succeeding years, memory has become cheaper, computers have become cheaper, and compilers have become much better at optimizing code. Additionally, many people have become programmers who probably never would have if they had been required to code in assembler. These people feel there is plenty of challenge in getting a COBOL system to run properly.

In the next section we define 4GLs. However, before we leave this section note that 4GLs today are in the same position that 3GLs were in during the mid-sixties. 4GLs exist, they are being used, and their usage is growing. Those who object to 4GLs today usually raise the same arguments that were raised against 3GLs during their early years—particularly the argument that 4GL programs tend to execute slowly. Ultimately, those arguments against 4GLs will very likely fail for the same reason they failed against 3GLs. In all probability, given the trend of the computer industry during the last 30 years, both hardware and software technology will continue to improve until it will become difficult to justify *not* using a 4GL for most applications.

WHAT IS A FOURTH GENERATION LANGUAGE?

A universally acceptable definition of a 4GL is elusive if not impossible to formulate. The following represent some of the proposed definitions:

■ A "non-procedural" language
■ An end-user language
■ A language which requires one-tenth the programming effort (or less) of a 3GL (Martin 1982).

Of course, none of these is really intended to be a definition. Rather, these are loose, descriptive phrases which are meant to convey general information about 4GLs. The last of these, in fact, was intended as an evaluation criterion. (That is, don't call it a 4GL unless it meets this criterion.)

Five Principles of 4GLs

The definition we shall give is not likely, nor is it intended, to settle the matter. In this book, our purpose is to identify and explore the fundamental principles that many, if not most, 4GLs utilize. These principles constitute our definition. 4GLs which incorporate these principles tend to improve system development time and incorporate non-procedural and end-user concepts. The following five principles constitute our "working definition" of 4GLs:

1. Database structures and programming (especially those of the relational model, which we shall emphasize in this book)
2. A centralized data dictionary
3. Visual programming
4. A graded-skill user interface
5. An interactive, integrated, multi-function programming environment

FIGURE 1.2   Principles of Fourth Generation Languages

Database Structures and Programming.   Although all five principles are optional, the most powerful 4GLs nearly always include Principle 1. Because of the central role that database processing plays in modern business systems, numerous approaches and refinements to these approaches have been developed to simplify manipulation of data in a database. We are specifically interested in the variety of 4GL approaches taken to facilitate database processing. Consequently, all of the systems which we shall consider have a heavy database orientation. As we examine specific 4GLs, we will focus primarily on how they facilitate database manipulation.

Data Dictionaries.   A data dictionary (Principle 2) is a central repository containing information about system components: screens, reports, data fields, records, files, programs, etc. It provides a means of controlling the technical aspects of systems and of eliminating duplication. Because we are primarily concerned with data manipulation, we shall give relatively minor consideration to Principle 2. Our discussion of data dictionaries will be integrated into our discussion of other 4GL principles throughout the book.

Visual Programming.   This principle refers to the system-supported capability which allows the user or programmer to instruct the system by visual means. This may involve structuring a data query table (as is done, for instance, in Query-by-Example), "painting" a screen form, or formatting a report. In each case the desired result is indicated pictorially. Visual programming may also include debugging aids which allow the programmer to "watch" the program execute and to "see" logic errors during the process.

Graded-Skill User Interface.   A graded-skill interface provides different access modes to users, depending on the level of their skill. Thus, it may provide a natural language interface for the naive user, a dialogue-based program generator for the more experienced user, an interactive command language for the advanced user, and a procedural programming language for the experienced programmer. R:BASE 5000 (covered later in the book) is an example of a system providing a graded-skill interface.

This principle is closely related to the visual programming principle. At the most elementary level, a graded-skill user interface is often visual. The interface may also employ "natural language" concepts. A "natural language" interface attempts to approximate common English usage as closely as possible while avoiding the ambiguities inherent in everyday usage. The system provides a base vocabulary which is supplemented by the user and the application database. Such interfaces give the user a great deal of flexibility in formulating expressions to query the system. This stands in stark contrast to the rigid rules of programming language syntax that programmers are accustomed to.

Interactive, Integrated, Multi-function Programming Environment. This principle includes features such as prompting forms, standardized approaches to common problems, and interactive access to a wide variety of system development tools. Examples of such tools are program editors, program and report generators, compilers, and screen generators. These features relieve the programmer of a considerable burden of memorization and resource manipulation.

The five principles of our 4GL definition are all ultimately concerned with the central problem of business data processing: the control and manipulation of data. Since there are already numerous texts available which treat the problems of database design, we have chosen to deal more thoroughly with the problem of data manipulation. In one way or another the majority of commercial 4GLs are built to facilitate the manipulation of data in databases. Hence, the theme underlying all of our discussion in subsequent chapters will be "database processing with fourth generation languages". We shall demonstrate how such database processing is accomplished via the various principles of our 4GL definition.

Contemporary 4GL Issues

Having specified a working definition of 4GLs, we now consider several issues surrounding 4GLs. Two of the debates we present concern the theoretical status of these languages. We then discuss practical issues of more immediate interest to prospective users and programmers: what are the pros and cons of 4GLs, and when is a 2, 3, or 4GL more suitable for an application?

Are 4GLs Really Languages?   The 18th century French philosopher Voltaire, once said that the Holy Roman Empire was "neither holy, nor Roman, nor an empire." Since the Holy Roman Empire was a loose confederation of German states, it was clearly neither Roman nor an empire. (We will leave it to others to decide if it was holy.)

In a more modern vein, 4GLs may be neither "fourth generation" nor "languages." We have already indicated that there is no universally accepted definition of what the fourth generation constitutes. But after seeing our working definition of 4GLs, you may also wonder whether 4GLs are really languages.

The answer to the question depends, of course, on what we mean by "language." Languages in the 2nd and 3rd generations are composed of words (or other symbolic expressions made up of characters found on the typewriter keyboard). We shall say that 2GLs and 3GLs are "verbal" languages. Now you will note that 4GLs include not only verbal elements but visual and interactive elements as well. Do these additional elements make it improper or inaccurate to refer to 4GLs as languages?

If a computer language is defined as a medium of communication between the human and the machine, then it is indeed accurate to refer to 4GLs as languages. The visual and the interactive elements of 4GLs significantly increase the probability of successful communication between user/programmer and machine, and therefore contribute important language elements that did not exist in earlier generations. These three elements (verbal, visual, and interactive) working together greatly increase the power of computer languages as tools for communication.

Are 4GLs "Non-Procedural" Languages?   As noted previously, 4GLs are sometimes defined as "non-procedural" languages. We shall now discuss two definitions of this term, and see how one definition is too broad and the other too narrow to characterize 4GLs.

Typically, a non-procedural language is defined as a language in which the programmer determines *what* is wanted, not *how* to get it. For example, the programmer might want to answer the query, "Which employees have salaries exceeding $30,000?" Using the appropriate syntax, the programmer restates this query in non-procedural language. The system would then make all decisions relative to accessing the appropriate file(s), selecting the appropriate records, and printing the list. All of this would be done *without further instruction from the programmer.* Thus, the programmer describes the end result desired, and the system handles all the details involved in bringing about that end result. A language which makes it possible for a programmer (or end-user) to do this is non-procedural. The programmer states what is wanted; the system determines how to get it.

If this definition is viewed in a broad sense, then 3GLs are also non-procedural. In a 3GL, the programmer codes statements which are compiled into machine code. (An example of such a statement would be "C = A + B" which we discussed when we compared 2GLs to 3GLs and 4GLs.) In translating such statements to machine code, the compiler decides *how* to accomplish the end result which the programmer has specified. In this sense then, 3GL statements are non-procedural. But since the term "non-procedural" was intended to specifically exclude 3GLs, it would appear that this definition is too broad.

In response to this criticism, it may be argued that non-procedural languages are intended to be at a high enough level to provide significant practical value to end-users in solving problems that end-users typically want to solve. Most end-users do not feel that the simple calculation facility available in 3GLs is nearly as valuable as the powerful query facility available in 4GLs. Thus, from an end-user perspective, 4 GLs have non-procedural capability, but 3GLs do not.

A non-procedural language can also be defined as a language in which the order of statements is not significant. While the previous definition was too broad, this definition is too narrow. It places a rather severe limitation on the types of problems that a non-procedural language can solve. Many important problems are *procedural;* that is, the order in which certain events take place is significant. Thus, a 4GL must have the ability to specify the order of processing in order to provide solutions to certain types of problems.

Many problems require a series of 4GL statements for their solutions. Such a series of statements typically includes control statements (IF. . THEN. . ELSE, DO WHILE) which cause conditional and iterative execution. This series of statements becomes a *procedural* solution to the problem.

On the other hand, single, non-procedural 4GL statements may be sufficient to solve some problems. The user-oriented interface provides the end-user with a non-procedural language which may be applied to problems that do not need to be solved in a specific sequence. Since many of the day-to-day questions that users ask concern problems of this nature, this non-procedural capability proves to be of great value.

Thus, in their application to a broad spectrum of problems, 4GLs can be viewed as procedural or as non-procedural, depending on the fundamental nature of the problems themselves. However, in developing more powerful languages for application development, the issue of procedurality versus non-procedurality is of less concern than the issue of separating logical processing problems from physical implementation problems. In other words, the goal is an environment in which the user, the programmer, the analyst, and the designer can concentrate exclusively on business problems and their logical solutions, while leaving the details of physical implementation to language systems. This ideal environment may never be attained, but 4GLs bring us closer to this goal.

Advantages of 4GLs. 4GLs have already provided significant benefits:

1. *Effective resource utilization.* Systems developed with 4GLs require a substantially smaller human resource expenditure than systems developed using 3GLs. This applies to programming, debugging, and post-installation maintenance.

2. *End-user computing.* 4GLs also provide a practical means for end-user computing, thus improving user satisfaction.

3. *Reduced back-log.* End-user computing decreases the application development burden on the DP staff.

4. *Reduced risk.* 4GLs significantly reduce the risk associated with long-term system development projects by making prototyping a feasible systems analysis technique. When users have the opportunity of interacting with working prototypes of applications systems, they are in a much stronger position to evaluate the adequacy of the undeveloped system than they are when traditional methods are used.

Disadvantages of 4GLs.   Current implementations of 4GLs have some rather significant shortcomings. Among them are:

1. *Lack of standardization.* Although SQL (Chapter 4) has been adopted as a standard by the American National Standards Institute (ANSI), no standards organization has adopted a general 4GL standard. Consequently, most 4GLs are proprietary commercial products and therefore run only on the machines for which their manufacturers have developed them or to which they have converted them. In theory, 4GLs should be portable. In practice, they are not at the present time.

2. *Lack of support for structured concepts.* The most serious omission in this area at present is the lack of parameter passing. With time it is certain that most 4GLs will include parameter passing as a standard feature.

3. *Slower execution times.* Programs written in 4GLs tend to execute more slowly than 3GL programs. However, several factors offset the seriousness of this shortcoming:

- Most 4GLs provide a means of compiling 4GL programs. Thus, although ad hoc queries are interpreted, and therefore run slowly, production programs are compiled to machine code and run much more efficiently.
- For many applications, speed of execution is not a significant shortcoming. Of course, if the application uses an excessive amount of computer time and degrades the response time of other users, then speed of execution is a problem.
- 4GLs are *relatively* immature products. As their manufacturers continue to develop them, their performance will improve.
- The performance of relational 4GLs can be influenced by the design of the database; 4GLs provide tools which allow data administrators to fine-tune the structure of the database (creating indexes, etc.) to improve performance.

Determining When to Use 4GLs

Data processing departments code systems in second or third generation languages whenever speed of execution is an issue of major importance for the application. The generation of language to be used in implementing a system often depends on which of the following factors is of greater importance:

- Labor costs (programming, testing, maintenance, etc.)
- Hardware costs (processor speed, memory size, etc.) in combination with user response time needs.

If labor costs are more important, then a 4GL would probably be the reasonable choice. If hardware costs are more important, then a traditional language should probably be used. Since labor costs tend to be rising, and hardware costs have consistently been decreasing, the long-term trends favor the ultimate use of 4GLs for most applications.

SUMMARY

4GLs represent a major step forward in application languages. While several important problems have yet to be fully resolved, existing commerical 4GLs are nonetheless capable of supporting a substantial portion of the application development workload in many organizations. Moreover, this portion is likely to increase significantly in the future.

4GLs utilize system development concepts associated with database processing, visual programming, and interactive programming that were virtually unknown in the batch environment of previous generations. These features significantly enrich the concept of a computer language, making it much more than just a verbal communication medium between humans and machines. Additionally, the verbal portion of computer languages has been substantially strengthened through the theoretical and practical development of high-level, non-procedural programming elements.

4GLs constitute an important step forward in application system development capability. It is anticipated that 4GLs and their analysis/design counterparts will have a revolutionary impact on methods of system development (Martin 1982, Martin and McClure 1985). Such a revolution will be possible only if sufficiently powerful tools are available. The power of 4GLs has been demonstrated in practice. In the remainder of this book we will examine the principles on which the power of 4GLs is based.

DISCUSSION QUESTIONS

1.1. Analyze the problems that are caused in data processing installations by the shortcomings of 3GLs. What characteristics of 4GLs help to alleviate these problems?

1.2. What differences between the four generations of programming languages justify the use of the term "generation" in differentiating between types of languages? Presumably, the "generation" changes only when there is a substantial difference between the new and the old. Are the differences between these languages substantial?

1.3.   Why are new generations of languages initially resisted? Why are they accepted eventually?

1.4.   All of the principles in our definition of 4GLs are optional. Are any of these principles of sufficient importance as to be made mandatory? Which, if any, should be required for a language to be considered a 4GL? Why?

1.5.   How can a system consisting of nonverbal elements be considered a "language"? What are the elements that make up a language (not just a computer language, but any language)? Can you think of other elements that are part of human communication that are not represented in our definition of 4GLs? Could these elements be applied in the design of a computer language?

1.6.   Review the chapter's discussion of non-procedural and procedural language. Do you feel the "ideal" computer language would be procedural or non-procedural? What limitations would have to be placed on a non-procedural language?

1.7.   Would natural language (e.g., English) be a good choice for a computer language? Give examples of English sentences that would be difficult for a computer to process. What kinds of sentences would it be reasonable to expect a computer to understand?

1.8.   Discuss the advantages and disadvantages of 4GLs. If you were the manager of a data processing installation would you want to use 4GLs for all of your applications? For none of them? What criterion would you use in deciding whether a 4GL should be the language for a particular application?

CHAPTER 2

FOURTH GENERATION LANGUAGES AND THEIR PHYSICAL ENVIRONMENT

In Chapter 1 we introduced the concept of fourth generation languages and differentiated them from earlier system development languages and techniques. The integration of a central data dictionary, relational database structures, and an interactive programming environment were emphasized as being key to the implementation of 4GLs.

The purpose of this chapter is to examine a typical database environment and introduce the system development technique known as prototyping. First we review the role of databases in business organizations and describe how a database language functions in systems architecture. We then depict the limitations of traditional 3GL system development projects in such an environment. With this framework established, we introduce prototyping and show how this technique (currently feasible and cost-effective using 4GLs) can improve the speed and quality of system design.

THE DATABASE ENVIRONMENT

The database environment as we wish to discuss it in this chapter provides the framework for two principal functions:

- Accessing data for processing and information purposes.
- Protecting data as an organizational resource.

Databases in large corporations often contain millions of records and billions of characters of data. They reside on large disk storage devices controlled by mainframe computers and may be physically accessed via many display terminals connected to the mainframe.

As part of their daily responsibilities, users working at terminals perform such tasks as using query languages to extract information, using preprogrammed routines to make on-line database updates, and initiating requests to run batch programs. After normal working hours, computer operators run batch cycles which carry out daily processing of business transactions, billing, report generation, and other common business functions requiring database access and update. A database processing system provides the means both for the user to access data on-line during the day and for the batch programs to access data at night.

Data being accessed by so many people for such a diversity of purposes is obviously a valuable corporate resource. The data is vulnerable to loss through physical system failure or human error. Additionally, it may be subject to abuse or fraud. Thus, an important aspect of any database environment is the protection of data.

In this chapter we shall discuss two mechanisms for data protection:

■ A physical mechanism, provided by a control environment for a database management system (DBMS).
■ An organizational mechanism, provided by a database administrator.

DBMSs (or their control environments) perform continual backup of database update transactions as well as providing methods, in the event of system failure, to recover the work that may have been lost. They also require that users log onto the system and allow them to work only on those portions of the database for which they have access authorization.

Database administrators control access to data by giving users authorization to read and update data. They also ensure the logical consistency of the database by controlling the design of its tables.

Query Management Facility (QMF)

To illustrate a system which provides end-user access to a relational database and supports data control and security, we consider IBM's Query Management Facility (QMF). The environment in this example has several interacting components as shown below:

1. *Organizational,* consisting of people, procedures, and policies.
2. *Hardware,* consisting of computers, disk drives, printers, terminals, etc.
3. *Data,* consisting of the tables and records in the database.
4. *Software,* consisting of:
   ■ The operating system, which is the control program that the user initially encounters.
   ■ QMF, which is also a control program. The user executes QMF by issuing a command to the operating system.
   ■ A relational language in which queries are formulated. SQL and QBE (Query-by-Example) are relational languages supported by QMF. These languages are discussed in detail in Chapters 4 and 11, respectively.

- The physical level DBMS which carries out the necessary accesses of the database in response to relational language queries.

Notice that the software component consists of layers as shown in Figure 2.1. First, the user interfaces with the operating system through the log-on process. This process identifies the user so that the operating system knows what the user has authority to do—which programs the user may run and which data may be accessed. The user executes the QMF program by giving an appropriate command to the operating system.

Second, after QMF is running, the user may formulate commands in a relational query language by giving the appropriate command to QMF.

Third, after a query has been formulated and translated, it is executed by the DBMS. If the user is not authorized to access the data requested in the query, access is denied, and appropriate messages are displayed. Otherwise, the data is retrieved and displayed to the user.

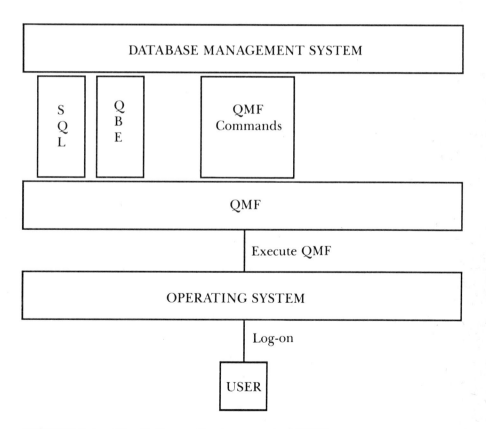

FIGURE 2.1 The Software Environment of QMF

A Sample QMF Session.   Suppose that you have logged onto the system and executed QMF. You now wish to retrieve information from the database in the form of a report. What are the steps you must take?

1. You ask QMF for a blank query screen. Since you are going to fill out a query, you must use one of the two query languages which QMF supports—SQL or QBE. QMF will display a screen for the language you request.
2. You type in your SQL or QBE query.
3. You issue the RUN command to QMF to execute the query. As QMF runs your query, it displays information indicating how long the query will take. If you decide that the query will take too long and consume too many system resources, you may cancel the query.
4. After the query is complete, QMF displays the result (that is, the data retrieved) on the screen. QMF will use a default report format, unless you requested otherwise. If you do not like the format used to display the result, you may specify some other format. QMF supports a wide variety of report formats. After you have specified the format, you can display the result again without re-running the query.
5. If you wish, you can issue a command to print the report.
6. You may permanently save the query, the result, and the report format. Then, if you wish to use the query again (perhaps with new data in the database) you can. You can also use the report format with this new data.
7. You can share your query with other users. If they are authorized to access the data retrieved by the query, they can use your query. Otherwise, the system prevents them from accessing this data.

You can also create your own data tables and enter, alter, or delete data. Moreover, if you are authorized, you may also make changes to data in tables which you have not created. Finally, you may authorize or restrict the access of others to view or change data in the tables which you have created.

Our discussion of QMF illustrated the features of a typical database environment. Although other systems are not identical to QMF, they do provide many similar capabilities.

Database Administration

The computer system and much of the data in a large organization is often centralized and therefore made accessible to many of the employees. Because data is an extremely valuable corporate resource it is important to control its use and structure carefully. Thus, many organizations use database administrators to oversee the design and maintenance of the database.

Database administrators are employees who carry the responsibility for protecting the company's database while at the same time making it available to all employees who need access to it to perform their jobs. They work with systems analysts to determine the logical structure of the database by deciding which tables should be created and which fields should reside in each table. They help to design database *views*, which are used to limit database access to particular rows and columns of designated tables. They are also involved in the allocation of the physical disk space on which the database tables reside.

An important aspect of the database administrator's job is ensuring the logical consistency of the database. The relational data model, as discussed in the next chapter, includes integrity constraints which, if observed, ensure in part that the database is logically consistent. Additionally, the database should be designed in such a way that redundant data is avoided. For example, maintaining a customer's address in more than one table is redundant. If the address changes, then all records in the database containing the address must be updated. If this does not happen, then the database is inconsistent. This problem can be avoided by eliminating data redundancies in the database design. As the person who has responsibility for and knowledge of all aspects of the database, the database administrator is able to oversee the changing design of the database and prevent the creation of data redundancies.

MOTIVATION FOR PROTOTYPING

4GLs make practical a powerful approach to system development known as prototyping. In the remainder of this chapter we discuss traditional system development techniques and explain their relationship to prototyping. We also show how the fast development methods made possible by 4GLs have resulted in modification to the traditional methods to allow the use of prototyping.

Early Systems

Systems which were designed and installed during the very early years of commercial computers were of necessity limited in their flexibility. The sophisticated, inexpensive equipment which we take for granted today was simply not available. Memory was expensive, large files were confined to cards or tape, and processing times were long. Moreover, third generation languages were either not available, or they consumed so many system resources that their power could not be fully realized. As a consequence, only the most basic of business processing needs could be addressed—those clerical functions for which a relatively clear-cut cost justification could be derived. Terms such as *management information systems* and *decision support systems* (MIS and DSS) referred to the future, not to current reality.

The relatively primitive nature of computer hardware also influenced the relationship of the data processing department to the rest of the company. The expensive computer had to have a room of its own with a special floor and dedicated air conditioning. Data processing personnel were required to be familiar with the complex technical aspects of computer equipment and software and had little time to become familiar with the details of their company's business. The rapidly changing technological world they were living in probably seemed more exciting than the more slowly changing world of their own company's business requirements. Since they worked in an isolated environment close to the computer, they tended to be physically as well as professionally separated from their fellow employees.

This environment of separation combined with the primitive state of programming had an important effect on the applications systems that were developed during those years: Data processing people made many of the decisions relating to what an applications system *would* do, since they were the authorities on what the computer *could* do. This was the day of the programmer. The user had relatively little influence on the details of system function. As a result, these application systems had minimal functionality, were difficult to use, and were difficult to change.

Advancing Technology and Emphasis on User Involvement.   With the advance of hardware and software technology, management began to insist on applications systems that were considerably more responsive to organizational needs. They began to dream of MIS and DSS and "complete automation" of their businesses. Naturally, this put a considerable amount of pressure on data processing departments to deliver systems that were substantively different from the systems they were used to delivering.

Partially as a result of this shift in emphasis, the "structured revolution" came about, resulting in concepts of structured programming, structured design, and structured analysis. The aim of these approaches was to turn the entire process of system development into an organized engineering discipline founded on principles of logic and rigor. In particular, structured analysis was intended to place the process of system requirements definition on a firm foundation so that the users' needs would be adequately served at the same time that the system developers were building precise documentation for use in system implementation.

System Development Life Cycle.   Formalization of the system development process resulted in a characterization of the phases which make up the System Development Life Cycle (SDLC). Although there are several different models of the SDLC, for use in our discussion we identify these phases as follows:

- Feasibility Study
- Requirements Definition (using structured analysis)
- System Design
- Programming and Testing

- Implementation and Training
- Evaluation and Maintenance

A project which follows the SDLC will carry out these phases in the order shown. In theory, if each phase is executed properly, a satisfactory, running system will be delivered.

A Typical 3GL System Project

We will now join Van Copple as he participates in his first major project as a programmer/analyst. Van had been promoted to programmer/analyst a year earlier and during that year had been responsible for the implementation of two very small systems. The first project had been less than satisfactory because he had prematurely embarked on programming. He had done an inadequate job of analyzing the user's needs, and when he attempted to install the completed system, the user requested a large number of substantial changes. These changes required him to redesign the system, rewrite a majority of the system modules, and write several additional modules. Since Van was an accomplished programmer and was anxious to please his customer, he was able to avoid disaster. He completed the task to the user's eventual satisfaction.

After this unpleasant experience, Van became familiar with the concepts of structured analysis. During the second project he applied the principles of structured analysis, carefully documenting the user's needs with data flow diagrams, process specifications, and a complete data dictionary. He painstakingly reviewed all of these documents with the user and then carefully designed, programmed, tested, and installed the system. The user was extremely pleased with the resulting system, and Van was promoted to a position on the project team for one of the company's most important application systems.

The project team to which Van was promoted consisted of four analysts who had been specifically assembled to carry out the project from the requirements definition phase through installation and training. All of them, including Van, were firm believers in the value of the structured methods. They were committed to do whatever was required to make this system a success. Because of the importance of this project to the company's business, management gave the team substantial support and encouragement. Of course, the team did not have unlimited time and money to complete the project. Nonetheless, an ample supply of both of these was promised.

Requirements Definition and System Design.   During the early weeks of requirements definition, the users were encouraged to be liberal in their requests for system functions. Additionally, when the users would suggest a need, one or more of the analysts would suggest possible system enhancements which would generalize the user's request and provide a more powerful system. At times Van questioned the value of some of the functions being identified, but since he was the youngest member of the team, he did not feel it appropriate for him to object. The requirements definition phase lasted considerably longer than anticipated, but the project team felt that the time was well spent since they were able to identify a complete set of user needs. They were sure that all needs had been identified, because they had a comprehensive set of data flow diagrams and other documentation, and they reviewed it with the users for correctness and completeness.

Several weeks into the system design phase of the project, the team began to realize that they were working with an extremely complex set of requirements and that a proper system design would take much longer than they had originally anticipated. They pushed ahead, of course, and with time they began to feel confidence in the ability of their designed system to handle the original user requirements. Unfortunately, the users continued to approach the team with additional functions they wanted to include in the system. Some of them were included quite readily, but some required significant modifications to the system design. Naturally, these extra functions extended the time devoted to system design.

As the design phase drew closer and closer to completion, the project team resisted the requests of the users more vigorously. They even began to refuse some of the users' requests. Eventually, they froze the requirements and would not entertain any more requests. Relations between the users and the members of the project team began to deteriorate during the design phase and continued to deteriorate until programming began, after which the users and team members rarely had contact with each other.

Programming and Implementation.   The requirements definition and design phases of the project had lasted so much longer than anticipated that management became uneasy. They were anxious to see at least the beginnings of a running system, but all they had up to this point were volumes of documentation and strained relationships between employees. They began to pressure the project team to produce a running system as quickly as possible.

By the time programming began, the system had become extremely complex and was very difficult to program and test. Nevertheless, because of management pressure, the team worked feverishly to complete the system. Of necessity, they cut corners and were less diligent in testing of system functions than they otherwise would have been.

More than two years after the beginning of the project, the system was ready to be installed. (Or at least the project team *said* it was ready.) There were many problems. The system itself had numerous bugs, since preinstallation testing had been superficial. In addition, the users found many aspects of the system difficult to use. There were a number of common situations which the system could handle only awkwardly. The users were familiar with these situations but had forgotten to bring them up during requirements definition. Many functions the users had assumed would be included in the system were not present. Moreover, many of the functions on which the system team had spent a great deal of design and programming time were not used or appreciated by the users. During the ensuing 18 months the project team made many design changes and system enhancements in order to make the system minimally acceptable to the users. Altogether, four years were spent on the project, and the system was only minimally acceptable.

What Went Wrong?   How could an experienced team of competent systems people have fallen so short of realizing their goal of a functional, timely, and cost-effective system implementation? Several contributing factors could be cited.

■ So much time elapsed between requirements definition and installation that business requirements changed. The initially installed system addressed business requirements which were over two years old.
■ The users took for granted that many functions would be present in the system. Moreover, it did not occur to them to mention some of the unusual situations which they encountered in their work with greater frequency than they realized.
■ The users had difficulty understanding the data flow diagrams and other documents produced during requirements definition. Not wishing to betray their ignorance, they mistakenly acknowledged the accuracy and completeness of this documentation.
■ Because of a lack of concrete results, management pressured project team members to move more rapidly. The team cut corners and produced a system that they themselves viewed as less than adequate.

Undoubtedly, the most important of the above points are the second and third, which suggest a serious communication gap between users and analysts. Unless this problem can be resolved, no amount of time and effort will produce satisfactory systems. User-analyst communication is clearly the weakest link in the requirements definition process.

WHAT IS A SYSTEM PROTOTYPE?

A prototype is a working model which attempts to incorporate the functions needed in a system. It is a key element in eliminating the user-analyst communication gap. There are many differences between a prototype and a production system, but for our purposes the essential difference is that the prototype is *not intended* to be a production system. Instead it is intended to give the users something concrete which they can "put their hands on" and criticize. Criticism in this mode is healthy and will lead ultimately to many concrete and practical recommendations for improvement. These recommendations can be implemented in a new prototype (*still* a prototype). The new prototype is then criticized and the cycle repeats. Eventually, a prototype worthy of being converted into a production system will emerge, and the requirements definition phase of the project will be complete. Functions of little value will probably not be included, and functions essential to genuine business needs very likely will be.

We note here that the system initially installed by Van Copple's project team was, in fact, a prototype. It provided the first concrete indication of what the analysts thought the users wanted and needed. Only after 18 months of additional work was the production system ready. A human relations problem occurred because neither the analysts nor the users *thought* that a prototype was being delivered. They all thought it was a production system, and this misconception fueled their disappointment.

Those who advocate prototyping argue that the first system delivered *will always be a prototype*. It cannot be avoided. The reason for this is that no one can be sure whether system needs have been identified until a running system is available. A user's reaction to any other form of requirements documentation will always be tentative. Thus, as Brooks (1975) puts it:

> In most projects, the first system built is barely usable. It may be too slow, too big, awkward to use, or all three. There is no alternative but to start again, smarting but smarter, and build a redesigned version in which these problems are solved. The discard and redesign may be done in one lump, or it may be done piece by piece. But all large-system experience shows that it will be done. Where a new system concept or new technology is used, one has to build a system to throw away, for even the best planning is not so omniscient as to get it right the first time.
>
> The management question, therefore, is not *whether* to build a pilot system and throw it away. You *will* do that. The only question is whether to plan in advance to build a throwaway, or to promise to deliver the throwaway to customers. Seen this way, the answer is much clearer. Delivering that throwaway to customers buys time, but it does so only at the cost of agony for the user, distraction for the builders while they do the redesign, and a bad reputation for the product that the best redesign will find hard to live down.
>
> Hence *plan to throw one away; you will, anyhow.*

Interestingly, as Boar (1984) notes, the creation of a prototype is standard procedure in virtually all engineering disciplines. Brooks expresses this fact as follows.

> Chemical engineers learned long ago that a process that works in the laboratory cannot be implemented in a factory in only one step. An intermediate step called the *pilot plant* is necessary to give experience in scaling quantities up and in operating in nonprotective environments. . . . Programming system builders have also been exposed to this lesson, but it seems to have not yet been learned. Project after project designs a set of algorithms and then plunges into construction of customer-deliverable software on a schedule that demands delivery of the first thing built.

We may ask then, why the structured methods did not include prototyping as an integrated technique. The answer is undoubtedly related to the difficulty of developing a prototype prior to the advent of 4GLs. We shall discuss this problem below. In connection with this, it should be mentioned that Brooks apparently felt that the language being used was irrelevant to the decision of developing a prototype. The passages cited above were written in 1975, before 4GLs became available.

4GLS and Prototyping

In the past, the prevailing argument against prototyping was that programming and testing were so difficult that it was unreasonable to require a preliminary model system. Although this argument was fallacious for the reasons cited above, it did nevertheless contain an element of truth: programming and testing were indeed difficult and expensive. Analysts hoped that by being sufficiently thorough during the requirements definition phase, they could eliminate a significant amount of unnecessary programming.

With the advent and widespread use of 4GLs, this argument can no longer be used. 4GLs provide the means for developing prototypes quickly. Boar (1984) gives a detailed description of 22 features essential to a programming system that is to be used for building prototypes. We may summarize these features by stating that in essence they give a detailed description of the five principles listed in Chapter 1 in our definition of 4GLs. Boar is, therefore, describing a powerful 4GL.

With such powerful language tools, prototypes can be developed very quickly. Boar feels that in order for the prototyping method to be effective, a prototype must be delivered within 2 months after fundamental business needs have been identified. If more than two months elapse, the user begins to lose interest and expects a working system rather than a model. 4GLs make feasible the delivery of models in such short periods of time.

The Problem Project Revisited

Let us now assume that Copple and his colleagues started their project with a powerful 4GL at their disposal, which they used from the beginning to provide a series of ever more functional prototypes. The requirements definition might then have proceeded as follows.

1. Individual team members sat side by side with users and interactively developed prototype data entry screens, data inquiry screens, and report formats. These were adjusted and refined until the user felt comfortable.
2. Using these data entry screens, the team members and users built small files in a prototype database. The data inquiry and report formats could then be demonstrated using data from the sample database.
3. The team members also demonstrated the query language facility of the 4GL in answering various queries posed by the users on the prototype database. They also demonstrated how users themselves could learn to express queries without help from systems personnel.
4. Separated from the users, the team members used the 4GL's integrated development environment to develop more sophisticated batch and on-line applications. These were developed in a relatively short period of time so that they could be demonstrated to users.
5. The structure of the emerging system was captured and documented by an integrated data dictionary facility. The team members and users supplemented this documentation with narratives, data flow diagrams, and other products of structure analysis. The emphasis was on describing the user needs that were to be implemented in the new system.

After a reasonable period, the final prototype and the requirements definition phase were complete. Decisions could now be made as to whether the project should continue, and if so, which portions of the prototype could feasibly be used in the production system, and which portions would need to be reprogrammed in a language that would execute more efficiently. With a more trustworthy conception of the genuine requirements of the system, the project steps following requirements definition could be carried out more readily.

It is important to note that prototyping makes it easier for the company's management to decide at a much earlier date whether it is feasible to continue a project. When concrete functions are being demonstrated, the effort needed to program those functions for a production system can be more accurately estimated. If the programming effort is deemed to be greater than the value of the functions, then the project can be terminated. In many cases, this is the best decision.

SUMMARY

As demonstrated in this chapter, the concept of 4GLs cannot be easily separated from either the environment in which systems are designed and implemented, or the system development process itself. The organizational hardware, data, and software components are all impacted when 4GLs are adopted.

Prototyping has changed the process by which systems are designed and implemented. We have seen that the prototyping approach to system development:

- Facilitates the communication process by giving users and analysts a concrete object for use in accurately assessing system requirements.
- Improves the relationship between users and analysts by giving users a clear conception of the proposed system and by giving them opportunity for seeing the results of requested revisions.
- Provides management with a reliable model for evaluating the benefit of the proposed system.

4GLs contribute substantively to these benefits. While some 4GLs are better suited to prototyping than others, it will be readily apparent from the 4GL products discussed in this book that changing system requirements are *expected* in the 4GL environment, rather than feared.

DISCUSSION QUESTIONS

2.1. Why is data a valuable corporate resource? In what ways could this resource be damaged or abused?

2.2. If you have access to a database management system, compare and contrast its features with those of QMF. What kind of security does it support? At what level is data security enforced (i.e., table, row, column, data item)? Are user views of data supported? Are multiple data manipulation languages supported? What user-oriented features are provided?

2.3. Discuss the database administrator's responsibilities. Does it seem feasible that a single person could carry out all of these tasks adequately? How should database administration be organized in a large company?

2.4. Why were Copple's first two projects successful? Why was the large project then not successful?

2.5. Why is it accurate to say that the system initially delivered to the users was a prototype? Is this true of the first system that Copple did on his own?

2.6. What portions of the SDLC are affected by the prototyping concept? How does prototyping cause the SDLC to be revised?

2.7. What factors have tended to work against the concept of prototyping in the past? Are these factors likely to pose problems in today's environment?

2.8. Are there reasons that a prototype should not be implemented as a production system? Are *all* aspects of a running system considered during the development of a prototype? Which aspects may be omitted? What needs to be done before a prototype system can be implemented?

PART TWO

RELATIONAL LANGUAGES

Database languages are the foundation for 4GLs. Since relational languages constitute the most powerful database languages from the standpoint of data manipulation, we give them primary emphasis throughout this book. Part Two introduces the theoretical concepts on which relational languages are based (Chapter 3) and then discusses two commercial implementations of these languages: SQL (Chapter 4) and QUEL (Chapter 5).

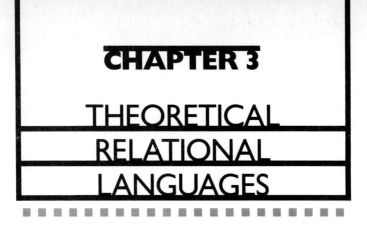

CHAPTER 3

THEORETICAL
RELATIONAL
LANGUAGES

The first principle in our working definition of 4GLs (Chapter 1) states that 4GLs include concepts of database processing—specifically, relational database processing. The purpose of this chapter is to define the relational data model and discuss its theoretical languages in detail. First we provide historical background for the motivation behind the development of relational database processing. Then, through database examples from a fictional company, we define and illustrate the relational data model. Continuing with the sample database we present the theoretical languages of relational algebra and relational calculus.

The relational data model and one or both of the theoretical relational languages provide the foundation for many commercial 4GLs. Because current 4GLs vary in the extent to which they implement the relational model, we conclude the chapter with criteria for evaluating whether a given 4GL is genuinely relational.

THE POWER OF THE RELATIONAL APPROACH

We discussed in Chapter 1 that the move from 2GLs to 3GLs was motivated by the need for languages that were problem-oriented rather than machine-oriented. Thus, for example, complex calculations could be expressed in 3GLs as formulas rather than as a series of register-oriented machine operations. In addition, 3GLs provided other features that made programming seem more natural (such as IF statements and other flow of control statements), with conditions stated in terms easily understood by the typical programmer. These functions combined to make 3GLs considerably more powerful for systems development than their predecessor languages.

Data Manipulation Without a Relational Model

In the area of data management, however, 3GLs continued to be oriented toward the physical arrangement of data. Files were processed sequentially, record by record, and sorted on a specified key. If two or more files needed to be processed simultaneously, the programmer had to provide logic assuring consistent processing of the files. As direct access storage devices became widely available, random access file processing was introduced. This included both direct access by record number and data-keyed access such as ISAM (Indexed Sequential Access Method).

Nevertheless, it was rapidly perceived that even the increased capability of random access was inadequate for many of the problems that users wanted to solve. What was needed was an easy way to relate data *across* file boundaries. For example, a retailer purchasing merchandise for resale is interested in relating specific items of merchandise to the vendors who sell those items. The retailer's system may include a file of merchandise items and a separate file of vendors with their names and addresses. But if the retailer were to ask, "What are the names and addresses of vendors who supply 21-inch color TVs?" it would be necessary to write a program combining data from the two files, since the vendor's address would probably not be available in the merchandise file. Of course, this is an expensive and time consuming way to answer a relatively simple question.

Questions like this, which required the combining of different types of data, were very common. It was clear that either: (1) data from different files must be combined into a single, large file, or (2) some kind of practical cross-file data access was needed. The first solution was impractical, since it would require enormous amounts of data to be recorded redundantly. In the example above, the vendor's name and address would be repeated in every merchandise record. Such data repetition would use significant storage space and cause update problems. (For example, if a vendor's address changes, it must be changed in every merchandise record.) The best approach to combining data, therefore, would be to provide a means for cross-file access. As a result, database processing was born.

The initial (pre-relational) approach to database processing utilized physical, more or less permanent, links and pointers to define relationships between records in different files. In order to relate data from two files, an appropriate link first had to be created. Then, the programmer had to write appropriate (and at times complex) code to navigate via the link mechanism from one record to another. The CODASYL DBTG model is a standardized version of this approach.

Although this approach provided capability not previously available, it was also severely limited for the following reasons:

1. Users could not ask questions for which the answers depended on links that had not been defined.

2. The programming task was still very complicated. The typical user could not be expected to understand the links and to navigate to the necessary records.

3. This method did not provide logical data independence. That is if the physical means of recording and controlling data relationships were changed, then programs had to be modified to reflect these changes. But programs should only be concerned about *logical* relationships between data and should not be affected by physical changes, such as changes to equipment or systems software.

The Relational Data Model

In several papers published during the early 1970s, E. F. Codd (1970, 1972) proposed the relational data model and two associated data manipulation languages—relational algebra and relational calculus. These and subsequent papers provided the theoretical basis for a very powerful and flexible approach to data management which was not possible using previous methods. Specifically, the relational data model provides:

- A simple yet comprehensive user view of data
- Independence between the logical (user) view of data and the physical format of data
- Powerful data manipulation operations which are multi-record rather than single-record oriented. These operations are independent of predefined relationships between files.

In order to illustrate relational concepts throughout this chapter, we now introduce a fictional company which uses two typical databases. Allied Construction has one database for construction projects and another for personnel. A portion of these databases is shown in Figure 3.1. Even though these databases may have originated independently as separate databases, the relational model allows us to consider them as one large database. With other database models it may not be possible to combine these two databases in all the ways we would like.

Tables and Relations.   Data in the relational model is represented very simply as values in tables. A table, consisting of rows and columns of data, is called a *relation*. There can be any number of relations in a database.

The projects database is used to identify which parts are used on which projects. For a given project, the total cost of materials can be calculated by determining the parts used on the project, mutiplying the quantity used of each part by its cost, and summing all of these products. This database was developed by project management to keep track of materials' costs. It consists of three relations: PROJECTS, PARTS, and PROJ-PARTS.

PROJECTS DATABASE

PROJECTS

PROJ NO	CUSTOMER	LOCATION
4	Adams	Telfs
2	Bern	Ester
3	Carney	Toole
1	Basel	Ester

PARTS

PART NO	VENDOR	COST
23	Beam	29.95
15	Rivers	3.00
87	Moberly	85.00

PROJ-PARTS

PROJ NO	PART NO	QTY
2	15	5
1	23	10
2	87	9
3	15	3
1	87	15

PERSONNEL DATABASE

DEPARTMENTS

DEPT NO	NAME
45	Assembly
25	Materials
83	Accounting

PERSONNEL

EMP NO	NAME	DEPT NO	PROJ NO	SALARY
333	Zendel	45	3	18000
212	Young	83	2	22000
456	Wilkes	45	1	15000
118	Unser	25	2	30000
782	Varen	25	1	45000
560	Welch	47	4	25000

FIGURE 3.1   Portion of Allied Construction Database

The personnel database was developed by the personnel department to identify which employees work in which departments. Current project number and salary are kept in the personnel relation for reference. There are two relations in the personnel database: DEPARTMENTS and PERSONNEL.

Recall that in a non-relational system it may be difficult to derive relationships between data in the two databases. For example, questions concerning the relationship between employees' salaries and the types of parts used on the projects these employees work on may be difficult to answer. In a relational system, however, these two databases can be treated as one large database (which we shall do), thus allowing a high degree of flexibility in the questions that can be asked. We will illustrate this as we continue.

Attributes and Domains.   Each column in a relation corresponds to an attribute of the relation. The name of the column is called the *attribute name*. We shall use the terms "attribute" and "attribute name" rather than "column" and "column name". The number of attributes in a relation is called the *degree* of the relation. For instance, if a relation has 5 attributes, then the relation is of degree 5.

It is assumed that there is no pre-specified order to the rows of a relation, and that no two rows have identical sets of values. Moreover, in order that the user not be required to remember the order of attributes in a relation, it is also assumed that the order of attributes is immaterial. However, in illustrating principles of relational languages we shall occasionally find it useful to specify an order for the attributes.

Using relations and attributes from Figure 3.1, the following illustrates the notation used to represent relations. Note that the relation name is followed in parentheses by the names of its attributes.

PROJECTS (Proj No, Customer, Location)
PARTS (Part No, Vendor, Cost)
PROJ-PARTS (Proj No, Part No, Qty)
DEPARTMENTS (Dept No, Name)
PERSONNEL (Emp No, Name, Dept No, Proj No, Salary)

The set of all possible values that an attribute may have is called the *domain* of the attribute. Two domains are the same only if they have the same meaning. Thus, *Part No, Proj No, Emp No,* and *Dept No* are all different domains, even though all of them consist of numbers. It is not necessary for an attribute name to be the same as its corresponding domain name.

Keys.   A *key* of a relation is a minimal set of attributes which will always uniquely define any row in the relation. By "minimal" we mean that no subset of the set of key attributes can be used as a key. For example, in the PROJECTS relation the attributes *Proj No, Customer,* and *Location* uniquely define any row in the relation. But this set of attributes is not minimal and therefore is not a key. In this example, *Proj No* by itself is a key, since any row in the relation is always uniquely identified by *Proj No.*

In the PROJ-PARTS relation, the key consists of the *Proj No* and the *Part No* attributes. Neither *Proj No* alone nor *Part No* alone uniquely identifies every row.

In any given relation, several different sets of attributes could be chosen as keys. We arbitrarily choose one of them and call this key the *primary key.*

Having introduced the concept of a key, we now need to amend the notation we use to identify a relation. The relations from Figure 3.1 are shown again below with their primary keys underlined.

PROJECTS (Proj No, Customer, Location)
PARTS (Part No, Vendor, Cost)
PROJ-PARTS (Proj No, Part No, Qty)
DEPARTMENTS (Dept No, Name)
PERSONNEL (Emp No, Name, Dept No, Proj No, Salary)

Let us now examine the PERSONNEL relation to illustrate an important concept. *Emp No* is the key of PERSONNEL, while the *Dept No* and *Proj No* attributes in PERSONNEL are keys in other relations. These attributes are called *foreign keys* within PERSONNEL. Foreign keys provide a means to connect data across relations. We note, however, that this is not the only means by which data can be connected across relations.

Integrity Rules

Suppose now that we are using a relational database management system to enter data into PERSONNEL records. (The traditional concept of a logical record corresponds approximately to the concept of a row in a relation.) When we come to employee Janet Ortiz we enter all of the data except the department, which we do not know. What happens next? Since we do not know the department, are we prohibited from adding the row to the relation? Of course not. We add the row, and the value for department is *null*. By null, we mean that the department is *unknown* or that no value from the domain has been entered. The department may be added later. In the meantime, the system makes note that the value for department is null.

In order for a system managing a large database to provide usable information, it is critically important that the data be internally consistent. This need leads directly to the formulation of two integrity rules:

■ *Entity Integrity.* No attribute in a key may be null.
■ *Referential Integrity.* Any value for a foreign key must either be null or must exist as a value of a primary key in another relation.

The underlying concept of entity integrity is that the key provides a means of uniquely identifying a row. We are saying that if any attribute in the key is null, then we do not know enough about the entity described by the row to identify it uniquely. The entity integrity rule prohibits us from entering a row in this case. It should be noted also that the concept of a key as a unique identifier prohibits us from entering the same key value for two different rows. Thus, a key must be entirely non-null and it must be unique within a relation.

Examine the row for employee Welch in the PERSONNEL relation of Figure 3.1. You will note that the department number for Welch is 47. Since this value for the foreign key *Dept No* does not exist in the DEPART-MENTS relation, this row violates the referential integrity rule.

In practice, referential integrity is supported by only a few commercial systems, and these support it only partially. This is undoubtedly because referential integrity has complex implications for a large database with many relations. To illustrate, suppose we add a row to the PERSONNEL relation. In order for the system to support referential integrity, it must examine both the PROJECTS and the DEPARTMENTS relations to verify that the project number and department number entered are keys in those two relations. If either of them is not a primary key, the system must notify us and prevent us from entering the row. We can then either change the value of the entry or give the attribute a null value. Similarly, we may want to change the value of *Proj No* in a PERSONNEL row. Again, the system must verify that the new value exists in the PROJECTS relation.

The worst situation occurs when we try to delete rows. For example, suppose we delete a row from the PROJECTS relation. Now the system must locate all relations that reference *Proj No* as a foreign key, and then locate all rows within those relations that use the *Proj No* value of the deleted row. In our example, suppose that project number 2 is deleted from the PROJECTS relation. Then the following rows in other relations are affected.

PROJ-PARTS			PERSONNEL		
PROJ NO	**PART NO**		**EMP NO**	**NAME**	**PROJ NO**
2	15		212	Young	2
2	87		118	Unser	2

What does the system do in this case? Prohibit the deletion? Issue a warning? Change the *Proj No* attribute in these rows to null? In most systems, if the user attempts an integrity violation the programmer must enforce referential integrity and implement the appropriate response (as determined by the organization using the system).

One of the most powerful features of relational languages is that they facilitate *set level* operations, which allow users to select, add, update, or delete *groups* of records which are chosen by some criterion. In the case of such a mass delete, however, the referential integrity problem is compounded by the number of records being deleted—a number which in some cases may be very large.

Although commercial systems do not presently support referential integrity in full, it is highly probable that they will eventually support it. Complete referential consistency is clearly of great value, and the marketplace will undoubtedly insist on support for it in commerical systems.

THEORETICAL RELATIONAL LANGUAGES

The two languages which Codd proposed for use with the relational model were relational algebra and relational calculus. These languages embody differences in programming language philosophy, the algebra being procedural and the calculus being non-procedural.

In 3GLs the programmer is limited to working on only one record at a time. In contrast, relational language statements work on entire relations, or multiple rows, at a time. Moreover, this multiple row manipulation is possible without the use of iterative looping logic. Thus, relational languages provide a substantial increase in programming power.

It should be noted that relational algebra (and relational calculus) were intended to be *sublanguages*, for data manipulation only, and not a complete programming language with instructions for computation, flow of control, etc. Codd intended that the proposed sublanguages be embedded in host languages which would provide the additional processing capability needed for full application development. This has been realized in practice. Some relational languages are embedded in 3GLs and others in 4GLs. Although our concern here is with relational languages as data sublanguages, we shall have occasion in subsequent chapters to examine the nature of the relationship between the sublanguage and the host language.

Relational Algebra

Relational algebra is procedural in the sense that the programmer accomplishes the desired goal through a set of sequential operations. These operations are mathematical in nature (union, intersection, product, difference, etc.) and work on *relations* to produce new relations. These new relations can then be the object of more operations.

Relational algebra consists of nine operations for manipulating relations: product, union, intersection, difference, projection, division, selection, join, and assignment. We will discuss these operations in detail and then consider several examples in which relational algebra is applied to practical problems.

Product. Suppose we split the DEPARTMENTS relation of Figure 3.1 into two relations as follows:

DEPTNO	DEPTNAME
DEPT NO	NAME
45	Assembly
25	Materials
83	Accounting

We can create the *product* (*) of these two relations by matching every row of DEPTNO with every row of DEPTNAME. This creates a relation of 9 rows which we will call DEPTPROD.

Result: DEPTPROD

DEPT NO	NAME
45	Assembly
45	Materials
45	Accounting
25	Assembly
25	Materials
25	Accounting
83	Assembly
83	Materials
83	Accounting

In general, the product of any two relations R and S is created by concatenating every row of S to every row of R. If R has m rows and S has n rows, then it is easy to see that the product of R and S (which we designate by R*S) will have m*n rows. Also, if the degree of R is j and the degree of S is k, then the degree of R*S is j + k.

As a second example of the Product operation, consider the PARTS and the PROJ-PARTS relations of Figure 3.1. We take the product of these two relations.

■ A = PARTS * PROJ-PARTS

Result: A

PART NO	VENDOR	COST	PROJ NO	PART NO	QTY
23	Beam	29.95	2	15	5
23	Beam	29.95	1	23	10
23	Beam	29.95	2	87	9
23	Beam	29.95	3	15	3
23	Beam	29.95	1	87	15
15	Rivers	3.00	2	15	5
15	Rivers	3.00	1	23	10
15	Rivers	3.00	2	87	9
15	Rivers	3.00	3	15	3

15	Rivers	3.00	1	87	15
87	Moberly	85.00	2	15	5
87	Moberly	85.00	1	23	10
87	Moberly	85.00	2	87	9
87	Moberly	85.00	3	15	3
87	Moberly	85.00	1	87	15

In this example we see that the product of the 3 rows of PARTS with the 5 rows of PROJ-PARTS yields a relation with 15 rows. Moreover, since each of the original relations had 3 attributes, the new relation has 6 attributes. Although this particular relation may not appear to be very useful, it provides an initial step toward the creation of another relation (the *join*) which is extremely useful.

Note that the DEPARTMENTS relation is a subset of the product of the domains of its attributes. In other words, DEPARTMENTS is a subset of DEPTPROD, which is the product of relations taken from the domains of DEPARTMENTS. In general, any relation is a subset of the product of the domains of its attributes. This fact will be important as we discuss other relational algebra operations.

Union.   Consider two relations similar to the PROJECTS relation of Figure 3.1.

ADAMS-PROJECTS

PROJ NO	CUSTOMER	LOCATION
14	Adams	Telfs
12	Adams	Ester
13	Adams	Box Elder

ESTER-PROJECTS

PROJ NO	CUSTOMER	LOCATION
18	Henrie	Ester
12	Adams	Ester
31	Carney	Ester
11	Basel	Ester

Suppose we want a relation giving all projects which are either for Customer Adams or are at Location Ester. We obtain such a relation by taking the union (∪) of these two relations. If we call the new relation R, we denote its creation by:

```
R = ADAMS-PROJECTS ∪ ESTER-PROJECTS
```

Result: **R**

PROJ NO	CUSTOMER	LOCATION
14	Adams	Telfs
12	Adams	Ester
13	Adams	Box Elder
18	Henrie	Ester
31	Carney	Ester
11	Basel	Ester

In general, the union of two relations consists of all rows which are in either (or both) of the relations. Note the following features of the union operation:

- Duplicate rows are eliminated in the new relation. The row (12, Adams, Ester) appeared in both of the original relations, but only once in the union. This is consistent with the rule that no two rows in a relation can have identical data values.
- The union operation can only be applied to two relations if they have the same degree and if the domains for corresponding attributes are the same. We say such relations are *union compatible*. (By "corresponding attributes," we mean attributes in the same columns of the two relations. We assume for convenience that the columns are numbered from left to right. Thus, the attributes in column 1 of both relations correspond, the attributes in column 2 correspond, etc.)

The union of mathematical set theory is similar but not identical to the union of relational algebra. Set theory union can be applied to any two sets. Relational algebra union applies only to special kinds of sets, and they must be union compatible.

Intersection.   Consider the same two relations we used in our discussion of union. Suppose we want a relation consisting of all rows describing projects for Customer Adams which are at Location Ester. Then we take the intersection (∩) of these two relations.

```
S = ADAMS-PROJECTS ∩ ESTER-PROJECTS
```

Result: S

PROJ NO	CUSTOMER	LOCATION
12	Adams	Ester

In general, the intersection of two relations consists of all rows which are in both of the relations. Of necessity, the two relations must be union compatible.

Difference.   Suppose we want a relation of all projects for Adams that are *not* in Ester. We use the difference (−) operation.

```
T = ADAMS-PROJECTS - ESTER-PROJECTS
```

Result: T

PROJ NO	CUSTOMER	LOCATION
14	Adams	Telfs
13	Adams	Box Elder

In general, if A and B are relations, the difference (A − B) is all rows in A which are not in B. Again, A and B must be union compatible.

We observed in our discussion of the product operation that all relations are subsets of the product of their domains. Note also that two relations are union compatible if and only if they are subsets of the same product.

Projection.   Many times it is useful to consider only some of the attributes in a relation. The projection operation allows us to create a new relation from an existing relation by choosing the desired attributes and ignoring the undesired attributes. The notation to indicate the projection of a given relation includes the relation name and the desired attributes. Thus,

```
A = PERSONNEL(Emp No, Salary)
```

is the projection of the PERSONNEL relation on the attributes Emp No and Salary. Using the data of Figure 3.1, this projection yields:

Result: **A**

EMP NO	SALARY
333	18000
212	22000
456	15000
118	30000
782	45000
560	25000

Note that, in this example, the projection has the same number of rows as the relation itself. This happened because the key was included in the attributes being projected. However, if the key is not included, then there will be fewer rows in the projection than in the original relation. Consider the projection:

```
B = PROJECTS(Location)
```

Result: **B**

LOCATION
Telfs
Ester
Toole

The PROJECTS relation has 4 rows while the new relation has only 3. The second occurrence of Ester is identical to the first, so it is omitted, since no two rows in a relation may be identical.

Division.   By analogy with arithmetic, the division operation is intended to be the inverse of the product operation. Thus, if A and B are two relations, then $A * B / B = A$, where "/" denotes division.

The division operation is more general than this, however. It can be applied to a relation which is not a product of two relations. For example, consider the following two relations:

PROJECTS	PROJ-PARTS	
PROJ NO	**PROJ NO**	**PART NO**
2	2	15
3	2	23
	2	87
	3	15
	3	87

Suppose we want to identify the parts that are used on *every* project. Then we divide PROJ-PARTS by PROJECTS. This yields a quotient relation which for this example we will call QUOTIENT:

Result: QUOTIENT

PART NO
15
87

To give a more general example, suppose that A and B are relations as follows:

A

v	w	x	y	z
5	3	2	4	q
4	1	2	4	q
5	3	8	8	t
4	1	2	0	p

B

x	y	z
2	4	q
8	8	t

Then the quotient relation $C = A / B$ is

Result: C

v	w
5	3

The quotient relation C in this example is constructed as follows:

1. The attributes of the quotient (C) are those attributes of the dividend (A) which are not in the divisor (B).

2. The rows of C are a subset of the projection of A on v and w, that is, A (v,w).

3. A row (v,w) is in C if and only if (v, w, x, y, z) is in the dividend (A) for *every* value of (x y, z) in the divisor (B). Thus, since

(5, 3, 2, 4, q)

(5, 3, 8, 8, t)

are both in A, then (5, 3) is in C.

This process can be extended to define division for relations in general. The only restriction is that the divisor be union compatible with a projection of the dividend. In the last example, the divisor (B) had attributes x, y, z and was therefore union compatible with a projection of the dividend (A) consisting of attributes v, w, x, y, z.

The division operation is not easy to understand or to use. However, either division or its equivalent in other operations is essential to make relational algebra *complete*. (We will define relational completeness below when we discuss relational calculus.) The essential characteristic of the division operation is that it provides a means of identifying rows in one relation that bear a certain relationship to *every* row in another relation.

Selection. Suppose we want all rows from the PERSONNEL relation such that the salary is over 25000. Then we apply the selection operation to PERSONNEL as follows:

```
R = sel(PERSONNEL : Salary > 25000)
```

This operation creates a new relation, R, which has the same attributes as PERSONNEL but fewer rows. It is a subset of PERSONNEL and of course is union compatible with it.

In general, the selection operation chooses rows from a relation if they satisfy a condition based on a comparison operator ($<$, $>$, $<=$, $>=$, $=$, not $=$) applied to two of its attributes or to one of its attributes and a constant. Selection thus creates a new relation which is a subset of the original relation.

If A and B are two relations created by applying the selection operation to a relation R, then A and B are both subsets of R and are union compatible. Therefore, it makes sense to talk about the union, intersection, and difference of A and B. For example, suppose that R is the PERSONNEL relation and:

```
A = sel (PERSONNEL : Salary > 25000)
B = sel (PERSONNEL : Proj No = 2)
```

Then:

```
A ∪ B = sel(PERSONNEL : Salary > 25000 or Proj No = 2),
A ∩ B = sel(PERSONNEL : Salary > 25000 and Proj No = 2),
A - B = sel(PERSONNEL : Salary > 25000 and not Proj No = 2).
```

We see, therefore, that the Boolean connectives (or, and, not) can be used in the condition of the selection operation.

Join.   Consider the PERSONNEL and PROJECTS relations from Figure 3.1, repeated here for convenience.

PERSONNEL

EMP NO	NAME	DEPT NO	PROJ NO	SALARY
333	Zendel	45	3	18000
212	Young	83	2	22000
456	Wilkes	45	1	15000
118	Unser	25	2	30000
782	Varen	25	1	45000
560	Welch	47	4	25000

PROJECTS

PROJ NO	CUSTOMER	LOCATION
4	Adams	Telfs
2	Bern	Ester
3	Carney	Toole
1	Basel	Ester

If we are interested in detailed information concerning the projects to which employees are assigned, we can *join* the PERSONNEL relation to the PROJECTS relation. Notationally, we indicate the join of these two relations by: join(PERSONNEL, PROJECTS : Proj No = Proj No). Our notation states that we join a PERSONNEL row to a PROJECTS row whenever the value of *Proj No* in the PERSONNEL row is equal to the value of *Proj No* in the PROJECTS row. This join is accomplished through three other algebraic operations as follows.

1. *Product:* to create a relation with 8 attributes, two of which are *Proj No.* The new relation also has 24 rows, most of which are useless to us.
2. *Selection:* to ignore all rows except those for which the two *Proj No* attributes are equal.
3. *Projection:* to eliminate repetition of the *Proj No* attribute.

The result of these operations is the *natural join* of PERSONNEL and PROJECTS. We will call it PPJOIN:

Result: PPJOIN

EMP NO	NAME	DEPT NO	PROJ NO	SALARY	CUSTOMER	LOC
333	Zendel	45	3	18000	Carney	Toole
212	Young	83	2	22000	Bern	Ester
456	Wilkes	45	1	15000	Basel	Ester
118	Unser	25	2	30000	Bern	Ester
782	Varen	25	1	45000	Basel	Ester
560	Welch	47	4	25000	Adams	Telfs

What is happening here? Essentially, we are taking each row in the PERSONNEL relation and looking up the associated row in the PROJECTS relation (i.e., the row with the same project number). Then we are adding the information in that PROJECTS row to the PERSONNEL row.

The power of the join operation lies in its ability to connect data across relations. In the example above, we were able to join the information about projects to the information about people on those projects in a single, set level operation.

In this example, the attributes on which the join takes place had the same name (*Proj No*) in both relations. This is not required, however. The only requirement is that the attributes be defined on the same domain and are therefore comparable.

This join was also based on the equality of the values of attributes in the two relations, but this need not be the case. We may also compare attributes using any of the comparison operators (<, >, <=, >=, =, not =). When we use the = operator, one of the attributes is superfluous and is eliminated through projection as indicated in Step 3 above. But if a different operator is used, then no attribute is superfluous and projection is skipped. We call the join based on equality the natural join. The natural join is the version of join most often used in practice.

You may wonder when a join other than the natural join may be used in a practical situation. The next example shows such a situation. It also shows the use of different attribute names for the attributes under comparison. Consider the following relations:

PERSONNEL

EMP NO	SALARY
333	18000
212	22000
456	15000
118	30000
782	45000
560	25000

POSITIONS

TITLE	START SALARY
Lift Operator	20000
Supervisor	25000

The second relation is a list of positions for which there are openings at the present time. Suppose we wish to identify employees who can fill the positions described in the POSITIONS relation. Since we would like the new position to be a promotion for the person selected, we are only interested in identifying those people who are not presently earning more than the starting salary for the position. Consequently, we formulate a join as follows:

```
A = join(PERSONNEL, POSITIONS : Salary <= Start Salary)
```

Result: A

EMP NO	SALARY	TITLE	START SALARY
333	18000	Lift Operator	20000
333	18000	Supervisor	25000
212	22000	Supervisor	25000
456	15000	Lift Operator	20000
456	15000	Supervisor	25000
560	25000	Supervisor	25000

Thus, with a single operation we have identified all employees who qualify for each of the positions available. Note also that the names of the two attributes being compared are different (Salary and Start Salary).

Assignment.   The operations of relational algebra create new relations from existing relations. Relational algebra operations may be applied in turn to the new relations. It is important, therefore, that we have a facility available to give names to new relations. *Assignment* provides this facility. Thus, if A and B are relations, then the statement $C = A \cup B$ assigns the name "C" to the union of A and B. Names are assigned to the results of other algebra operations in the same way; in fact, we have been doing it throughout this section.

You may have observed that some of the 9 relational algebra operations can be derived from the others. For example, the join is nothing more than the combination of product, selection, and (sometimes) projection. The question arises, therefore, as to why such "redundant" operations are included in relational algebra. The answer is that the object is not to provide a *minimal* set of relational algebra operations, but rather, a *useful* set of operations. Combination operations, such as the join, have proven extremely useful in practice, and so they clearly belong in the set we are seeking to build.

Sample Applications of Relational Algebra.   Having defined the operations of relational algebra, we are now in a position to illustrate both the power and the limitations of this data sublanguage. The next few examples assume the database of Figure 3.2.

PROJECTS

PROJ NO	CUSTOMER	LOCATION
4	Adams	Telfs
2	Bern	Ester
3	Carney	Toole
1	Basel	Ester

PARTS

PART NO	VENDOR	COST
23	Beam	29.95
15	Rivers	3.00
87	Moberly	85.00

PROJ-PARTS

PROJ NO	PART NO	QTY
2	15	5
1	23	10
2	87	9
3	15	3
1	87	15

FIGURE 3.2   Portion of Allied Construction Database

QUERY: What vendor or vendors supply parts for projects located in Toole?

In this query, the requested information (vendor name) is in the PARTS relation; the condition (Location = "Toole") is in the PROJECTS relation. Since the only connection between these two relations is the PROJ-PARTS relation, we must work with all three relations. We give two solutions to this query. The first solution creates four new relations, A, B, C, and D. Note that relation B is the natural join of all three relations from Figure 3.2 (PROJECTS, PROJ-PARTS, and PARTS). We then select the desired rows from B to create relation C.

```
A = join(PROJECTS, PROJ-PARTS : Proj No = Proj No)
```

Result: A

PROJ NO	PART NO	QTY	CUSTOMER	LOCATION
2	15	5	Bern	Ester
1	23	10	Basel	Ester
2	87	9	Bern	Ester
3	15	3	Carney	Toole
1	87	15	Basel	Ester

```
B = join(A, PARTS : Part No = Part No)
```

Result: B

PROJ NO	PART NO	QTY	CUSTOMER	LOCATION	VENDOR	COST
2	15	5	Bern	Ester	Rivers	3.00
1	23	10	Basel	Ester	Beam	29.95
2	87	9	Bern	Ester	Moberly	85.00
3	15	3	Carney	Toole	Rivers	3.00
1	87	15	Basel	Ester	Moberly	85.00

```
C = sel(B : Location = "Toole")
```

Result: C

PROJ NO	PART NO	QTY	CUSTOMER	LOCATION	VENDOR	COST
3	15	3	Carney	Toole	Rivers	3.00

```
D = C(Vendor)
```

Result: D

VENDOR
Rivers

The second solution also creates four new relations, but we perform the selection operation first, as shown below:

```
R = sel(PROJECTS : Location = "Toole")
```

Result: R

PROJ NO	CUSTOMER	LOCATION
3	Carney	Toole

```
S = join(R, PROJ-PARTS : Proj No = Proj No)
```

Result: S

PROJ NO	CUSTOMER	LOCATION	PART NO	QTY
3	Carney	Toole	15	3

```
T = join(S, PARTS : Part No = Part No)
```

Result: T

PROJ NO	CUSTOMER	LOCATION	PART NO	QTY	VENDOR	COST
3	Carney	Toole	15	3	Rivers	3.00

```
U = T(Vendor)
```

Result: U

VENDOR
Rivers

There is a significant difference in efficiency between these two solutions. Relations A and B of solution 1 have 5 rows, while relations R and S of solution 2 both have 1 row. This difference is not meaningful in the small database of our example; however, in a large production database, the amount of time and space required to carry out the first approach could be excessive. In practical terms, the first solution would be very costly. Because of the large number of records involved in a join operation, it is usually advisable to do selection operations before joins, if logically possible.

The next example uses the PROJECTS and PROJ-PARTS relations of Figure 3.2, duplicated below.

PROJECTS

PROJ NO	CUSTOMER	LOCATION
4	Adams	Telfs
2	Bern	Ester
3	Carney	Toole
1	Basel	Ester

PROJ-PARTS

PROJ NO	PART NO	QTY
2	15	5
1	23	10
2	87	9
3	15	3
1	87	23

QUERY: Which parts are used on all projects in Ester?

You may recognize this query as a revised version of the first example given for the division operation. To illustrate the flexibility of relational algebra, we give two solutions.

For the first solution we first create B, which is a list of the project numbers for all projects in Ester. C is the PROJ-PARTS relation with the *Qty* attribute deleted so that we can perform division properly. Then we divide to obtain the desired list of parts (D).

```
A = sel(PROJECTS : Location = "Ester")
B = A(PROJ NO)
C = PROJ-PARTS(Proj No, Part No)
D = C / B
```

Result:

B	C		D
PROJ NO	**PROJ NO**	**PART NO**	**PART NO**
2	2	15	87
1	1	23	
	2	87	
	3	15	
	1	87	

It is not necessary to assign an intermediate relation name to the result of every operation; operations can be nested. Thus, we could have avoided use of B and C altogether by merely writing:

```
D = PROJ-PARTS(Proj No, Part No) / A(Proj No)
```

To avoid confusion as to which operations are performed first we are using intermediate relations. Hereafter, we shall nest operations when confusion seems unlikely.

A commercial implementation of relational algebra may not include the division operation. Consequently, we give here a second solution which does not use division. For this approach we use the fact that division can be expressed in terms of product, subtraction, and projection (Codd 1972).

First we create relation R, which is a list of project numbers in Ester. Relation S is a list of all part numbers used on some project. A row of relation T consists of a project number in Ester together with a part number *not* used on that project. U is a list of part numbers not used on at least one project in Ester. Relation V, containing all part numbers used on every project in Ester, is the solution to the query.

```
R = sel(PROJECTS : Location = "Ester") (Proj No)
S = PROJ-PARTS(Part No)
T = (R * S) - PROJ-PARTS(Proj No, Part No)
U = T(Part No)
V = S - U
```

Result:

R		S
PROJ NO		**PART NO**
2		15
1		23
		87

T		U
PROJ NO	**PART NO**	**PART NO**
2	23	23
1	15	15

V
PART NO
87

This query and its solution illustrate a fundamental weakness in relational algebra as a programming language—a weakness which relational calculus attempts to address. The two solutions are difficult to comprehend, and the second solution is particularly difficult to develop. Most programmers who have not previously encountered a query like this struggle to derive a solution in relational algebra. With practice, a programmer can learn to develop algebra solutions using the division operation, but the process tends to be very mechanical, and the programmer frequently does not understand what is happening.

The difficulty in the present example is posed by the condition used for selection of part numbers. The condition states that a part number is placed in the new relation only if it is used on all projects in Ester. The word *all*, stating in effect that every row in some relation must be examined, is the source of the difficulty. Relational algebra is poorly equipped to handle such queries, providing either the division operation or a double application of the subtraction operation (as shown in the last example). Relational calculus, on the other hand, provides the powerful facility of quantifiers, whose meanings are well-established in traditional symbolic logic, and which can provide more comprehensible solutions to such queries.

The previous examples both deal with queries, a particular area of strength for relational languages. However, many applications involve other aspects of data processing as well. We shall now look at a traditional master-transaction report problem to analyze the contribution that relational algebra makes to its solution. Consider the problem of printing monthly statements for revolving charge accounts. We have two relations:

MASTER

ACCT NO	NAME	ADDRESS	BALANCE
3434	Black	333 N. Main	250.00
1212	Brown	890 5th St.	100.00

TRANSACTION

ACCT NO	DATE	TYPE	AMOUNT
1212	5/13	Charge	17.00
3434	5/7	Charge	23.95
3434	5/1	Charge	10.00
1212	5/2	Payment	50.00
1212	5/28	Charge	85.00
3434	5/23	Payment	200.00

We are to process the two relations sequentially and produce a separate printed statement for each account. Each statement should display the customer's name and address, all transactions in order by date, and a beginning and ending balance. Charges are added to the balance, and payments are subtracted.

Let us list some of the functions which any solution to this problem must perform:

1. Each master row must be associated with all of its corresponding transaction rows.
2. All of the rows for one account (both master and transactions) must be grouped together so that the information in the rows can be printed.
3. The transaction rows for a given account must be in order by date.
4. A new balance must be calculated for printing.
5. Data must be formatted properly on the printed document.

How many of these functions can be carried out by operations in relational algebra? Unfortunately, only the first. A natural join on the two relations will attach master rows to transaction rows. But the new relation created by this join will not have any order defined on its rows, and ordering is essential for functions 2 and 3. Moreover, since relational algebra is a *data sublanguage* and therefore does not include computational operations, function 4 cannot be performed via relational algebra. Function 5 is clearly outside the realm of relational algebra as well. Finally, even though the first of these functions can be handled via a relational join, this solution is not wholly satisfactory. There are other ways of handling master-transaction relationships which are more natural than the join.

As we shall see in subsequent chapters, all of the capabilities needed to carry out the functions listed above are found in 4GLs. Relational languages are an integral part of 4GLs, but their power must be, and has been, supplemented by many other tools to provide full applications development capability.

The above problem was intentionally stated to highlight the limitations of data sublanguages. We note, however, that in more complex versions of this problem, the power of relational concepts may be utilized. For example, suppose we were interested in extracting data from 3 or 4 relations instead of only 2. Also, suppose we were interested in printing statements for only a selected group of customers—e.g., those whose balance is over $1000. In cases like these, relational operations would constitute a larger portion of the solution to the problem.

Relational Calculus

Relational algebra is procedural. The programmer specifies a sequence of operations which results in a relation containing the desired data. Relational calculus, on the other hand, is non-procedural. The programmer specifies the data desired (including conditions the data satisfies), and the system creates the operations needed to produce a relation containing the data.

Our treatment of relational calculus will be informal, with the concepts illustrated by many examples. If you desire a more formal treatment, refer to Codd (1972) or Ullman (1982).

Row Variables.   Our first example uses the relation shown below to illustrate row variables.

PROJ-PARTS

PROJ NO	PART NO	QTY
2	15	5
1	23	10
2	87	9
3	15	3
1	87	15

QUERY: Create a relation containing the numbers of all projects using part number 15.

This query can be divided into two pieces. First, the list of attributes in the new relation is defined. In this case the list consists of only one attribute, *Proj No.* Second, the condition or conditions the data must satisfy is defined. In this query, the part number must be equal to 15.

The problem is to create a relational calculus expression which: (1) captures the list of attributes, the conditions, and the logical relationship between them, and (2) is in a format that can be comprehended by a computer.

These two conditions can be met by using a *row variable* in the relational calculus expression. A row variable is a symbol which represents an arbitrary row in a specified relation. Thus, suppose r is a row variable in PROJ-PARTS. Then the above query can be expressed in relational calculus as follows:

```
(r.Proj No) : r in PROJ-PARTS and
              r.Part No = 15
```

This relational calculus expression may be read: the *Proj No* in row r, where r is a row in PROJ-PARTS and the *Part No* of r is 15. More specifically, a row is selected in PROJ-PARTS and labeled r. If the part number for that row is 15, then a row is created in the new relation consisting of the value of the project number in row r. If the value of *Part No* in r is not 15, no action is needed. After all elements in the row are examined, a new row is selected and labeled r. Then the process is repeated until all the rows of PROJ-PARTS have been examined.

Notice that the list of attributes is to the left of the colon and the condition is to the right. The logical connection between the attributes and the condition is expressed by the use of the row variable r. If we call the new relation A, then:

Result: A

PROJ NO

2
3

The relational algebra equivalent of the calculus statement is:

```
A = sel(PROJ-PARTS : Part No = 15) (Proj No)
```

This algebra version is very similar to the calculus version—the only difference, aside from syntax, is the row variable. As we proceed to more complicated queries, however, the significant differences between algebra and calculus will become evident.

The next example uses the PROJ-PARTS relation above, along with the PARTS relation of Figure 3.2, duplicated below:

PARTS

PART NO	VENDOR	COST
23	Beam	29.95
15	Rivers	3.00
87	Moberly	85.00

QUERY: Retrieve the part numbers and costs for all parts used on project 2.

```
(r.Part No, s.Cost) : r in PROJ-PARTS and
                      s in PARTS and
                      r.Proj No = 2 and
                      r.Part No = s.Part No
```

In this statement:

- r and s are row variables in PROJ-PARTS and PARTS, respectively.
- A row is created in the new relation if the *Proj No* of r is 2 and the *Part No* of r equals the *Part No* of s. The attributes of this row in the new relation will be the *Part No* from r and the *Cost* from s.
- The above process is repeated for all possible combinations of rows r and s.

Result: B

PART NO	COST
15	3.00
87	85.00

Target Lists and Qualification Expressions.   The last two examples illustrate three basic principles of relational calculus, as summarized below.

1. The first part of the calculus statement lists the attributes of the new relation. These attributes are attributes in existing relations, each of them prefixed by a row variable identifying the relation from which the attribute is taken. This list of attributes in the new relation is called the *target list*.

2. The second part of the statement specifies a condition that rows in the new relation must satisfy. This condition is called the *qualification expression* and consists of:

- Definitions of row variables, including the relation over which they range (e.g., "r in PROJ–PARTS").
- Comparison terms (e.g., r.Part No = s.Part No), which define a relationship between two attributes or between an attribute and a constant. Comparison operators may be $<$, $>$, $<=$, $>=$, $=$, not $=$. Each comparison term evaluates to *true* or *false*.
- Expressions containing quantifiers (to be explained shortly). Quantifiers are of two types: Existential ("there exists") and universal ("for every" or "for all"). Quantified expressions also evaluate to "true" or "false".
- Boolean connectives which connect the row variable definitions, the comparison terms, and the quantified expressions. The Boolean connectives are *and, or,* and *not*. These connectives make it possible to determine a true or false value for the qualification expression as a whole.

3. If the qualification expression as a whole evaluates to true for given values of the row variables, then a row is created in the new relation using the attributes in the target list, taking their values from the values of the row variables. While the row variables in the target list must appear in the qualification expression, it is not necessary for the attributes in the target list to appear in the qualification expression. Both of the examples above illustrate this.

Quantifiers.   The relational calculus queries we have looked at so far are relatively simple. The conditions in these queries only require the examination of a single row per relation at a time. However, many queries require the examination of all the rows in a relation in order to decide whether or not the qualification expression is true. In relational calculus this is accomplished by means of quantifiers.

   We shall consider a number of examples of queries solved by quantifiers. In the early examples the solutions are simple. However, the solutions will become more complex as we proceed to more difficult queries. The first example is given to illustrate the use of quantified expressions. It uses both the PROJECTS and PROJ-PARTS relations from Figure 3.2, duplicated below.

PROJECTS

PROJ NO	CUSTOMER	LOCATION
4	Adams	Telfs
2	Bern	Ester
3	Carney	Toole
1	Basel	Ester

PROJ-PARTS

PROJ NO	PART NO	QTY
2	15	5
1	23	10
2	87	9
3	15	3
1	87	23

QUERY: Produce a list of customers who are using part number 15.

   Another way of stating this query is that a row in PROJECTS will be selected if there is a row in PROJ-PARTS having the same project number and also having a part number of 15. Queries like this are best handled by calculus statements using the existential quantifier ("there exists"):

```
(r.Customer) : r in PROJECTS and
               there exists s in PROJ-PARTS
               (r.Proj No = s.Proj No and
               s.Part No = 15)
```

The expression in parentheses is read: ". . . such that r.Proj No = s.Proj No and s.Part No = 15." This calculus statement may be read as "Create a relation of customers taken from all rows r of PROJECTS having the property that there is a row s in PROJ-PARTS with the same *Proj No* as r and with a *Part No* of 15."

This statement is almost identical to the wording in the paragraph immediately preceding the calculus statement. Thus, the calculus statement is very close to the statement of the problem itself. Hence, we say that relational calculus is non-procedural.

Note how the quantifier gives us a simple way of handling a complex query. In this example, examining each row in PROJECTS requires (potentially) a look at every row in PROJ-PARTS to decide whether or not to select the row from PROJECTS. To accomplish this we would ordinarily need to set up complex processing logic. But the quantifier eliminates this requirement. It provides a simple way of stating the condition. The system must then determine whether the row satisfies the condition.

Result: **C**

CUSTOMER

Bern
Carney

Now we will illustrate the universal quantifier ("for every") with an example using the PARTS relation.

PARTS

PART NO	VENDOR	COST
23	Beam	29.95
15	Rivers	3.00
87	Moberly	85.00

QUERY: Identify the part or parts with the lowest cost.

This query may be rephrased as: "Which part or parts have a cost that is less than or equal to the cost of *every* other part?"

```
(r.Part No) : r in PARTS and
             for every s in PARTS
             (r.Cost <= s.Cost)
```

Again, the calculus statement is nearly identical to the rephrasing of the original query. Also, note that each time we examine a row r in PARTS we must examine *every* row in PARTS to determine whether the qualification expression is true. The universal quantifier gives us a simple way of doing this. Of course, part 15 will be the result.

These examples of quantified expressions illustrated that a quantified expression consists of a quantifier, a row variable, and a logical expression which uses the quantified row variable. A quantified expression evaluates to true or false. The quantified row variable (s in these examples) is said to be *bound* (by the quantifier). Any row variable which is not bound is said to be *free* (r in these examples). Row variables appearing in the target list of a relational calculus statement will always be free.

The existential quantifier, when applied to a relation, states that there is at least one row in the relation for which the following statement—the logical expression—is true. The universal quantifier states that the logical expression is true for all the rows in the relation. The next example, which uses the PROJECTS relation above, may use either quantifier.

QUERY: List the locations having only one project.

In this query, for each row we examine we must also examine every other row in the relation to see whether or not another row has the same value for *Location*. The first solution uses the universal quantifier, while the second uses the negation of the existential quantifier to accomplish the same result.

```
(r.Location) : r in PROJECTS and
               for every s in PROJECTS
               (s = r or
               s.Location not = r.Location)
```

This statement says: Choose a *Location* from a row r if every row s in PROJECTS is either equal to r or has a *Location* that is not equal to the value of *Location* in r. This is illustrated below. Think of r as identifying a row in one copy of PROJECTS, while s ranges over the rows of a second copy of PROJECTS. If r refers to the first row in PROJECTS, then *Location* in r (Telfs) will be selected if every value of s has a different location—except when s = r. Since Telfs does not occur in any row except r, it is selected. Toole will also be selected, but Ester will not, since it occurs in two rows.

PROJECTS

	PROJ NO	CUSTOMER	LOCATION
r	4	Adams	Telfs
	2	Bern	Ester
	3	Carney	Toole
	1	Basel	Ester

PROJECTS

	PROJ NO	CUSTOMER	LOCATION
s	4	Adams	Telfs
s	2	Bern	Ester
s	3	Carney	Toole
s	1	Basel	Ester

```
(r.Location) :  r in PROJECTS and
                there does not exist s in PROJECTS
                (s not = r and
                 s.Location = r.Location)
```

This second statement says: Choose a *Location* from a row r if there is no row s in Projects which is different from r and which has the same value for *Location* as r. This is illustrated below. In this case the row r we are illustrating has a location of Ester. Since there exists an s which is different from r and which has the same value for *Location*, we will not choose Ester. Only when there does *not* exist such an s will we choose the location in row r.

PROJECTS

	PROJ NO	CUSTOMER	LOCATION
	4	Adams	Telfs
r	2	Bern	Ester
	3	Carney	Toole
	1	Basel	Ester

PROJECTS

	PROJ NO	CUSTOMER	LOCATION
	4	Adams	Telfs
	2	Bern	Ester
	3	Carney	Toole
s	1	Basel	Ester

Both of these statements satisfy the requirements of the query and are therefore equivalent. Moreover, it is true that we can always eliminate the universal quantifier by using an appropriate negation of the existential quantifier. Conversely, we can always eliminate the existential quantifier by using an appropriate negation of the universal quantifier (Suppes, 1957). This fact will be applied in later chapters when we discuss the implementation of quantifiers in commerical 4GLs.

Existential and universal quantifiers may both appear in a single calculus expression as we shall now see. Let us take another look at one of the examples from the previous section on relational algebra. The PARTS, PROJECTS, and PROJ-PARTS relations from Figure 3.2 are used in this example.

QUERY: Which parts are used on all projects in Ester?

You will recall that we took a somewhat roundabout approach to solving this query with relational algebra. The operations used were not easily related to the statement of the problem itself. Consider now the following relational calculus solution to the same query:

```
(r.Part No) : r in PARTS and
              for every s in PROJECTS
              (s.Location not = Ester or
              there exists t in PROJ-PARTS
                   (t.Proj No = s.Proj No and
                   t.Part No = r.Part No))
```

The quantified expression may be read "For every row s in PROJECTS either: (1) s.Location not = Ester, or (2) there exists a row t in PROJ-PARTS such that t.Proj No = s.Proj No and t.Part No = r.Part No."

The process for a single row r is illustrated below. We have shown two rows s that have Location = Ester. There exists a row t corresponding to each of these rows s. Row t_1 corresponds to s_1, and row t_2 corresponds to s_2.

PARTS

	PART NO	VENDOR	COST
	23	Beam	29.95
	15	Rivers	3.00
r	87	Moberly	85.00

PROJECTS

	PROJ NO	CUSTOMER	LOCATION
	4	Adams	Telfs
s_1	2	Bern	Ester
	3	Carney	Toole
s_2	1	Basel	Ester

PROJ-PARTS

	PROJ NO	PART NO	QTY
	2	15	5
	1	23	10
t_1	2	87	9
	3	15	3
t_2	1	87	15

Summary of Relational Calculus.   Relational calculus provides a descriptive (non-procedural) means of defining new relations from existing relations.

GENERAL SYNTAX

```
A = {(target list) : qualification expression}
```

This may be read as "The relation A is defined to be the set of all rows made up of the indicated list of attributes (the target list) such that the qualification expression, related to the target list by row variables, is true."

Many commercial implementations of relational languages are versions of relational calculus. We shall consider several of them in this book.

The queries we have used in this section to illustrate the features of relational calculus have been progressively more difficult. Specifically, those queries requiring universal quantifiers, at times in combination with existential quantifiers, are especially difficult to comprehend, even though they appear to be straightforward at a purely logical level. Although one would think that relational calculus, being non-procedural, should be easier to use than a procedural language, research has shown that this is not necessarily true (Ehrenreich 1981). Quantifiers have been shown to be especially troublesome. Thus, it is still an open question as to whether the relational algebra approach or the relational calculus approach is superior. While the relational calculus solution is usually more directly related to the statement of the problem than is the algebra solution, it is, nevertheless, somewhat difficult to comprehend. It is likely that future research will develop more effective ways to handle such queries.

RELATIONAL VS. QUASI-RELATIONAL SYSTEMS

Seemingly every database management system (DBMS) on the market today is described in its promotional literature as being in some way "relational"—"truly relational", "relational like", "post-relational", etc. As relational systems are being introduced, and as their power for application development is being demonstrated in practice, the desire to jump onto the relational bandwagon has become irresistible. However, a system described as relational may or may not be genuinely relational. In this section we discuss criteria for determining the degree to which a system conforms to the requirements of the relational model.

In the 1981 ACM Turing Award Lecture, E. F. Codd (1982) gave defining criteria for a relational DBMS. He later summarized these criteria (Codd 1983). Our discussion here is based on Codd's criteria, which defines the relational model as consisting of three parts, defined below. Codd defines as *fully relational* any DBMS which supports all three parts of the relational model.

- *Structure.* In the relational model, all data is represented as values in tables.
- *Manipulation.* A data manipulation language is provided which is based on relational algebra or relational calculus.
- *Integrity.* Data in relations adheres to the two integrity rules (entity integrity and referential integrity, defined earlier in this chapter).

Codd (1972) showed that relational algebra and relational calculus are equivalent. In particular, any relation that can be defined via a statement in relational calculus can be duplicated via operations in relational algebra. He called any language that is equivalent to relational calculus in this sense *relationally complete*. Thus, relational algebra (and, of course, relational calculus) is relationally complete. Relational algebra and relational calculus were recommended as yardsticks by which other relational languages may be measured.

A DBMS is defined as *minimally relational* if:

■ It assumes relational structure for its data.
■ It supports the selection, projection, and join operations of relational algebra.
■ It does not require the programmer to use iterative loops or navigation links between tables to perform any of these operations (selection, projection, join).

Thus, we have three terms for relational DBMS (in order of decreasing power): fully relational, relationally complete, and minimally relational. Any DBMS which does not meet the requirements of a minimally relational DBMS should not be called relational.

SUMMARY

Concepts of relational database processing provide the foundation for 4GLs. This foundation consists of a simple tabular view of data in combination with equivalent set-at-a-time data sublanguages—relational algebra (procedural) and relational calculus (non-procedural). Commercial products supporting the relational view of data and one of the relational languages usually include other processing features as well. In succeeding chapters we shall examine how specific features of the relational model have been implemented, as well as how they are combined with other processing features to provide for application system development.

DISCUSSION QUESTIONS

3.1. Discuss some of the reasons why database processing originated. What are some difficulties with the prerelational approach to database processing?
3.2. How is data viewed in the relational model?
3.3. Define the following terms:
■ Attribute
■ Domain
■ Key

3.4. What do entity integrity and referential integrity mean? Why are they needed? What are null values?

3.5. In what ways are relational algebra and calculus more powerful than 3GL data manipulation techniques?

3.6. What are the three features of the relational model?

3.7. What is meant by the terms "fully relational," "relationally complete," and "minimally relational"?

EXERCISES

3.1. Using the database shown below, write sequences of relational algebra statements and relational calculus statements which produce relations with the characteristics described. Sample rows for each of these relations are given in Figure 3.1. However, for these exercises, assume that each relation could consist of many more rows than those shown in Figure 3.1.

PROJECTS (Proj No, Customer, Location)
PARTS (Part No, Vendor, Cost)
PROJ-PARTS (Proj No, Part No, Qty)
DEPARTMENTS (Dept No, Name)
PERSONNEL (Emp No, Name, Dept No, Proj No, Salary)

   a. A list of all customers.
   b. A list of all customers in Martinsville.
   c. For the next three lists, the algebra solution should *not* contain Boolean connectives (and, or, not)—in the selection condition.
      (1). A list of part numbers from vendor Smith costing between $25 and $100.
      (2). A list of names of employees other than Jones who are making over $40,000 in salary.
      (3). A list of department numbers of people who are on project number 5 or who are making over $30,000.
   d. A list of names of employees in Accounting who are making less than $20,000.
   e. A list of vendors who supply parts for all projects in Outland.
   f. A list of all employees in the Accounting Department whose salary is larger than the salary of at least one employee in the Marketing Department. (Hint for algebra: Use the JOIN.)

3.2. The database shown below gives information about independent insurance agents who place insurance policies with a variety of different companies. Write relational algebra and relational calculus solutions to the following queries.

POLICY (<u>Policy No</u>, Insured, Agent No, Company No, Amount, Premium)
AGENT (<u>Agent No</u>, Agent Name, State)
COMPANY (<u>Company No</u>, Company Name, Commission Rate, Revenue)

    a. A list of all companies with revenue exceeding $100 million who offer a commission rate of less than 15%.

    b. A list of policies written by agents in Illinois.

    c. A list of companies having policies with amounts between $50,000 and $100,000.

    d. A list of agents getting a commission rate exceeding 20% on any of their policies.

    e. All the companies that Sam Stone writes policies for.

    f. Agents who have written policies for every company.

    g. Companies which do business with all agents in Iowa.

    h. The maximum policy amount written by an agent in Georgia.

3.3. Use the databases for exercises 3.1 and 3.2 to write relational calculus solutions for the following queries.

    a. Projects which have at least one employee from every department.

    b. Locations, all of whose projects get their parts from a single vendor.

    c. Agents who are the only agents in their state.

    d. Companies, none of whose policies are for an amount over $1,000,000.

CHAPTER 4

STRUCTURED QUERY LANGUAGE (SQL)

■ ■

Structured Query Language (SQL, pronounced like *sequel*) is a commercial relational language based on the relational calculus. SQL, originally known as SEQUEL, was implemented in IBM's System R project. The purpose of this project was to validate the usefulness of the relational data model by having users interact with a running (though experimental) system (Chamberlin 1980). Encouraged by the success of the System R project, IBM proceeded with the development of commercial products based on SQL. Subsequently, IBM introduced SQL/DS, DB2, and QMF, all of which use SQL, for various operating environments.

A number of other vendors have introduced products which use the SQL language (Date 1986). Among these other vendors are Relational Technology, Inc., whose QUEL language we shall consider in the next chapter, and Oracle, which introduced the first commercial version of SQL. In addition, SQL has received final approval by the American National Standards Institute (ANSI) as a relational language standard. Obviously, SQL is, and will increasingly be, a database language of substantial importance.

The SQL data manipulation language consists of four basic statements: SELECT (for queries), INSERT (for adding data to a relation), UPDATE (for changing the value of existing data), and DELETE (for removing data). Since the SELECT statement best demonstrates the power of a relational language for making complex database queries, we shall spend most of our time discussing SELECT and its features. We shall give explanations of the other three statements toward the end of the chapter.

Throughout this chapter, our examples refer to the database given in Figure 4.1. The examples are oriented to the implementation of SQL that runs under IBM's Query Management Facility (QMF). The solutions of queries in the examples may vary slightly in other implementations. For additional information on the concepts of this chapter, refer to the bibliography (IBM 1983, 1984).

APPLIANCE DATABASE

APPLIANCES

INVENTORY

ID	TYPE	VENDOR	COST	PRICE
100	Refrigerator	22	150.00	250.00
150	Television	27	225.00	340.00
110	Refrigerator	20	175.00	300.00
200	Microwave Oven	22	120.00	180.00
300	Washer	27	200.00	325.00
310	Washer	22	280.00	400.00
400	Dryer	20	150.00	220.00
420	Dryer	22	240.00	360.00

VENDORS

VENDOR	CITY	STATE	RATING
22	Orem	Utah	8
20	Davis	Calif	6
27	Urbana	Illinois	9

SALESPEOPLE

NAME	ADDRESS	COMM RATE	BASE SALARY	SUPV
Linda	Box 23, Middleton	15%	1200	Anne
Anne	14 S. Elm	12%	1800	
Charles	1933 Eisenhower	10%	1150	Anne
Hank	103 Royal Arms	18%	1700	Anne

SALES

DATE	SP NAME	INV ID	QTY
10/01	Anne	150	1
10/05	Hank	110	1
10/03	Charles	110	2
10/13	Anne	100	1
10/25	Linda	150	2
10/22	Linda	100	2
10/12	Charles	150	3
10/14	Hank	100	1
10/15	Linda	300	1
10/03	Charles	200	2
10/31	Charles	310	1
10/05	Anne	420	1
10/15	Hank	400	2

FIGURE 4.1   Appliance Database

SIMPLE QUERIES

To illustrate SQL statements and capabilities, we begin with simple queries. These simple SQL statements can be modified by means of *clauses*. After presenting some of these clauses and demonstrating how they work, we proceed to more complex queries on multiple relations.

Select

Every SQL query contains lines having the following format:

GENERAL SYNTAX

```
SELECT attribute-list
FROM relation-list
```

The *relation-list* designates a list of relation names separated by commas. The *attribute-list* designates a list of attribute names taken from the relations in the relation-list. Thus, the example below is a syntactically valid query using the database of Figure 4.1.

```
SELECT TYPE
FROM APPLIANCES
```

This query commands the system to create (for display) a new relation from the rows of the APPLIANCES relation. Each row of the new relation will have the single attribute *Type*. This query is almost equivalent to the following statements in relational calculus and algebra.

Relational Calculus

(r.Type) : r in APPLIANCES

Relational Algebra

APPLIANCES(Type)

Result: **TYPE**

Refrigerator
Television
Refrigerator
Microwave Oven
Washer
Washer
Dryer
Dryer

Why is this SQL query *almost* equivalent to the respective calculus and algebra queries? The SQL query will not eliminate duplicate rows from the resulting set. In order to make the SQL query equivalent, we must add the keyword DISTINCT:

```
SELECT DISTINCT TYPE
FROM APPLIANCES
```

Result: **TYPE**

Refrigerator
Television
Microwave Oven
Washer
Dryer

A SQL query will not eliminate duplicate rows from the resulting relation unless the keyword DISTINCT appears immediately after SELECT.

If we desire to see both the type and price of all appliances, we enter:

```
SELECT TYPE, PRICE
FROM APPLIANCES
```

If we want to see all available information from the APPLIANCES relation we enter:

```
SELECT *
FROM APPLIANCES
```

The asterisk (*) means *the entire row.* This query will give us the entire APPLIANCES table as shown in Figure 4.1.

The next query creates the relational algebra product of the APPLIANCES and VENDORS relations. That is, the result of this query will be a new relation consisting of every possible combination of a row from APPLIANCES placed next to a row from VENDORS.

```
SELECT APPLIANCES.*, VENDORS.*
FROM APPLIANCES, VENDORS
```

The expression *APPLIANCES.** means *an entire row from APPLIANCES.* Here APPLIANCES qualifies the asterisk, indicating which relation the entire row is taken from. Any attribute name may be similarly qualified by preceding it with the name of the relation from which it is taken, followed by a period.

The WHERE Clause

The queries we have seen so far are very simple. They are given in relational calculus format and simulate the relational algebra operations of projection and product. Naturally, we are interested in much more powerful queries. The next two queries introduce the WHERE clause, and are equivalent to relational algebra's selection operation.

QUERY: Display the inventory ID, type, vendor number, cost, and price of all televisions in stock.

```
SELECT * FROM APPLIANCES
WHERE TYPE = 'Television'
```

Result:

INVENTORY ID	TYPE	VENDOR	COST	PRICE
150	Television	27	225.00	340.00

QUERY: Display the same information for all appliances with a price of over $250.

```
SELECT * FROM APPLIANCES
WHERE PRICE > 250
```

Result:

INVENTORY ID	TYPE	VENDOR	COST	PRICE
150	Television	27	225.00	340.00
110	Refrigerator	20	175.00	300.00
300	Washer	27	200.00	325.00
310	Washer	22	280.00	400.00
420	Dryer	22	240.00	360.00

The following query combines a selection with a projection by listing only the attributes desired in the resulting relation. Note that the WHERE condition references an attribute (Vendor) which is not in the final relation.

QUERY: Display only the type and price of all appliances from vendor number 20.

```
SELECT TYPE, PRICE FROM APPLIANCES
WHERE VENDOR = 20
```

Result:

TYPE	PRICE
Refrigerator	300.00
Dryer	220.00

As we shall see, much of the power of SQL lies in the wide variety of conditions that can be specified using the WHERE clause. For the remainder of this section we shall discuss queries in which the FROM clause references only a single relation. In succeeding sections of this chapter we shall discuss and illustrate multi-relation queries. Both single and multiple relation queries make heavy use of the various capabilities of the WHERE clause.

Figure 4.2 lists simple relational operators which can be used to compare two elements in a WHERE clause. We have already given examples using the = and > operators. We now illustrate the less familiar operators *between, in, like,* and *null.*

OPERATOR	MEANING
=	is equal to
¬=	is not equal to
>	is greater than
>=	is greater than or equal to
¬>	is not greater than
<	is less than
<=	is less than or equal to
¬<	is not less than
BETWEEN. . .AND	(value 1) is between (value 2) and (value 3)
IN	is in the set
LIKE	compares equally with the string [possibly using wildcard characters*]
IS (NOT) NULL	has (does not have) a null value

* Wildcard characters are:
  % meaning "any number of characters" (including 0).
  _ (underscore) meaning "any single character".

FIGURE 4.2   Simple Relational Operators

QUERY: Display all salespeople with a base salary between $1000 and $1500, inclusive.

```
SELECT NAME, BASESALARY FROM SALESPEOPLE
WHERE BASESALARY BETWEEN 1000 AND 1500
```

Result:

NAME	BASE SALARY
Linda	1200
Charles	1150

QUERY: Display the appliances available from vendors 20 and 27.

```
SELECT INVENTORYID, TYPE, VENDOR FROM APPLIANCES
WHERE VENDOR IN (20, 27)
```

Result:

INVENTORY ID	TYPE	VENDOR
150	Television	27
110	Refrigerator	20
300	Washer	27
400	Dryer	20

QUERY: Display all salespeople with Middleton in their addresses.

```
SELECT NAME, ADDRESS FROM SALESPEOPLE
WHERE ADDRESS LIKE '%MIDDLETON%'
```

Result:

NAME	ADDRESS
Linda	Box 23, Middleton

QUERY: Display all salespeople whose name begins with L.

```
SELECT NAME FROM SALESPEOPLE
WHERE NAME LIKE 'L%'
```

Result:

NAME
Linda

QUERY: Display vendors located in cities with 4 letters in their names, the first two of which are "Or".

```
SELECT VENDOR, CITY, STATE FROM VENDORS
WHERE CITY LIKE 'Or__'
```

Result:

VENDOR	CITY	STATE
22	Orem	Utah

QUERY: Display vendors located in cities with at least 3 letters in their names, the first of which is "U".

```
SELECT VENDOR, CITY, STATE FROM VENDORS
WHERE CITY LIKE 'U__%'
```

Result:

VENDOR	CITY	STATE
27	Urbana	Illinois

QUERY: Display all salespeople for whom no supervisor has been entered.

```
SELECT NAME FROM SALESPEOPLE
WHERE SUPV IS NULL
```

Result: <u>NAME</u>

Anne

QUERY: Display the names and supervisors for those salespeople who *do* have a supervisor entered.

```
SELECT NAME, SUPV FROM SALESPEOPLE
WHERE SUPV IS NOT NULL
```

Result:

NAME	SUPV
Linda	Anne
Charles	Anne
Hank	Anne

The forms *WHERE RATING = NULL* and *WHERE RATING ¬= NULL* are invalid in SQL. To identify records on the basis of null values in one of their attributes, the format in the previous examples must be used.

Boolean Operators.   Frequently, it is desirable to use more than one selection condition in a single query. Conditions may be combined through the use of the Boolean operators *AND* and *OR*. The operator *NOT* is used to negate the truth value of a condition. It is advisable to use parentheses to eliminate ambiguity when multiple conditions are used.

QUERY: Display all information for refrigerators that are either from vendor 20 or cost less than $160.

```
SELECT * FROM APPLIANCES
WHERE (VENDOR = 20 OR COST < 160) AND
      (TYPE LIKE 'Ref%')
```

Result:

INVENTORY ID	TYPE	VENDOR	COST	PRICE
100	Refrigerator	22	150.00	250.00
110	Refrigerator	20	175.00	300.00

Arithmetic Expressions.   Many of the SQL queries illustrated to this point have a version in relational algebra and calculus. However, SQL has many functional capabilities which cannot be duplicated in the theoretical languages. One of these is the capability to perform and display the results of calculations on retrieved data. For example, the SALESPEOPLE relation in our sample database contains base salary, which is a monthly salary. If we are interested in listing all salespeople together with their *annual* salary, we simply multiply base salary by 12.

```
SELECT NAME, BASESALARY * 12
FROM SALESPEOPLE
```

Result:

NAME	
Linda	14400
Anne	21600
Charles	13800
Hank	20400

Note that the calculated column has no heading. In the QMF implementation, SQL provides headings for columns taken directly from data. But there are no natural names for calculated values, so the headings are left blank. Depending on the implementation, such headings may be provided.

In the SELECT clause shown above, *BASESALARY * 12* is an *expression*. In general, an expression is a combination of data elements and constants, which uses the arithmetic operators +, −, *, /. Expressions may consist entirely of constants and may include character strings. Thus, the query above could have been written:

```
SELECT NAME, " has an annual salary of ", BASESALARY * 12
FROM SALESPEOPLE
```

Result:

NAME		
Linda	has an annual salary of	14400
Anne	has an annual salary of	21600
Charles	has an annual salary of	13800
Hank	has an annual salary of	20400

Expressions may also be used in WHERE clauses. For example, we may want to restrict the preceding query by specifying:

```
SELECT NAME, " has an annual salary of ", BASESALARY * 12
FROM SALESPEOPLE
WHERE BASESALARY * 12 > 10000
```

The ORDER BY Clause

The rows of relations do not have any predefined order. Thus, when a query is printed, the rows will be in whatever order the system happens to put them. However, if a large relation is printed on a report, the report may be difficult to use with rows that are helter-skelter. Suppose that we want the result of the query above to be printed in alphabetical order by salesperson's name. SQL provides for the ordering of printed results via the ORDER BY clause. In the example below, the system places the rows in *ascending* order by value of the salesperson's name.

```
SELECT NAME, " has an annual salary of ", BASESALARY * 12
FROM SALESPEOPLE
ORDER BY NAME
```

Result:

NAME		
Anne	has an annual salary of	21600
Charles	has an annual salary of	13800
Hank	has an annual salary of	20400
Linda	has an annual salary of	14400

We may order the report by any column in the SELECT clause, and we may choose the order to be ascending (the default) or descending (DESC). To order the report by annual salary with the highest salary first, we enter this query:

```
SELECT NAME, " has an annual salary of ", BASESALARY * 12
FROM SALESPEOPLE
ORDER BY 3 DESC
```

Since the annual salary is a calculated expression, we cannot refer to it by name. In this case we referred to it by the number of the column it occupies. Annual salary in this example occupies the third column, so we specified that the report should be in descending order of the value in column 3.

Result:

NAME		
Anne	has an annual salary of	21600
Hank	has an annual salary of	20400
Linda	has an annual salary of	14400
Charles	has an annual salary of	13800

We may order the report on multiple columns. If we desire to order the example alphabetically by name within descending order of annual salary, we enter this query:

```
SELECT NAME, " has an annual salary of ", BASESALARY * 12
FROM SALESPEOPLE
ORDER BY 3 DESC, NAME
```

Names will be in descending order by annual salary. If several people have the same salary, their names will be ordered alphabetically (that is, ascending).

MULTIPLE TABLE QUERIES

In the preceding section we stated that the following query would produce the relational algebra product of the APPLIANCES and VENDORS relations.

```
SELECT APPLIANCES.*, VENDORS.*
FROM APPLIANCES, VENDORS
```

Such a product is usually a very long relation and has little application. You will recall, however, that taking the product of two relations was the first step in creating their natural join. The next step was to select those rows in which an attribute from the first relation was equal to an attribute from the second relation. To do this in SQL for the above example (joining on the attribute *Vendor*), we add the appropriate WHERE clause as follows:

```
SELECT APPLIANCES.*, VENDORS.*
FROM APPLIANCES, VENDORS
WHERE APPLIANCES.VENDOR = VENDORS.VENDOR
```

The result of this query will almost, but not quite, be the natural join, since it will have two vendor attributes, each having the same value for any given row. This join is called the *equijoin*. To obtain the natural join we need to project out the superfluous vendor attribute.

Suppose we wish to list all appliances together with their vendor information. However, we don't want to see all of the information from these two relations. We can indicate the attributes we wish to see by listing them in the SELECT clause.

```
SELECT INVENTORYID, TYPE, VENDORS.VENDOR, STATE
FROM APPLIANCES, VENDORS
WHERE APPLIANCES.VENDOR = VENDORS.VENDOR
```

This is a projection of the natural join of the APPLIANCES and VENDORS relations. Note that the *Vendor* attributes in the SELECT and WHERE clauses had to be qualified, since the same attribute name appears in two relations.

Result:

INVENTORY ID	TYPE	VENDORS.VENDOR	STATE
100	Refrigerator	22	Utah
150	Television	27	Illinois
110	Refrigerator	20	Calif
200	Microwave Oven	22	Utah
300	Washer	27	Illinois
310	Washer	22	Utah
400	Dryer	20	Calif
420	Dryer	22	Utah

Examples of Join Queries

The following query combines a join with a selection. This is accomplished by merely adding another condition to the WHERE clause.

QUERY: Display inventory and vendor information for refrigerators.

```
SELECT INVENTORYID, TYPE, VENDORS.VENDOR, STATE
FROM APPLIANCES, VENDORS
WHERE APPLIANCES.VENDOR = VENDORS.VENDOR
    AND TYPE = 'Refrigerator'
```

Result:

INVENTORY ID	TYPE	VENDORS.VENDOR	STATE
100	Refrigerator	22	Utah
110	Refrigerator	20	Calif

QUERY: Display information for refrigerators costing over $160.

```
SELECT INVENTORYID, TYPE, VENDORS.VENDOR, STATE
FROM APPLIANCES, VENDORS
WHERE APPLIANCES.VENDOR = VENDORS.VENDOR
    AND TYPE = 'Refrigerator'
    AND COST > 160
```

Result:

INVENTORY ID	TYPE	VENDORS.VENDOR	STATE
110	Refrigerator	20	Calif

QUERY: List sales of refrigerators with total sale price.

```
SELECT SALES.INVID, TYPE, QTY, QTY * PRICE
FROM SALES, APPLIANCES
WHERE TYPE = 'Refrigerator'
    AND APPLIANCES.INVENTORYID = SALES.INVID
```

Result:

SALES.INVID	TYPE	QTY	(QTY * PRICE)
110	Refrigerator	1	300.00
110	Refrigerator	2	600.00
100	Refrigerator	1	250.00
100	Refrigerator	2	500.00
100	Refrigerator	1	250.00

Note that the (Qty * Price) label is shown for explanatory purposes only, as it is not displayed in the QMF implementation of SQL.

QUERY: List sales with profits for Anne's sales of refrigerators.

```
SELECT SPNAME, QTY, ' Profit = ', QTY * (PRICE - COST)
FROM SALES, APPLIANCES
WHERE TYPE = 'Refrigerator'
      AND APPLIANCES.INVENTORYID = SALES.INVID
      AND SPNAME = 'Anne'
```

Result:

SPNAME	QTY	
Anne	1	Profit = 100.00

The next query is a combination of two joins, a selection, and a projection. Note that we do not qualify any of the names since all the names we use are unique. However, we could qualify names, if we wish.

QUERY: List sales and commissions for salespeople whose commission rate is 10% or less.

```
SELECT NAME, TYPE, ' Commission = ',
       COMMRATE * QTY * PRICE
FROM SALESPEOPLE, APPLIANCES, SALES
WHERE COMMRATE <= 10%
      AND NAME = SPNAME
      AND INVID = INVENTORYID
```

Result:

NAME	TYPE		
Charles	Refrigerator	Commission =	60.00
Charles	Television	Commission =	102.00
Charles	Microwave Oven	Commission =	36.00
Charles	Washer	Commission =	40.00

The names of our tables are so long that qualifying attribute names may be tedious. Thus, we qualify names only when absolutely necessary. However, we can give *aliases* (alternate, shorter names) to the table names if we wish. We do this by adding the alias to the table name in the FROM clause. This is illustrated by the following modified version of an earlier query.

```
SELECT AP.INVENTORYID, AP.TYPE, V.VENDOR, V.STATE
FROM APPLIANCES AP, VENDORS V
WHERE AP.VENDOR = V.VENDOR
      AND AP.TYPE = 'Refrigerator'
      AND AP.COST > 160
```

At times it may be necessary to join a table to itself. In such a case it is essential to use aliases and to qualify attribute names. Suppose, for example, that we desire to compare a salesperson's commission rate with that of his or her supervisor. We could use the letters A and B to distinguish the two commission rates as shown below.

```
SELECT A.NAME, A.COMMRATE, B.NAME, B.COMMRATE
FROM SALESPEOPLE A, SALESPEOPLE B
WHERE A.SUPV = B.NAME
```

Conceptually, this query makes two copies of the SALESPEOPLE relation and joins them. We can think of the B copy as containing information about the supervisor, while the A copy contains information about the employee.

BUILT-IN FUNCTIONS

SQL provides an extension to the theoretical relational languages in the form of functions which calculate values associated with entire relations. There are five such functions, called *built-in functions:* COUNT, SUM, AVG, MAX, MIN. These functions are very useful in providing values commonly needed in applications. The arguments of these functions may be column names or calculated expressions using column names and constants. In the case of COUNT, an asterisk (*) may be the argument, where the asterisk means the entire row. In this section, we shall discuss and illustrate the use of built-in functions in the SELECT clause of the SELECT statement.

COUNT.   The COUNT function calculates the number of elements of the type specified in the argument. As an example, the next statement calculates the number of rows in the APPLIANCES relation.

```
SELECT COUNT(*)
FROM APPLIANCES
```

If we wish to know the number of different types of appliances, we must write DISTINCT before the column name.

```
SELECT COUNT(DISTINCT TYPE)
FROM APPLIANCES
```

Whereas the answer to the first query is 8 (8 rows in the APPLIANCES table), the answer to the second query is 5, since there are only 5 distinct types of appliances.

WHERE clauses can be used in queries with built-in functions. For example, to count how many people have base salaries over $1500, we would write the following statement.

```
SELECT COUNT(*) FROM SALESPEOPLE
WHERE BASESALARY > 1500
```

Result: 2

SUM.   The SUM function calculates the total value of a given column or expression in the rows satisfying the WHERE clause. To count sales of inventory id 100 refrigerators, we would use:

```
SELECT SUM(QTY) FROM SALES
WHERE INVID = 100
```

Result: 4

If we want to know the total annual base salary paid to salespeople, we use an expression (BASESALARY * 12) as the argument:

```
SELECT SUM(BASESALARY * 12)
FROM SALESPEOPLE
```

Result: 70200

AVG, MAX, MIN.   The AVG function computes the average value of its argument over the rows selected. The MAX function computes the maximum value; the MIN function computes the minimum value.

```
SELECT AVG(BASESALARY), MAX(COMMRATE), MIN(NAME)
FROM SALESPEOPLE
```

Result: 1462.50, 18%, Anne

This example illustrates that multiple built-in functions can be used in a single SELECT statement, that they can apply to different attributes, and that MIN and MAX apply both to numeric and to string fields. In our example, MIN(NAME) is Anne because *Anne* is the first (or smallest) in an alphabetical listing of salespeople names.

SUBQUERIES

Consider the following query:

QUERY: List names and commission rates of salespeople who have sold televisions.

This query requires information from three tables: SALESPEOPLE, SALES, and APPLIANCES. It can be solved by using a join query on those three tables. However, there is another approach that may be easier to understand. Conceptually, we divide the query into two steps as follows.

1. Identify the salespeople who have sold televisions. This requires the use of the tables SALES and APPLIANCES.
2. Obtain the commission rates of these salespeople from the SALESPEOPLE table.

Step 1 can be handled by the following query.

```
SELECT SPNAME FROM SALES, APPLIANCES
WHERE INVID = INVENTORYID
      AND TYPE = 'Television'
```

Result: **SPNAME**

　　　　Anne
　　　　Linda
　　　　Charles

We use the above query as a subquery to perform step 2.

```
SELECT NAME, COMMRATE FROM SALESPEOPLE
WHERE NAME IN (SELECT SPNAME
               FROM SALES, APPLIANCES
               WHERE INVID = INVENTORYID
                 AND TYPE = 'Television')
```

The subquery creates the set of salespeople who have sold televisions. This set is then used with the IN operator of the WHERE clause of the main query. A row from SALESPEOPLE is selected if the *Name* attribute in that row is in the set created by the subquery.

What is a subquery? A subquery is a query nested within the WHERE clause of a query. A subquery can in turn have another subquery nested within its WHERE clause. We shall refer to the topmost (unnested) query as the *main* query.

The query of our last example illustrates the concept of a subquery using the IN operator. The IN operator was necessary because the subquery produced a set of elements for comparison. If the subquery is to produce only a single value, as in the next example, then any of the numerical comparison operators ($<$, $>$, $<=$, $>=$, $=$, $\neg=$, $\neg<$, $\neg>$) can be used.

QUERY: List salespeople who have a commission rate higher than Anne's rate.

```
SELECT NAME FROM SALESPEOPLE
WHERE COMMRATE >    (SELECT COMMRATE
                     FROM SALESPEOPLE
                     WHERE NAME = 'Anne')
```

Since *Name* is the key of SALESPEOPLE we can be sure that the subquery will produce only one element. Therefore, it is appropriate for the WHERE clause of the main query to compare a single element using ">" with the result of the subquery.

Comparison using a subquery is perhaps more powerful when built-in functions are used. Consider the query: "List all washers whose price is above the average for washers."

```
SELECT * FROM APPLIANCES
WHERE TYPE = 'Washer'
    AND PRICE > (SELECT AVG(PRICE)
                FROM APPLIANCES
                WHERE TYPE = 'Washer')
```

The subquery in this example produces a single number—the average price for washers. This number is then used for comparison in the WHERE clause of the main query.

Correlated Subqueries.   The subqueries we have seen so far generate a single set or element which is plugged-in to the main query. In these examples, the subquery produces the same result regardless of which row is being examined by the main query. For example, in the preceding query the subquery calculated the average price for washers, and this number was used by the main query in examining every row of the APPLIANCES relation. A (washer) row whose price was above this average was selected, and all other rows were not selected. Regardless of the washer row being examined, the average price for washers remained constant.

Suppose, however, that we have a query with the property that the subquery produces a different result for every row of the main query. Consider this query:

QUERY: List appliances whose price is above average for appliances of their type.

We can paraphrase this query as: "Select a row from the APPLIANCES table if its price is above the average price for all appliances having the same type as this row." This query can be expressed in SQL as follows:

```
SELECT A.* FROM APPLIANCES A
WHERE A.PRICE >    (SELECT AVG(PRICE)
                FROM APPLIANCES B
                WHERE B.TYPE = A.TYPE)
```

Note first of all that APPLIANCES is given the alias A in the main query and the alias B in the subquery. Note also that the subquery contains a reference (A.TYPE) to the alias A. Conceptually, we may consider the query as being carried out in the following manner: The main query causes each row in APPLIANCES to be examined separately. The row currently being examined by the main query is called "A". For each value of A, the subquery is executed, producing an average price for all appliances having the same type as A. Thus, if A.TYPE = 'Refrigerator', then the subquery produces the average price for refrigerators. The row A is selected if its price is above the average price calculated by the subquery. The main query then moves on to the next row and A assumes the value of this row. If A.TYPE = 'Microwave Oven', then the subquery calculates the average price for microwave ovens.

This subquery is *correlated* because its value depends on, or is correlated with, the value of the row being examined by the main query. Another way of saying this is that the value of the subquery is a function of the row being examined by the main query.

Let's look at more examples of correlated subqueries.

QUERY: List appliances sold by more than one salesperson.

```
SELECT A.INVID FROM SALES A
WHERE 1 < (SELECT COUNT(DISTINCT B.SPNAME)
           FROM SALES B
           WHERE B.INVID = A.INVID)
```

QUERY: List appliance types having the property that at least 10 appliances of that type have been sold.

```
SELECT A.TYPE FROM APPLIANCES A
WHERE 10 <= (SELECT SUM(QTY)
           FROM SALES
           WHERE INVID IN
               (SELECT B.INVENTORYID
               FROM APPLIANCES B
               WHERE B.TYPE = A.TYPE))
```

In this example we have a subquery nested in a subquery, and the innermost subquery refers to the row being examined by the main query. The innermost subquery identifies the set of Inventory ID's having the same Type as row A. The subquery on the level above then calculates the total quantity sold of all of these Inventory ID's. Row A is selected by the main query if the total quantity sold is 10 or larger. (In our sample database, none of the types would be selected by this query.)

The EXISTS Operator.   SQL provides an EXISTS operator which corresponds to the existential quantifier of relational calculus. We illustrate its usage with the first subquery that we demonstrated.

QUERY: List names and commission rates of salespeople who have sold televisions.

```
SELECT NAME, COMMRATE FROM SALESPEOPLE A
WHERE EXISTS (SELECT SPNAME
               FROM SALES B, APPLIANCES C
               WHERE A.NAME = B.SPNAME
               AND B.INVID = C.INVENTORYID
               AND C.TYPE = 'Television')
```

EXISTS is an operator which returns "true" if the relation resulting from the subquery on which it is operating is not empty. If the result of the subquery is empty, EXISTS returns false. Thus, in this example a row is selected from SALESPEOPLE by the main query if EXISTS returns a true value, or in other words if the result of the subquery is not empty. Note that the subquery is a correlated subquery, so that its value depends on the value of row A.

Result:

NAME	COMMRATE
Anne	12%
Linda	15%
Charles	10%

The principal usage of the EXISTS operator, however, is in its negated form (NOT EXISTS). In the negated form, EXISTS fills the role of the universal quantifier. In the section on quantifiers in Chapter 3 we saw two equivalent formulations of a query—one using the universal quantifier and the other using the negation of the existential quantifier. In this discussion of SQL, we use the negation of EXISTS in solving queries which would require the universal quantifier in relational calculus.

QUERY: List appliance types for which there is only one inventory ID.

```
SELECT TYPE FROM APPLIANCES A
WHERE NOT EXISTS
     (SELECT * FROM APPLIANCES B
     WHERE B.TYPE = A.TYPE
        AND B.INVENTORYID ¬= A.INVENTORYID)
```

Result:

TYPE
Television
Microwave Oven

This query can be translated as "Select the type from row A if there does not exist another row having the same type." The need for the universal quantifier is not obvious in this query. In fact, either the universal or the existential quantifier would seem to serve equally well. However, there are many problems for which the universal quantifier would seem to be the obvious choice, such as the next example.

QUERY: List appliance types supplied by every vendor.

```
SELECT TYPE FROM APPLIANCES A
WHERE NOT EXISTS
(SELECT * FROM VENDORS B
 WHERE NOT EXISTS
     (SELECT * FROM APPLIANCES C
      WHERE C.VENDOR = B.VENDOR
          AND C.TYPE = A.TYPE))
```

This can be literally translated as "Select the Type from row A if there is no Vendor B for which there is not an appliance row C having Vendor B as its vendor and Type A as its type." A simpler translation would be "Select an appliance type if there is no vendor who does not supply an appliance of that type." In the example database, no appliances qualify under these criteria.

The query is difficult to understand because it uses a double negative (that is, two nested NOT EXISTS operators). Despite this difficulty, the EXISTS operator is useful in solving a number of queries which cannot be handled with any other available facility.

The GROUP BY Clause

We showed earlier that the built-in functions can operate on entire relations or on subsets of relations determined by WHERE conditions. In addition, SQL provides a facility for splitting a relation into groups, and then allowing the built-in functions to operate on each of the groups. For example, suppose we are interested in knowing the average price of each appliance type. We state our query as follows:

```
SELECT TYPE, AVG(PRICE) FROM APPLIANCES
GROUP BY TYPE
```

In this query the GROUP BY clause says to divide the APPLIANCES relation into groups according to *Type*. SQL will then logically group the rows of APPLIANCES so that all rows having the same value for *Type* will be grouped together. The SELECT clause tells SQL to calculate the average price for each type and to display the result of this calculation together with the type.

Result:

TYPE	
Refrigerator	275.00
Television	340.00
Microwave Oven	180.00
Washer	362.50
Dryer	290.00

We can restrict the rows before placing them in groups by using the WHERE clause. Suppose we are interested only in rows having a price over $250:

```
SELECT TYPE, AVG(PRICE) FROM APPLIANCES
WHERE PRICE > 250
GROUP BY TYPE
```

It is important to note that the WHERE clause is executed before the GROUP BY clause. That is, the rows are selected based on the WHERE condition, and then they are divided into groups and the average price is calculated.

Result: **TYPE**

Refrigerator	300.00
Television	340.00
Washer	362.50
Dryer	360.00

After the groups have been formed we may want to restrict consideration to groups which satisfy certain conditions. For example, suppose we only want to consider groups that contain more than one row:

```
SELECT TYPE, AVG(PRICE) FROM APPLIANCES
WHERE PRICE > 250
GROUP BY TYPE HAVING COUNT(*) > 1
```

The HAVING clause is used to place conditions on groups. It applies only to groups, whereas the WHERE clause applies only to rows. When this query is executed, the rows are selected first using the WHERE clause criterion. Next, the groups are formed by type, and the groups having more than one row are selected. Finally, the average price of each remaining group is calculated, and the type and average price for each type are displayed.

Result: **TYPE**

Washer	362.50

The following query references more than one relation in the FROM clause, although rows from only one relation are grouped.

QUERY: List salespeople together with their average commission on sales, excluding sales of refrigerators.

```
SELECT SPNAME, AVG(COMMRATE * QTY * PRICE)
FROM SALESPEOPLE, SALES, APPLIANCES
WHERE TYPE ¬= 'Refrigerator'
     AND NAME = SPNAME
     AND INVID = INVENTORYID
GROUP BY SPNAME
```

Result:

NAME	AVERAGE COMMISSION
Linda	51.25
Anne	42.00
Charles	59.33
Hank	79.20

Before closing this section, it is important to note the following additional points:

1. More than one attribute can be listed in a GROUP BY clause. Groups are formed of rows having identical values for *all* of the attributes listed.
2. If GROUP BY is used, the SELECT clause should contain *all and only those* attributes listed in the GROUP BY clause. If an attribute not listed in the GROUP BY clause appears in the SELECT clause, what value would it have? The system has no way of determining which one of the many possible values of that attribute should be listed.
3. Multiple built-in functions may appear in the SELECT clause.

UNION

Although SQL is based for the most part on relational calculus, it does include the UNION operator from relational algebra. In this sense it is a hybrid language. Certainly, however, the SELECT statement is far more powerful in its application than is the UNION operator, so we may think of SQL as being primarily a calculus-based language.

The following is an example of the application of UNION to combine data from two different relations.

QUERY: List the inventory ID's of all washers and of all appliances sold by Linda.

```
SELECT INVID FROM SALES
WHERE SPNAME = 'Linda'
UNION
SELECT INVENTORYID FROM APPLIANCES
WHERE TYPE = 'Washer'
```

DATABASE MODIFICATION: INSERT, UPDATE, AND DELETE

Changes to the database can be effected through the INSERT, UPDATE, and DELETE statements, which are described in this section.

INSERT

The INSERT statement is used to add rows to an existing table. This may or may not be a table with data already in it. After a table is created, it exists but has no data in it. The INSERT statement has two formats:

GENERAL SYNTAX

```
INSERT INTO table-name
              [(list of column names)]
      VALUES  (list of values)
```

```
INSERT INTO table-name
              [(list of column names)]
      SELECT column name(s)
      FROM table-name(s)
      [WHERE conditions]
      etc.
```

Several notational conventions are used in the formats above. Words in uppercase are to be typed precisely as shown. Words in lowercase are variables for which actual table names, column names, and conditions are to be substituted. Items in brackets ([. . .]) are optional.

Following are two examples using the first format:

```
INSERT INTO VENDORS
        (VENDOR, CITY, STATE)
    VALUES   (25, Athens, Georgia)
```

```
INSERT INTO VENDORS
    VALUES   (25, Athens, Georgia, NULL)
```

Both of these statements have the same effect. That is, if a column name (*Rating,* in this case) is not specified in the column name list, SQL will automatically set that column to null.

The second format uses the SELECT statement as a subquery and is consequently far more powerful than the first format. Virtually any feature of the SELECT statement can be used. The UNION operator, however, cannot be used. As an example of the application of this format, suppose we desire a table containing the names and statistical sales data for the salespeople. Assuming the table SALSTAT has been created, we insert data into it by:

```
INSERT INTO SALSTAT
        (SPNAME, TOTAL, HIGH, LOW, AVERAGE)
     SELECT SPNAME, SUM(QTY * PRICE), MAX(QTY * PRICE),
               MIN(QTY * PRICE), AVG(QTY * PRICE)
     FROM SALES, APPLIANCES
     WHERE INVID = INVENTORYID
     GROUP BY SPNAME
```

Result:

SPNAME	TOTAL	HIGH	LOW	AVERAGE
Anne	950	360	250	316.67
Hank	990	440	250	330
Charles	2380	1020	360	595
Linda	1505	680	325	501.67

UPDATE

The UPDATE statement is used to change existing data values in specified columns and rows of a table.

GENERAL SYNTAX

```
UPDATE table-name
   SET field-name 1 = expression 1,
       [field-name 2 = expression 2, ...]
[WHERE conditions]
```

Just as in the SELECT statement, the WHERE clause is used to identify rows to be changed. If the WHERE clause is omitted, then all rows in the table are changed. The term *field-name* refers to column or attribute name. The following statement increases the cost of every appliance from vendor 22 by 15%:

```
UPDATE APPLIANCES
   SET COST = 1.15 * COST
WHERE VENDOR = 22
```

DELETE

The DELETE statement is used to remove entire rows from a table.

GENERAL SYNTAX

```
DELETE
   FROM table-name
[WHERE conditions]
```

If the WHERE clause is omitted, all rows will be deleted from the named table. The table will still exist although it will be empty. The following statement removes all of the appliances of vendor 22:

```
DELETE
   FROM APPLIANCES
WHERE VENDOR = 22
```

VIEWS

A database for a large organization may contain many tables consisting of many rows and columns of data—much more data, in fact, than any single user may need to have access to. In order to restrict access to confidential data and to simplify data manipulation by providing users with essential data in a familiar format, relational systems commonly provide facilities for constructing *user views* of data.

Let us clarify this concept with some examples. Suppose Joan has the responsibility of maintaining the SALESPEOPLE table, except for salary and commission information (which is Anne's responsibility). Joan makes address changes, supervisor changes, and adds records to or deletes records from the SALESPEOPLE table. Joan's view of the SALESPEOPLE table should look like this:

Result:	NAME	ADDRESS	SUPV
	Linda	Box 23, Middleton	Anne
	Anne	14 S. Elm	
	Charles	1933 Eisenhower	Anne
	Hank	103 Royal Arms	Anne

But if Joan has access to the SALESPEOPLE table as a whole, then she would have access to confidential financial information. Thus, some means is needed for SQL to restrict access to specified columns of a table.

Marvin is responsible for working with appliances from vendor 22 and *only* from vendor 22. Appliance information from other vendors is not necessarily confidential, but Marvin is not interested in seeing it, since it does not pertain directly to his job. The following is a typical query that Marvin would enter:

```
SELECT * FROM APPLIANCES
WHERE VENDOR = 22
```

Since nearly every query that Marvin types is exclusively concerned with vendor 22, Marvin feels that it is wasteful and tedious to type "WHERE VENDOR = 22" over and over throughout the day. Thus, Marvin needs some means within SQL of automatically selecting only those rows in which he is generally interested.

In Joan's case we are interested in restricting access to certain columns in the table. In Marvin's case we wish to restrict access to certain rows. Other users will be interested in other types of data restrictions and combinations. To satisfy such requirements SQL provides the *view* facility.

The tables in the database which actually contain the data are referred to as *base tables*. For example, in our sample database of Figure 4.1 we have four base tables. User views are called *virtual tables,* which means that they don't actually exist in real storage, but are created and updated dynamically, in response to references by the user. As an illustration, consider the statement used to create Joan's view of the SALESPEOPLE table:

```
CREATE VIEW SPMAINT
    AS SELECT NAME, ADDRESS, SUPV
      FROM SALESPEOPLE
```

This statement defines the view named SPMAINT. It creates a virtual table with three columns of data (NAME, ADDRESS, SUPV) taken from the SALESPEOPLE table. However, at the time the view is defined, no data is actually retrieved. Data retrieval and manipulation take place only when this view is referred to in a SELECT, INSERT, UPDATE, or DELETE statement. For example, if Joan wants to see the current contents of Hank's record she uses a SELECT statement as follows:

```
SELECT * FROM SPMAINT
WHERE NAME = 'Hank'
```

The system uses the original CREATE VIEW statement to identify the base table from which the data is to be retrieved. In this case, the base table is SALESPEOPLE. It then retrieves the record from SALESPEOPLE which contains "Hank" in the *NAME* column, and displays the entire row as defined in the view SPMAINT. In SPMAINT the row is defined as consisting of the columns NAME, ADDRESS, and SUPV.

Result:

NAME	ADDRESS	SUPV
Hank	103 Royal Arms	Anne

For Marvin's benefit we define the following view:

```
CREATE VIEW VEND22APP  (INVID, TYPE, CST, PRC)
    AS SELECT INVENTORYID, TYPE, COST, PRICE
      FROM APPLIANCES
      WHERE VENDOR = 22
```

In this example, we have given new names to some of the columns in the view. The column names are specified in parentheses immediately after the name of the view. In the first example above (SPMAINT), we did not specify names for columns in the view, so they *inherited* the names they had in the base table (Date 1984). In this second example you will note that we have also omitted the vendor column, since every appliance will have the same vendor.

GENERAL SYNTAX

```
CREATE VIEW  view-name
        [list of view column names]
AS SELECT list of column names from base tables or views
    FROM base table or view names
  [WHERE conditions]
  [other SELECT statement clauses]
    [WITH CHECK OPTION]
```

We note these points:

1. A view is a relation defined by the subquery (the SELECT statement) in the CREATE VIEW statement.

2. A view may be defined in terms of one or more base tables, one or more other views, or combinations of base tables and views.

3. The view definition may not include the UNION operator.

4. With exceptions to be noted below, views defined by the CREATE VIEW statement may be referenced in SELECT, INSERT, UPDATE, or DELETE statements.

The WITH CHECK OPTION clause requires some explanation. Consider the following view:

```
CREATE VIEW COSTLYAPP
AS SELECT * FROM APPLIANCES
    WHERE COST > 200
```

This view contains all columns in the APPLIANCES relation, but only those rows whose cost exceeds $200. Suppose we added a row to COST-LYAPP by using the INSERT statement:

```
INSERT INTO COSTLYAPP
        (INVENTORYID, TYPE, VENDOR, COST, PRICE)
    VALUES (500, Mixer, 27, 35.00, 60.00)
```

The cost of the appliance being added to COSTLYAPP in this example is $35. But $35 is less than the cost required for an appliance to be in COSTLYAPP. Consequently, if we added this appliance to COSTLYAPP we would not be able to retrieve it again with a SELECT statement. It would disappear.

The WITH CHECK OPTION clause prohibits this from happening. When WITH CHECK OPTION is specified in the CREATE VIEW statement, then changes or additions to data in the view are not allowed if such changes would result in the data no longer satisfying the conditions required by the view. In essence, WITH CHECK OPTION specifies that the conditions of the WHERE clause are to be used as validation criteria for INSERT and UPDATE operations.

Examples

1. Create a view giving the average cost of appliances from each vendor.

```
CREATE VIEW VENDAVG (VENDOR, AVGCOST)
    AS SELECT VENDOR, AVG(COST)
        FROM APPLIANCES
      GROUP BY VENDOR
```

2. Create a view giving names of salespeople getting more than 10% commission, together with the types of appliances they have sold.

```
CREATE VIEW SPAPPS (SPERSON, APPTYPE)
    AS SELECT DISTINCT NAME, TYPE
        FROM SALESPEOPLE, SALES, APPLIANCES
      WHERE NAME = SPNAME
      AND INVID = INVENTORYID
      AND COMMRATE > 10%
```

As stated earlier, the CREATE VIEW statement merely defines a virtual table. No data is retrieved until data manipulation takes place. Using the above example:

```
SELECT *
FROM SPAPPS
```

Result:

SPERSON	APPTYPE
Anne	Television
Hank	Refrigerator
Anne	Refrigerator
Linda	Television
Linda	Refrigerator
Linda	Washer
Anne	Dryer
Hank	Dryer

Restrictions on View Updates

Since views do not actually contain data, any updates to views must in actuality be updates to their underlying base tables. Consider now Example 1 above which gave a view of the average appliance cost by vendor. Suppose we were to attempt the following update:

```
UPDATE VENDAVG
    SET AVGCOST = 195.00
WHERE VENDOR = 27
```

Since the average cost is calculated from the values of Cost in the base table APPLIANCES, this update would only make sense if we could appropriately update the *Cost* field for each of the individual rows where Vendor = 27. But the update statement contains no information as to how these individual rows are to be updated. Nor could it. The problem lies in the fact that the VENDAVG view contains summary information, and the detail information from which the summary was derived is not available in the VENDAVG view. The only possible way to change the average cost is by accessing the APPLIANCES table directly.

This example illustrates why updates to certain types of views are prohibited. Date (1984) lists several types of views on which updating is not allowed. The major categories of such views are: (1) views which contain multiple tables in the FROM clause, (2) views which use built-in functions, (3) views which use GROUP BY, (4) views which use DISTINCT, and (5) views containing calculated fields.

In some cases, certain retrieval operations may also be prohibited. For more information see Date (1984).

EMBEDDED SQL

Throughout this chapter we have assumed an environment in which queries are developed interactively and executed on-line. It is important to note, however, that SQL can also be used in a batch environment. The relational languages developed by Codd were proposed as sublanguages to form the data manipulation portion of larger languages. Languages such as SQL and QUEL can be embedded as data sublanguages in 3GLs such as COBOL. Commands to accomplish this, in combination with the standard SQL commands, form *embedded* SQL.

The primary problem with embedding relational languages in 3GLs is that 3GLs work with data one record at a time, while relational languages utilize multi-record operations. How can these two characteristics be reconciled?

Suppose we wish to send form letters to all vendors with a rating exceeding 8. We use a relational selection capability to identify such vendor records; then we use a 3GL to generate the form letter, inserting data from each vendor record at appropriate places in the letter. This can be accomplished as follows:

■ An SQL statement is used to identify the vendors.

```
SELECT * FROM VENDORS
WHERE RATING > 8
```

This statement identifies a set of records, or what would normally be a file in, say, COBOL. An embedded SQL statement would give a name to this file. We then would use this file in a COBOL program as if it were a normal COBOL file, except that we would use different statements to open, read, detect end-of-file, etc.

■ The program we write to do the above would be a hybrid COBOL-SQL program. As an example, in the IBM environment it would be compiled in two steps (Date 1984). First, the program would be processed by a pre-compiler program which would identify the SQL statements and replace them with CALLs to subroutines. Then the revised program would be compiled as a normal COBOL program.

A weakness of embedded SQL as a data sublanguage is that we continue to be restricted by the basic weaknesses of 3GLs. However, considering the widespread usage of COBOL, as well as the large number of people with COBOL training and experience, the embedded SQL approach is probably the wisest for making the ultimate transition to full-fledged 4GLs. Since 3GLs will continue to have a distinct advantage in processing efficiency for some time to come, it seems likely that embedded relational languages will be of continuing importance in business processing systems.

EXERCISES

For all exercises, write SQL statements which will produce the required result. For the following exercises use the appliance database whose structure is as follows:

APPLIANCE DATABASE

APPLIANCES (Inventory id, Type, Vendor, Cost, Price)
VENDORS (Vendor, City, State, Rating)
SALESPEOPLE (Name, Address, Comm_rate, Base_salary, Supv)
SALES (Date, Sp_name, Inv_id, Qty)

Although this is the database used in the text of the chapter, many of the queries refer to information not shown in the sample data of Figure 4.1.

4.1. Create statements to answer these simple queries:
   a. List all the supervisors.
   b. List supervisors with duplicates eliminated.
   c. List everything about Richard's sales.
   d. List salespeople with a commission rate between 10% and 18%, inclusive.
   e. Identify vendors located in states whose names begin with the letter N.
   f. Who are the salespeople for whom the database has no address?
   g. List the inventory_id and profit (price − cost) on mixers from vendor 77.
   h. List vendors in Indiana in ascending order by rating.

4.2.   Write statements to create results for the multiple table queries below.
   a. List the inventory_id, the vendor, and the vendor's city and state for all appliances in the database.
   b. Create the following queries for the salesperson named Sam:
      (1). List Sam's sales, together with his commission rate on each sale.
      (2). Include the price of each item on the list of Sam's sales.
      (3). Include the commission on each item on the list of Sam's sales.
      (4). What is the profit (price − cost − commission) on each of Sam's sales?
   c. List salespeople having a base salary higher than their supervisor.

4.3.   Use built-in functions and GROUP BY clauses to answer the queries below.
   a. What is the total base salary being paid each month?
   b. What is the average profit margin (price − cost) of appliances?
   c. How may different states are the vendors located in?
   d. What is the highest price for a television? What is the lowest price?

4.4.   Use subqueries in statements to solve the following queries.
   a. List names and ratings of vendors who sell toasters.
   b. List appliances having a cost under the average cost of appliances from vendor 86.
   c. List inventory id's for which the total quantity sold is greater than 20.
   d. Who supervises the salesperson with the highest base salary?

4.5.   Write statements using EXISTS to obtain the following lists.
   a. List inventory id's sold by every salesperson.
   b. List appliance types supplied by every vendor in Vermont.

4.6.   Using UNION, list vendors located in Kansas or who supply dishwashers.

4.7.   Use INSERT, UPDATE, and DELETE as needed to accomplish the following tasks.
   a. Assume a table exists named VENDAVG, which contains the columns: Vendor, Type, Average_Cost, Average_Price. The last two columns are the average cost and average price of appliances supplied by the vendor of the designated type. Write an INSERT statement which places rows in VENDAVG containing average costs and prices of refrigerators for each vendor.
   b. Increase the base salary of all salespeople reporting to Anne by 10%.
   c. Remove all sales from the SALES table which occurred in October.

4.8.   Create a view of inventory id's, types, and prices of appliances whose price is under $1000.

Use the following database for the next group of exercises. This database gives information about independent insurance agents who place insurance policies with a variety of different companies. These exercises were given in Chapter 3. Compare the SQL solutions with the relational calculus and algebra solutions.

POLICY DATABASE

POLICY (<u>Policy No</u>, Insured, Agent No, Company No, Amount, Premium)
AGENT (<u>Agent No</u>, Agent Name, State)
COMPANY (<u>Company No</u>, Company Name, Commission Rate, Revenue)

4.9.   Create statements to answer the following queries.
   a. List companies with revenue exceeding $100 million who offer a commission rate of less than 15%.
   b. List policies written by agents in Illinois.
   c. List companies having policies with amounts between $50,000 and $100,000.
   d. List agents getting a commission rate exceeding 20% on any of their policies.
   e. List the companies that Sam Stone writes policies for.
   f. List agents who have written policies for every company.
   g. List companies which do business with all agents in Iowa.
   h. Find the maximum policy amount written by an agent in Georgia.

CHAPTER 5

QUEL

QUEL (QUEry Language) is the interactive query language of the INGRES relational database management system. INGRES (INteractive Graphics and REtrieval System) was originally developed as a teaching and research system at the University of California, Berkeley (Schmidt and Brodie 1983). In 1980, Relational Technology, Inc. was formed to market INGRES, and to develop and market related products.

QUEL is based on the relational calculus, and is a more faithful implementation of the calculus than SQL. Because of the power of QUEL as a relational language, other companies are offering data manipulation products that utilize an approach similar to QUEL's (Date 1986).

The four basic data manipulation statements of QUEL are: RETRIEVE (for queries), APPEND (for adding data to a relation), REPLACE (for changing the value of existing data), and DELETE (for removing data). The RETRIEVE statement is the most general of these and will be our primary focus initially. As with SQL we shall discuss the database update statements after discussing the RETRIEVE statement. Throughout this chapter we shall refer for our examples to the database shown in Figure 5.1 (which is a copy of the database we used in Chapter 4). For additional information on the concepts of this chapter, refer to the bibliography (Relational Technology 1982).

SIMPLE QUERIES

As in Chapter 4, we will introduce a number of concepts using simple queries before proceeding to more complex queries.

APPLIANCE DATABASE

APPLIANCES (A)
INVENTORY

ID	TYPE	VENDOR	COST	PRICE
100	Refrigerator	22	150.00	250.00
150	Television	27	225.00	340.00
110	Refrigerator	20	175.00	300.00
200	Microwave Oven	22	120.00	180.00
300	Washer	27	200.00	325.00
310	Washer	22	280.00	400.00
400	Dryer	20	150.00	220.00
420	Dryer	22	240.00	360.00

VENDORS (V)

VENDOR	CITY	STATE	RATING
22	Orem	Utah	8
20	Davis	Calif	6
27	Urbana	Illinois	9

SALESPEOPLE (SPL)

NAME	ADDRESS	COMM RATE	BASE SALARY	SUPV
Linda	Box 23, Middleton	15%	1200	Anne
Anne	14 S. Elm	12%	1800	
Charles	1933 Eisenhower	10%	1150	Anne
Hank	103 Royal Arms	18%	1700	Anne

SALES (SLS)

DATE	SPNAME	INVID	QTY
10/01	Anne	150	1
10/05	Hank	110	1
10/03	Charles	110	2
10/13	Anne	100	1
10/25	Linda	150	2
10/22	Linda	100	2
10/12	Charles	150	3
10/14	Hank	100	1
10/15	Linda	300	1
10/03	Charles	200	2
10/31	Charles	310	1
10/05	Anne	420	1
10/15	Hank	400	2

FIGURE 5.1   Appliance Database

The RANGE Statement

In order to identify the tables from which data is retrieved, QUEL requires the use of row variables (as in relational calculus) to qualify column names. Row variables may be explicitly declared via RANGE statements; or they may be relation names, which are automatically row variables by default. In our examples, APPLIANCES, VENDORS, SALESPEOPLE, and SALES are default row variables. In addition, we can declare other row variables by using the RANGE statement:

```
RANGE OF A IS APPLIANCES
RANGE OF V IS VENDORS
RANGE OF SPL IS SALESPEOPLE
RANGE OF SLS IS SALES
```

In the examples which follow, we assume these four row variable declarations (which are also noted in Figure 5.1). From our examples, you will deduce that the general syntax of the RANGE statement is:

GENERAL SYNTAX

```
RANGE OF range-variable IS table-name
```

The RETRIEVE Statement

The simplest form of a QUEL RETRIEVE statement is as follows:

GENERAL SYNTAX

```
RETRIEVE (target-list)
```

Here *target-list* designates a sequence of data items separated by commas; each item in the sequence may have one of the three formats:

range-variable.column-name

range-variable.all

result-column-name = expression

We shall discuss the last of these formats later when we present *expressions*. The second format is shorthand for typing all of the column names in the table. Thus, A.ALL (where A is a previously declared range variable for the APPLIANCES table) is shorthand for:

```
(A.INVENTORYID, A.TYPE, A.VENDOR, A.COST, A.PRICE)
```

An example of the first format (*range-variable.column-name*) is given in the query:

```
RETRIEVE (APPLIANCES.TYPE)
```

Here APPLIANCES is the row variable, and TYPE is the column name. We could have also used A as the row variable. This query will create a new relation from the rows of the APPLIANCES relation. Each row of the new relation will have the single attribute *Type*. This query is equivalent to the SQL query:

```
SELECT TYPE
FROM APPLIANCES
```

Result: **TYPE**

Refrigerator
Television
Refrigerator
Microwave Oven
Washer
Washer
Dryer
Dryer

Note that if the result of a query is intended for display on the terminal screen, QUEL (just as SQL) will not eliminate duplicate rows unless the keyword UNIQUE is inserted:

```
RETRIEVE UNIQUE (APPLIANCES.TYPE)
```

Result: **TYPE**

Refrigerator
Television
Microwave Oven
Washer
Dryer

Suppose, however, that the user's intent is to create a new relation of appliance types. In this case the query can be constructed to send its result to a new relation which, for our example, we shall call TYPES:

```
RETRIEVE INTO TYPES (APPLIANCES.TYPE)
```

This query will cause a new relation TYPES to be created, and its contents are the rows shown in the prior result. Notice that UNIQUE is not required in this case. QUEL always eliminates duplicate rows from defined relations.

If we desire to see both the Type and Price of all APPLIANCES we can enter the following query (where A has previously been declared as a range variable for the APPLIANCES relation):

```
RETRIEVE (A.TYPE, A.PRICE)
```

If we want to see all available information from the APPLIANCES relation we enter:

```
RETRIEVE (A.ALL)
```

A.ALL means *the entire row*. This query will give us the entire APPLIANCES table as shown in Figure 5.1.

The following query will create the relational algebra product of the APPLIANCES and VENDORS relations. That is, the result of this query will be a new relation consisting of every possible combination of a row from APPLIANCES placed next to a row from VENDORS.

```
RETRIEVE (A.ALL, V.ALL)
```

The WHERE Clause

The next two queries introduce the WHERE clause:

```
RETRIEVE (A.ALL)
WHERE A.TYPE = 'Television'
```

Result:

INVENTORY ID	TYPE	VENDOR	COST	PRICE
150	Television	27	225.00	340.00

```
RETRIEVE (A.ALL)
WHERE A.PRICE > 250
```

Result:

INVENTORY ID	TYPE	VENDOR	COST	PRICE
150	Television	27	225.00	340.00
110	Refrigerator	20	175.00	300.00
300	Washer	27	200.00	325.00
310	Washer	22	280.00	400.00
420	Dryer	22	240.00	360.00

We combine a selection with a projection by listing only the attributes desired in the resulting relation. Note that the WHERE condition in this query references an attribute (Vendor) which is not in the final relation.

```
RETRIEVE (A.TYPE, A.PRICE)
WHERE A.VENDOR = 20
```

Result:

TYPE	PRICE
Refrigerator	300.00
Dryer	220.00

In the queries given so far, the similarities between QUEL and SQL are obvious. RETRIEVE corresponds to SELECT; the range variables correspond to the FROM clause; and both languages have a WHERE clause. As with SQL, much of the power of QUEL lies in the wide variety of conditions that can be specified using the WHERE clause. We will use many of the same examples to illustrate QUEL that we used in illustrating SQL. Also, we shall follow a similar organization of our material in that we shall first study single relation queries, and then we shall study multiple relation queries. We shall compare and contrast the two languages frequently. In some cases we shall slightly alter QUEL syntax to make it uniform with SQL syntax in order to ease your burden of learning new concepts.

QUEL supports the standard six relational operators ($=$, $\neg=$, $<$, $<=$, $>$, $>=$) in the WHERE clause. In addition, it allows wildcard characters in comparisons involving strings. The wildcard characters supported are listed in Figure 5.2. The next few examples illustrate their application.

*	any number of characters (including no characters)
?	any single character
[ ]	any of the characters in the brackets

FIGURE 5.2   Wildcard Characters

QUERY: Select all salespeople with Middleton in their address.

```
RETRIEVE (SPL.ALL)
WHERE SPL.ADDRESS = "*Middleton*"
```

QUERY: Select vendors located in cities with 4 letters in their names, the first two of which are "Or".

```
RETRIEVE (V.ALL)
WHERE V.CITY = "Or??"
```

QUERY: Select vendors located in cities with at least 3 letters in their names, the first of which is "C," "D," or "O."

```
RETRIEVE (V.ALL)
WHERE V.CITY = "[CDO]??*"
```

QUERY: Select vendors located in cities in the first half of the alphabet. (This example illustrates a range feature used within the brack-·ets. "A-M" means "any of the letters between A and M, inclusive".)

```
RETRIEVE (V.ALL)
WHERE V.CITY = "[A-M]*"
```

Null Values.   QUEL does not support null values as such. Whenever a row is added to the table with no values entered for some fields, QUEL places a zero or blanks in the field depending on whether the field is numeric or character. To select rows based on the condition that a given field is null, the user must enter *field = 0* or *field = " "*, depending on whether the field is a numeric or a character field.

Boolean Operators.   Frequently, it is desirable to use more than one selection condition in a single query. Conditions may be combined through the use of the Boolean operators *AND* and *OR*. The operator *NOT* is used to negate the truth value of a condition. These operators have their standard meanings in QUEL. It is advisable to use parentheses to eliminate ambiguity when multiple conditions are used, for instance:

```
RETRIEVE (A.ALL)
WHERE (A.VENDOR > 20 OR A.COST < 200) AND
     (A.TYPE = "Ref*")
```

Expressions.   QUEL, as SQL, has many functional capabilities which cannot be duplicated in the theoretical languages. One of these is the capability to perform and display the results of calculations on retrieved data. For example, the SALESPEOPLE relation in our sample database contains Base Salary, which is a monthly salary. Suppose we are interested in listing all salespeople together with their *annual* salary. We would multiply Base Salary by 12.

```
RETRIEVE (SPL.NAME, ANNUALSAL = SPL.BASESALARY * 12)
```

Result:

NAME	ANNUALSAL
Linda	14400
Anne	21600
Charles	13800
Hank	20400

Note that the calculated column has the heading ANNUALSAL, which was defined in the target list. At the beginning of this section, when we defined target list, we indicated that a data item in the target list may have the format *result-column-name = expression*. We have deferred discussion of this format until now. The syntax of QUEL provides the capability of giving names to derived expressions. ANNUALSAL of the present example is an instance of such an expression. The above query creates a new relation with two columns. The first column in the new relation inherits the name NAME from the relation SPL. The second column, however, is a calculated expression and therefore has no name to inherit. Consequently, the user specifies a name for this column by entering *ANNUALSAL =* before the calculated expression. If the RETRIEVE statement above had included an

INTO table-name clause, then a new table would have been created, and the result of this query would have been placed in it. The new table would have two columns named NAME and ANNUALSAL.

In the RETRIEVE clause shown above, *SPL.BASESALARY * 12* is an *expression*. In general, an expression is any result calculated from data elements and constants, which uses the arithmetic operators $+$, $-$, $*$, $/$, or $**$ (exponentiation). A constant or a column name without an arithmetic operator is also an expression. Parentheses may also be used in expressions. The $+$ may also be used to concatenate character strings. For example, we may want to modify the above query so that the output is more descriptive:

```
RETRIEVE (DESCR = SPL.NAME + " has an annual salary of ",
          ANNUALSAL = SPL.BASESALARY * 12)
```

Result:	DESCR	ANNUALSAL
	Linda has an annual salary of	14400
	Anne has an annual salary of	21600
	Charles has an annual salary of	13800
	Hank has an annual salary of	20400

Expressions may also be used in WHERE clauses. For example, we may want to restrict the preceding query by specifying:

```
RETRIEVE (DESCR = SPL.NAME + " has an annual salary of ",
          ANNUALSAL = SPL.BASESALARY * 12)
WHERE SPL.BASESALARY * 12 > 10000
```

Aggregate operators and functions (to be discussed below) may also be used in expressions.

The SORT BY Clause

SQL orders the retrieved rows of relations through the ORDER BY clause. QUEL uses the SORT BY clause. Suppose that we want the result of the query above to be printed in alphabetical order by salesperson's name:

```
RETRIEVE (DESCR = SPL.NAME + " has an annual salary of ",
          ANNUALSAL = SPL.BASESALARY * 12)
SORT BY DESCR
```

Result:	DESCR	ANNUALSAL
	Anne has an annual salary of	21600
	Charles has an annual salary of	13800
	Hank has an annual salary of	20400
	Linda has an annual salary of	14400

Note that the sort column is specified by using the *result name*. The system placed the rows in *ascending* order by value of the DESCR field. Incidentally, if the result of a query is sorted, then duplicate rows are deleted, even if UNIQUE is not specified.

We may order the report by any column in the RETRIEVE clause, and we may choose the order to be ascending (the default) or descending (:D). Suppose we want to order the report by annual salary with the highest salary first. Since we have chosen a descending sort order, we must specify ":D" immediately after the column name on which we desire to sort:

```
RETRIEVE (DESCR = SPL.NAME + " has an annual salary of ",
          ANNUALSAL = SPL.BASESALARY * 12)
SORT BY ANNUALSAL:D
```

Result:

DESCR	ANNUALSAL
Anne has an annual salary of	21600
Hank has an annual salary of	20400
Linda has an annual salary of	14400
Charles has an annual salary of	13800

We may order the report on multiple columns. If we desire to order the example alphabetically by DESCR within descending order of annual salary, we enter:

```
RETRIEVE (DESCR = SPL.NAME + " has an annual salary of ",
          ANNUALSAL = SPL.BASESALARY * 12)
SORT BY ANNUALSAL:D, DESCR
```

General Syntax of RETRIEVE Statement

We summarize the information discussed so far by giving the general syntax of the RETRIEVE statement:

GENERAL SYNTAX

```
RETRIEVE [[INTO] result-name]|
[UNIQUE] (target-list) [WHERE conditions]
[SORT [BY]] column-name1 [:sort-order]
     {, column-name-n [:sort-order]}]
```

The notational conventions for this general syntax statement are as follows.

1. Items in uppercase (e.g., RETRIEVE) are to be entered exactly as they stand. Items in lowercase represent names to be determined by the user.
2. Square brackets ([]) indicate optional items.
3. A vertical line (|) indicates a separation of mutually exclusive choices.
4. Braces ({}) indicate multiple items of the type within the braces.

MULTIPLE TABLE QUERIES

The following QUEL and SQL queries are equivalent in that both produce the relational algebra product of the APPLIANCES and VENDOR relations:

QUEL:

```
RETRIEVE (A.ALL, V.ALL)
```

SQL:

```
SELECT APPLIANCES.*, VENDORS.*
FROM APPLIANCES, VENDORS
```

The query below will produce the equijoin in QUEL, which is the natural join with a superfluous vendor column. To obtain the natural join we must project out the superfluous vendor attribute.

```
RETRIEVE (A.ALL, V.ALL)
WHERE A.VENDOR = V.VENDOR
```

To create a projection of the natural join of the APPLIANCES and VENDORS relations, we list specified columns for all appliances and their corresponding vendors:

```
RETRIEVE (A.INVENTORYID, A.TYPE, V.VENDOR, V.STATE)
WHERE A.VENDOR = V.VENDOR
```

Result:

INVENTORYID	TYPE	VENDOR	STATE
100	Refrigerator	22	Utah
150	Television	27	Illinois
110	Refrigerator	20	Calif
200	Microwave Oven	22	Utah
300	Washer	27	Illinois
310	Washer	22	Utah
400	Dryer	20	Calif
420	Dryer	22	Utah

QUERY: Display inventory and vendor information for refrigerators.

```
RETRIEVE (A.INVENTORYID, A.TYPE, V.VENDOR, V.STATE)
WHERE A.VENDOR = V.VENDOR
    AND A.TYPE = 'Refrigerator'
```

Result:

INVENTORYID	TYPE	VENDOR	STATE
100	Refrigerator	22	Utah
110	Refrigerator	20	Calif

Note that we are combining a join query with a selection. As with SQL this is accomplished by merely adding another condition to the WHERE clause.

QUERY: Display information for refrigerators costing over $160.

```
RETRIEVE (A.INVENTORYID, A.TYPE, V.VENDOR, V.STATE)
WHERE A.VENDOR = V.VENDOR
      AND A.TYPE = 'Refrigerator'
      AND A.COST > 160
```

Result:

INVENTORYID	TYPE	VENDOR	STATE
110	Refrigerator	20	Calif

QUERY: List sales of refrigerators with total sale price.

```
RETRIEVE (SLS.INVID, A.TYPE, SLS.QTY,
          TOTPRICE = SLS.QTY * A.PRICE)
WHERE A.TYPE = 'Refrigerator'
      AND A.INVENTORYID = SLS.INVID
```

Result:

INVID	TYPE	QTY	TOTPRICE
110	Refrigerator	1	300.00
110	Refrigerator	2	600.00
100	Refrigerator	1	250.00
100	Refrigerator	2	500.00
100	Refrigerator	1	250.00

QUERY: List sales with profits for Anne's sales of refrigerators.

```
RETRIEVE (SPL.SPNAME, SLS.QTY,
          PROFIT = SLS.QTY * (A.PRICE - A.COST))
WHERE A.TYPE = 'Refrigerator'
      AND A.INVENTORYID = SLS.INVID
      AND SLS.SPNAME = 'Anne'
```

Result:

SMNAME	QTY	PROFIT
Anne	1	100.00

QUERY: List sales and commissions for salespeople whose commission rate is 10% or less (this query is a combination of two joins, a selection, and a projection).

```
RETRIEVE (SPL.NAME, A.TYPE,
         COMMISSION = SPL.COMMRATE * SLS.QTY * A.PRICE)
WHERE SPL.COMMRATE <= 10%
      AND SPL.NAME = SLS.SPNAME
      AND SLS.INVID = A.INVENTORYID
```

Result:

NAME	TYPE	COMMISSION
Charles	Refrigerator	60.00
Charles	Television	102.00
Charles	Microwave Oven	36.00
Charles	Washer	40.00

At times it may be necessary to join a table to itself. Such a join would be impossible without the use of range variables or their equivalent (aliases in SQL). Suppose, for example, that we desire to compare a salesperson's commission rate with that of the supervisor:

```
RANGE OF X IS SALESPEOPLE
RANGE OF Y IS SALESPEOPLE
RETRIEVE (X.NAME, X.COMMRATE, Y.NAME, Y.COMMRATE)
WHERE X.SUPV = Y.NAME
```

Conceptually, this query makes two copies of the SALESPEOPLE relation and joins them. For this query we can think of the Y copy as containing information about the supervisor, while the X copy contains information about the employee.

Aggregate Operators and Functions

The QUEL analogue to the built-in functions and GROUP BY clause of SQL are *aggregate* operators and functions. The aggregate operators correspond to SQL built-in functions, and the aggregate functions correspond to the GROUP BY clause used in combination with built-in functions.

There are nine aggregate operators: COUNT, COUNTU, SUM, SUMU, AVG, AVGU, MAX, MIN, and ANY. These operators are useful in providing values commonly needed in applications.

GENERAL SYNTAX

```
aggregate-operator(expression
      [WHERE conditions])
```

Aggregate-operator is one of the nine operators listed above. The evaluation of an aggregate operator occurs in two steps as illustrated in the next examples:

1. A set of values is built by evaluating *expression* once for each set of values of column-names used in *expression* and satisfying the WHERE clause.
2. The aggregate operator is applied to the set of values built in step 1.

COUNT. The COUNT operator calculates the number of elements of the type specified in the argument (i.e., within the parentheses following the operator). Thus, the following statement calculates the number of rows in the APPLIANCES relation.

```
RETRIEVE (NUMROWS = COUNT(A.TYPE))
```

If we wish to know the number of *different* types of appliances we must use COUNTU (count unique):

```
RETRIEVE (NUMTYPES = COUNTU(A.TYPE))
```

Thus, whereas the answer to the first query is 8 (8 rows in the APPLIANCES table), the answer to the second query is 5, since there are only 5 distinct types of appliances.

QUERY: How many salespeople have a base salary above $1500?

```
RETRIEVE (HISALS = COUNT(SPL.NAME
           WHERE SPL.BASESALARY > 1500))
```

Result: 2

SUM. The SUM operator calculates the total value of an expression in the rows satisfying the WHERE clause.

QUERY: How many refrigerators having inventory id 100 have been sold?

```
RETRIEVE (TOTQTY = SUM(SLS.QTY WHERE SLS.INVID = 100))
```

Result: 4

If we want to know the total annual base salary paid to salespeople, we use a calculated expression (SPL.BASESALARY * 12) as the argument:

```
RETRIEVE (TOTSALS = SUM(SPL.BASESALARY * 12))
```

Result: 70200

AVG, MAX, MIN.   The AVG operator computes the average value of its argument over the rows selected. The MAX operator computes the maximum value; the MIN operator computes the minimum value.

```
RETRIEVE (AVGSAL = AVG(SPL.BASESALARY),
          HIPRICE = MAX(A.PRICE WHERE  A.TYPE = 'Dryer'),
          LOWQTY = MIN(SLS.QTY WHERE
             SLS.SPNAME = 'Anne'))
```

Result: 1462.50, 360.00, 1

This example illustrates that multiple aggregate operators can be used in a single RETRIEVE statement, that they can apply to different attributes in different tables, and that WHERE clauses can be applied individually to the aggregate operators. Note that this cannot be done in SQL because the conditions in the WHERE clause must apply to the entire SELECT statement.

As with SQL the MIN and MAX aggregate operators can apply to character strings. The MIN of a set of character strings is the first string in alphabetical order. The MAX is the last string in alphabetical order.

Aggregate operators can also be used in the WHERE clause of the RETRIEVE statement as the next example illustrates.

QUERY: List salespeople whose base salary is above average.

```
RETRIEVE (SPL.NAME, SPL.BASESALARY)
WHERE SPL.BASESALARY > AVG(SPL.BASESALARY)
```

This query illustrates an important aspect of QUEL syntax. The range variable SPL appears four times in this query. The first three occurrences of SPL refer to a fixed row in the SALESPEOPLE table. However, the meaning of SPL in the AVG aggregate is local to that aggregate. That is, it is not connected to the three previous occurrences of SPL. This can be made more clear by restating the query:

```
RANGE OF S IS SALESPEOPLE
RETRIEVE (SPL.NAME, SPL.BASESALARY)
WHERE SPL.BASESALARY > AVG(S.BASESALARY)
```

This version differs from the previous version in that the range variable in the AVG aggregate is now S instead of SPL. The result, however, is the same in both queries. In general, it is true that range variables within the argument of an aggregate operator are not connected to range variables with the same names outside of the aggregate.

The SUMU and AVGU operators function precisely as the SUM and AVG operators, respectively, except that duplicate values are eliminated before these operators are applied.

Aggregate Functions.   The following SQL query creates a list of appliance types together with the average price for each type.

```
SELECT TYPE, AVG(PRICE)
FROM APPLIANCES
GROUP BY TYPE
```

We accomplish the same thing in QUEL via:

```
RETRIEVE (A.TYPE, AVPRICE = AVG(A.PRICE BY A.TYPE))
```

Result:

TYPE	AVPRICE
Refrigerator	275.00
Television	340.00
Microwave Oven	180.00
Washer	362.50
Dryer	290.00

The last portion of the RETRIEVE statement above contains an *aggregate function*: AVG(A.PRICE BY A.TYPE). An aggregate function may be thought of as an aggregate operator with a "BY clause" (Relational Technology 1982). The column name (or names) following BY identifies the groups (in a manner similar to SQL's GROUP BY) to be acted on by the aggregate operator. In this example we have grouped appliance records by Type.

An aggregate function creates a set of values—one for each value of the variable or variables following BY. In this example, the AVG aggregate function calculates a different average for each value of A.TYPE. This value is equal to the average price for all the records in the APPLIANCES table which have a given value of A.TYPE. For example, the value calculated by the aggregate function for *A.TYPE = "Television"* is the same as the value of the aggregate operator:

```
AVG(A.PRICE WHERE A.TYPE = "Television")
```

The RETRIEVE statement above will cause the various appliance types to be listed, together with their average price. Notice that the variable following BY is *not* local to the aggregate function. That is, A.TYPE has the same meaning inside the AVG function as it does outside. In general, variables following BY in an aggregate function are global.

We can also restrict the rows before placing them in groups by using the WHERE clause. Suppose we are interested only in rows having a price over $250:

```
RETRIEVE (A.TYPE, AVPRICE = AVG(A.PRICE BY A.TYPE WHERE
                                        A.PRICE > 250)
```

Result:

TYPE	AVPRICE
Refrigerator	300.00
Television	340.00
Washer	362.50
Dryer	360.00

After the groups have been formed we may want to restrict consideration to groups which satisfy certain conditions. For example, suppose we want to consider only those groups that contain more than one row:

```
RETRIEVE (A.TYPE, AVPRICE = AVG(A.PRICE BY A.TYPE WHERE
                                        A.PRICE > 250)
WHERE COUNT(A.INVENTORYID BY A.TYPE WHERE A.PRICE > 250) > 1
```

Result:

TYPE	AVPRICE
Washer	362.50

Notice that we actually need three WHERE clauses, two that are used within aggregate functions, and one that applies to the RETRIEVE statement as a whole. SQL, on the other hand, uses a WHERE clause and a HAVING clause. This example illustrates a basic difference in philosophy between the two languages. In this case, QUEL appears to be somewhat more cumbersome. In other cases, however, QUEL appears to have more flexibility than SQL.

The following query references more than one relation, although only rows from one relation are grouped.

QUERY: List salespeople together with their average commission on sales, excluding sales of refrigerators.

```
RETRIEVE (SLS.SPNAME,
            AVCOMM = AVG(SPL.COMMRATE * SLS.QTY * A.PRICE
                BY SLS.SPNAME
                WHERE A.TYPE ¬= 'Refrigerator'
                AND SPL.NAME = SLS.SPNAME
                AND SLS.INVID = A.INVENTORYID))
```

Notice that the lengthy WHERE clause is part of the AVG aggregate function, which is part of the target list. This is done so that the correct average commission for each salesperson will be calculated. Perhaps the easiest way to visualize what is happening is to think of the average calculation as taking place on one giant relation which is the product of the three relations SALESPEOPLE, SALES, and APPLIANCES. The WHERE clause then selects only those rows which apply to the specified salesperson and which are not for refrigerators.

QUERY: Calculate the highest sales dollar volume among all salespeople.

```
RETRIEVE (MAXSALES = MAX(SUM(SLS.QTY * A.PRICE BY SLS.SPNAME
                WHERE SLS.INVID = A.INVENTORYID)))
```

Result: 2380

This query illustrates the nesting of aggregates. The inner aggregate (SUM) causes a column of values to be calculated—one value for each value of SPNAME. The outer aggregate (MAX) then selects the maximum of this column of values.

Examples.   We now give several sample queries using the aggregate operators and aggregate functions. You may note that these examples are taken from those used in the SQL section on subqueries. Although QUEL does not provide the facility of subqueries, these sample queries can be handled using the QUEL facilities already discussed.

QUERY: List washers whose price is above the average for all washers.

```
RETRIEVE (A.ALL)
WHERE A.TYPE = "Washer"
      AND A.PRICE > AVG(A.PRICE  WHERE A.TYPE = "Washer")
```

This example also illustrates the concept of nesting. The query contains a WHERE clause within an aggregate within another WHERE clause. In general QUEL allows such nesting to any level.

QUERY: List appliances whose price is above average for appliances of their type.

```
RANGE OF B IS APPLIANCES
RETRIEVE (A.ALL)
WHERE A.PRICE >
      AVG(B.PRICE  BY A.TYPE WHERE B.TYPE = A.TYPE)
```

We use two range variables (A and B) in the argument of AVG. The A variable communicates with the outside world (that is, A is global)—while B is local to the aggregate. For a particular value of A.TYPE, e.g., A.TYPE = "Television", the RETRIEVE statement would look like this:

```
RETRIEVE (A.ALL)
WHERE A.PRICE >
  AVG(B.PRICE WHERE B.TYPE = A.TYPE AND A.TYPE =
      "Television")
```

QUEL repeats this procedure for each possible value of A.TYPE.

QUERY: List appliances sold by more than one salesperson.

```
RETRIEVE (SLS.INVID)
WHERE  COUNTU(SLS.SPNAME BY SLS.INVID) > 1
```

QUERY: List appliance types having the property that at least 10 appliances of that type have been sold.

```
RETRIEVE (A.TYPE)
WHERE
  SUM(SLS.QTY BY A.TYPE WHERE A.INVENTORYID =
      SLS.INVID) > 10
```

The ANY Function.   QUEL's ANY function works as an existential quantifier and corresponds to the EXISTS operator of SQL. Its syntax is the same as the syntax of the other aggregate functions:

GENERAL SYNTAX

```
ANY(expression BY column-name(s)
    WHERE conditions)
```

However, with the ANY operator the emphasis is on the WHERE clause. ANY evaluates to 1 if there is any combination of rows in the referenced tables which satisfy the WHERE clause. It evaluates to 0 otherwise. We illustrate its usage with the following query:

QUERY: List names and commission rates of salespeople who have sold televisions.

```
RETRIEVE (SPL.NAME, SPL.COMMRATE)
WHERE ANY(SLS.SPNAME BY SPL.NAME
                    WHERE SLS.SPNAME = SPL.NAME
                    AND SLS.INVID = A.INVENTORYID
                    AND A.TYPE = 'Television') = 1
```

A name and commission rate will be retrieved whenever the ANY function evaluates to 1. For example, suppose we are considering whether Linda and her commission rate should be retrieved. Then SPL.NAME = "Linda".

If we set the other variables within the ANY function to values as follows:

```
SLS.SPNAME = "Linda"
SLS.INVID = 150
A.INVENTORYID = 150
```

then there are rows in the database that have the necessary values to satisfy the WHERE clause of the ANY function. In particular, the row in the SALES table:

DATE	SPNAME	INVID	QTY
10/25	Linda	150	2

and the row in the APPLIANCES table:

INVENTORY ID	TYPE	VENDOR	COST	PRICE
150	Television	27	225.00	340.00

provide the necessary values. Thus, ANY evaluates to 1 for this value of
SPL.NAME, and Linda and her commission rate are retrieved.

Of course, this query can be handled in a more straightforward manner
by using a simple join, without the ANY function. The principal usage of
the ANY function comes, as it does with SQL's EXISTS operator, when it
is used as the negation of the existential quantifier. It then fills the role of
the universal quantifier. This is accomplished by setting the ANY function
equal to 0, as our next example illustrates.

QUERY: List appliance types supplied by every vendor.

```
RANGE OF B IS APPLIANCES
RETRIEVE (A.TYPE)
WHERE ANY (V.VENDOR BY A.TYPE
         WHERE ANY(B.INVENTORYID BY V.VENDOR, A.TYPE
             WHERE B.VENDOR = A.VENDOR
             AND B.TYPE = A.TYPE) = 0) = 0
```

This solution is based on a rephrased version of the original query: Select
an appliance type if there is no vendor who does not supply an appliance
of that type. The main part of the query consists of an ANY function nested
within another ANY function. The expression containing the inner ANY
function looks like this:

```
ANY(B.INVENTORYID BY V.VENDOR, A.TYPE
         WHERE B.VENDOR = A.VENDOR
         AND B.TYPE = A.TYPE) = 0
```

This expression asserts that for a given value of V.VENDOR and A.TYPE
there are no rows of B having that Vendor value and that Type value. The
expression containing the outer ANY function asserts that for a given value
of A.TYPE there are no vendors who satisfy the expression containing the
inner ANY function. The combination of these two ANY functions corresponds to the rephrased version of the query.

This query is difficult to understand because it uses a double negative—
i.e., two nested ANY functions. Thus, the fundamental complexity in expressing queries using universal quantifiers exists in QUEL as well as in
the languages we have previously studied. QUEL changes the syntax, but
the problem remains.

DATABASE MODIFICATION: APPEND, REPLACE, AND DELETE

Changes to the database can be effected through the APPEND, RE-PLACE, and DELETE statements, which are described in this section.

APPEND

The APPEND statement is used to add data to an existing table. This may or may not be a table with data already in it. After a table is created, it exists but it has no data in it.

GENERAL SYNTAX

```
APPEND [TO] table-name (target list)
       [WHERE conditions]
```

We give several examples of the APPEND statement:

```
APPEND TO VENDORS (VENDOR = 25, CITY = "Athens",
                   STATE = "Georgia")
```

This statement will insert a single row into the VENDORS table. Three of the columns are given values by this statement. The fourth column is set to QUEL's version of NULL (0 for numeric columns, blanks for character strings).

```
APPEND TO SALES (10/30, Linda, INVID = A.INVENTORYID, 2)
          WHERE A.TYPE = "Dryer" AND A.PRICE = 220.00
```

This statement illustrates the use of the WHERE clause. Of course, if more than one row in APPLIANCES satisfies the WHERE clause, then more than one new row will be added to SALES.

```
APPEND TO SALSTAT
    (SPNAME = SLS.SPNAME,
     TOTAL = SUM(SLS.QTY * A.PRICE BY SLS.SPNAME
         WHERE SLS.INVID = A.INVENTORYID),
     HIGH = MAX(SLS.QTY * A.PRICE BY SLS.SPNAME
         WHERE SLS.INVID = A.INVENTORYID),
     LOW = MIN(SLS.QTY * A.PRICE BY SLS.SPNAME
         WHERE SLS.INVID = A.INVENTORYID),
     AVERAGE = AVG(SLS.QTY * A.PRICE BY SLS.SPNAME
         WHERE SLS.INVID = A.INVENTORYID))
```

This example illustrates the use of expressions (aggregates in this case) in the target list of the APPEND statement. The result below shows the contents of the table SALSTAT after this APPEND operation has been executed.

Result:	SPNAME	TOTAL	HIGH	LOW	AVERAGE
	Anne	950	360	250	316.67
	Hank	990	440	250	330
	Charles	2380	1020	360	595
	Linda	1505	680	325	501.67

REPLACE

The REPLACE statement is used to change existing data values in specified columns and rows of a table.

GENERAL SYNTAX

```
REPLACE range-variable (target list)
        [WHERE conditions]
```

Just as in the RETRIEVE statement, the WHERE clause is used to identify rows to be changed. If the WHERE clause is omitted, then all rows in the table are changed. The target list need only include those columns to be changed.

The following statement increases the cost of every appliance from vendor 22 by 15%:

```
REPLACE APPLIANCES (COST = 1.15 * APPLIANCES.COST)
WHERE APPLIANCES.VENDOR = 22
```

DELETE

The DELETE statement is used to remove entire rows from a table.

GENERAL SYNTAX

```
DELETE range-variable [WHERE conditions]
```

If the WHERE clause is omitted, all rows will be deleted from the named table. The table will still exist although it will be empty. The following statement removes all of the appliances of vendor 22:

```
DELETE A WHERE A.VENDOR = 22
```

Disjoint Queries

If the REPLACE and DELETE statements in the examples above had been written slightly differently they would have altered or deleted all of the rows in the APPLIANCES relation. Thus, consider these two statements:

```
REPLACE A (COST = 1.15 * A.COST)
WHERE APPLIANCES.VENDOR = 22

DELETE APPLIANCES WHERE A.VENDOR = 22
```

The first statement will increase the cost of *all* appliances by 15%. The second statement will delete all rows from the APPLIANCES relation. The problem in both cases is the same: Two different range variables are being used. The two range variables (A and APPLIANCES) refer to two copies of the same relation. Consequently, they do not point to the same row. The WHERE condition being stated in terms of one range variable will have no effect on the operation defined in terms of the other variable. This effectively eliminates the WHERE clause from the statement and causes the operation to act on *all* of the rows of the table. Disjoint queries can be avoided by taking care that the range variable in the WHERE condition is the same as that identified in the main part of the statement.

VIEWS

The capability of creating views is provided by QUEL for the same reason it is provided by SQL—to restrict access to confidential data, and to simplify data manipulation by providing only essential data. QUEL's view creation facility is similar to SQL's.

To define a view that restricts access within the SALESPEOPLE table to non-financial data we can enter:

```
DEFINE VIEW SPMAINT (SPL.NAME, SPL.ADDRESS, SPL.SUPV)
```

This statement defines the view named SPMAINT. It creates a logical table with three columns of data (NAME, ADDRESS, SUPV) taken from the SALESPEOPLE table. As with SQL the view definition causes no data to be retrieved. Data retrieval and manipulation take place only when the view is referred to in a RETRIEVE, APPEND, REPLACE, or DELETE statement. For example, to see the current contents of Hank's record we enter a RETRIEVE statement as follows:

```
RANGE OF X IS SPMAINT
RETRIEVE X.ALL WHERE X.NAME = "Hank"
```

Notice that a RANGE statement is needed to define a range variable for the view. The RETRIEVE statement is then written as if the view were a base table. The system uses the original DEFINE VIEW statement to identify the base table from which the data is to be retrieved. In this case, the base table is SALESPEOPLE. It then retrieves the record from SALESPEOPLE which contains "Hank" in the NAME column, and displays the entire row as defined in the view SPMAINT. This row consists of the columns NAME, ADDRESS, and SUPV.

Result:	NAME	ADDRESS	SUPV
	Hank	103 Royal Arms	Anne

To define a view of appliances from vendor 22:

```
DEFINE VIEW VEND22APP
          (INVID = A.INVENTORYID, A.TYPE, CST = A.COST,
                                        PRC = A.PRICE)
       WHERE A.VENDOR = 22
```

In this example, we have given new names to some of the columns in the view by specifying the columns in the target list in the *result-name = expression* format. In the first example above (SPMAINT), we did not specify names for columns in the view, so they "inherited" the names they had in the base table. In this second example we have omitted the vendor column, since every appliance will have the same vendor.

GENERAL SYNTAX

```
DEFINE VIEW view-name (target list)
      [WHERE conditions]
```

We note these points:

1. The format of the DEFINE VIEW statement is identical to that of the RETRIEVE INTO statement. Indeed, the only difference between the two is that DEFINE VIEW creates a *virtual* relation while RETRIEVE INTO creates a *real* relation. That is, DEFINE VIEW creates the logical structure for a relation, but no actual data is retrieved until the relation is referenced in a data manipulation statement.
2. A view may be defined in terms of one or more base tables, one or more other views, or combinations of base tables and views.
3. With exceptions to be noted later, views defined by the DEFINE VIEW statement may be referenced in RETRIEVE, APPEND, REPLACE, or DELETE statements.

Examples

1. Create a view giving the average cost of appliances from each vendor.

```
DEFINE VIEW VENDAVG
          (A.VENDOR, AVGCOST = AVG(A.COST BY A.VENDOR))
```

2. Create a view giving names of salespeople getting more than 10% commission together with the types of appliances they have sold.

```
DEFINE VIEW SPAPPS
          (SPERSON = SPL.NAME, APPTYPE = A.TYPE)
       WHERE SPL.NAME = SLS.SPNAME
       AND SLS.INVID = A.INVENTORYID
       AND SPL.COMMRATE > 10%
```

The following RETRIEVE statement causes the table shown below to be displayed.

```
RANGE OF SPP IS SPAPPS
RETRIEVE SPP.ALL
FROM SPAPPS
```

Result:

SMAN	APPTYPE
Anne	Television
Hank	Refrigerator
Anne	Refrigerator
Linda	Television
Linda	Refrigerator
Hank	Refrigerator
Linda	Washer
Anne	Dryer
Hank	Dryer

Restrictions on View Updates

When we discussed SQL views in the previous chapter, we noted that certain types of views cannot be updated. QUEL has similar restrictions. In general the following types of updates are not allowed:

1. Updates to views which have more than one base table.
2. Updates to columns referenced in the WHERE clause of the view definition.
3. Updates to columns in the view definition's target list which are not simply column names (i.e., are defined by some kind of computation).

As a rule of thumb, if the update to the view would be identical to the update to the underlying base table, then the update is permitted (Relational Technology 1982).

EXERCISES

The following exercises are identical to those given in Chapter 4 for SQL. Since some of the features of SQL are different from those of QUEL, some of the topical exercises from Chapter 4 are included in exercises 5.7 and 5.8.

For all exercises write QUEL statements which will produce the required result. For the following exercises use the appliance database with the structure shown below. Although this is the same database as that used in the text of the chapter, many of the queries refer to information not shown in the sample data of Figure 5.1.

APPLIANCE DATABASE

APPLIANCES (<u>Inventory id</u>, Type, Vendor, Cost, Price)
VENDORS (<u>Vendor</u>, City, State, Rating)
SALESPEOPLE (<u>Name</u>, Address, Comm_rate, Base_salary, Supv)
SALES (Date, Sp_name, Inv_id, Qty)

5.1. Write appropriate statements to create results for the following simple queries.

   a. List all the supervisors.
   b. List supervisors with duplicates eliminated.
   c. List everything about Richard's sales.
   d. List salespeople with a commission rate between 10% and 18%, inclusive.
   e. Identify vendors located in states whose names begin with the letter N.
   f. Who are the salespeople for whom the database has no address?
   g. List the inventory_id and profit (price − cost) on mixers from vendor 77.
   h. List vendors in Indiana in ascending order by rating.

5.2. Write appropriate statements to create results for the multiple table queries below.

   a. List the inventory_id, the vendor, and the vendor's city and state for all appliances in the database.
   b. Create the following queries for the salesperson named Sam:
      (1). List Sam's sales together with his commission rate on each sale.
      (2). Include the price of each item on the list of Sam's sales.
      (3). Include the commission on each item on the list of Sam's sales.
      (4). What is the profit (price − cost − commission) on each of Sam's sales?
   c. List salespeople having a base salary higher than their supervisor.

5.3. Use statements with aggregate operators and functions to solve the following queries.

   a. What is the total base salary being paid each month?
   b. What is the average profit margin (price − cost) of appliances?
   c. How many different states are the vendors located in?
   d. What is the highest price for a television? What is the lowest price?

5.4. Create statements for the following queries using ANY.

   a. List inventory id's sold by every salesperson.
   b. List appliance types supplied by every vendor in Vermont.

5.5. Use APPEND, REPLACE, and DELETE to write QUEL statements for the queries below.

   a. Assume a table exists named VENDAVG, which contains the columns: Vendor, Type, Average_Cost, Average_Price. The last two columns are the average cost and average price of appliances supplied by the vendor of the designated type. Write an INSERT statement which places rows in VENDAVG containing average costs and prices of refrigerators for each vendor.

b. Increase the base salary of all salespeople reporting to Anne by 10%.

c. Remove all sales from the SALES table which occurred in October.

5.6. Create a view of inventory id's, types, and prices of appliances whose price is under $1000.

5.7. Write QUEL statements to answer the following queries about the APPLIANCE database.

a. List names and ratings of vendors who sell toasters.

b. List appliances having a cost under the average cost of appliances from vendor 86.

c. List inventory id's for which the total quantity sold is greater than 20.

d. Who supervises the salesperson with the highest base salary?

e. List vendors located in Kansas or who supply dishwashers.

Use the following database for the next exercise. This database gives information about independent insurance agents who place insurance policies with a variety of different companies. This exercise was given in Chapter 3. Compare the QUEL solutions with the relational calculus and algebra solutions.

POLICY DATABASE

POLICY (Policy No, Insured, Agent No, Company No, Amount, Premium)
AGENT (Agent No, Agent Name, State)
COMPANY (Company No, Company Name, Commission Rate, Revenue)

5.8. Write QUEL statements using the POLICY database shown above.

a. List companies with revenue exceeding $100 million who offer a commission rate of less than 15%.

b. List policies written by agents in Illinois.

c. List companies having policies with amounts between $50,000 and $100,000.

d. List agents getting a commission rate exceeding 20% on any of their policies.

e. List the companies for which Sam Stone writes policies.

f. List agents who have written policies for every company.

g. List companies which do business with all agents in Iowa.

h. Find the maximum policy amount written by an agent in Georgia.

PART THREE

INTERACTIVE PROGRAMMING ENVIRONMENTS

A major strength of 4GLs in comparison to previous generations of languages is the environment they provide. By integrating many of the features commonly needed in systems development (editors, debuggers, report generators, etc.) into an interactive environment which utilizes database concepts, they accelerate the development process considerably. In Part Three we examine two such interactive environments in detail: R:BASE 5000 and dBASE III PLUS. Chapters 6 and 7 are devoted to various aspects of R:BASE 5000, while Chapters 8 and 9 handle similar aspects of dBASE III PLUS. Chapter 10 discusses IDEAL—a programming language utilized with a database system implemented in the mainframe computer environment.

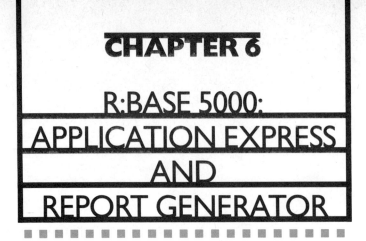

CHAPTER 6

R:BASE 5000:
APPLICATION EXPRESS
AND
REPORT GENERATOR

R:BASE 5000, a product of Microrim, Inc., is a microcomputer-based relational database management system which provides a powerful multifaceted environment for application development. Its features include (among others) a database definition and manipulation language, a procedural programming language, program, report, and screen generators, a compiler, and a file interface for communication with other systems. It supports interactive and batch command execution; it provides a natural language facility, CLOUT, for data extraction; and it uses visual programming concepts in several of its programs. In short, R:BASE embodies, at least to some extent, all of the features of our definition of a 4GL.

The present chapter demonstrates how the Application EXPRESS and the R:BASE report generation facility can be used to rapidly develop an application or prototype. Chapter 7 will cover the R:BASE command language. We shall cover CLOUT in Chapter 13.

R:BASE 5000 consists of several separately executable programs which can be used together to create end-user application systems. All of the facilities covered in Chapters 6 and 7 are included in just two of these programs: *express* and *rbase*. *Express* contains the facilities of the Application EXPRESS. *Rbase* contains the facilities of report generation and of the R:BASE 5000 command language.

THE APPLICATION EXPRESS

The Application EXPRESS is an application generator. That is, it generates files of R:BASE commands as a result of interactive instructions from the programmer. These command files can then be executed as application programs by the R:BASE system.

Throughout this chapter we shall use the database defined in Figure 6.1 as the basis for building a retail management system. This sytem will provide processing services for Halliday's, a fictitious department store. The system's services include monthly commission statements for salespeople, an inventory report, batch update of the inventory master, and a variety of database queries in support of management functions.

The Application EXPRESS provides support both in defining the database and in generating the application system which processes the database. The extent of this support will be illustrated in the following pages as we define Halliday's database and build portions of the retail management system.

Defining Halliday's Database

The database of Figure 6.1 consists of 5 tables, each of which has a number of columns. To develop an application system using this database we must first define the database to the system. Database definition in the EXPRESS consists of three steps: (1) naming the database, (2) defining the tables, and (3) defining the columns in the tables. EXPRESS provides a visual approach to data definition, which will be illustrated as we develop our database.

Before we begin, we note that database names must be no longer than 7 characters, the first of which must be alphabetic. Column names begin with an alphabetic character and may have up to 8 characters. Screen form names and report names may also be up to 8 characters in length.

We begin database definition by selecting choice 1, "Define a new database," from the EXPRESS Main menu.

```
                        Application EXPRESS
         Copyright (c) 1985 by Microrim, Inc. (Ver. 1.01 PC-DOS)

            ══════════Select option - [F10] for help══════════
         (1)   Define a new database
         (2)   Change an existing database definition
         (3)   Define a new application
         (4)   Change an existing application
         (5)   Display file directory
         (6)   Exit
```

EXPRESS then prompts us for a database name, and for this example we respond by entering RETAIL. EXPRESS now displays a table definition form with an expanded cursor in the box in the upper lefthand corner. We will use this form to define the tables and columns of the RETAIL database.

RETAIL MANAGEMENT DATABASE

INVENTORY MASTER (invmast)*	COLUMN NAME	DATA TYPE
Inventory Identification	invid	text 3 char
Inventory Category	invcat	text 10 char
Inventory Name	invname	text 10 char
Quantity in Stock	qtystk	integer
Price	price	dollar

SALESPERSON MASTER (spmast)*	COLUMN NAME	DATA TYPE
Salesperson Identification	spid	text 3 char
Salesperson Name	spname	text 8 char
Commission Rate	commrate	real

CUSTOMER MASTER (custmast)*	COLUMN NAME	DATA TYPE
Customer Identification	custid	text 3 char
Customer Name	custname	text 15 char
Customer Address	custaddr	text 30 char
Customer Balance	custbal	dollar

SALES TRANSACTIONS (saltx)*	COLUMN NAME	DATA TYPE
Date	saldate	date
Time	saltime	time
Salesperson Identification	spid	
Customer Identification	custid	
Cash/Charge	cashchg	text 1 char
Inventory Identification	invid	
Quantity	salqty	integer
Sale Price	salprice	dollar

PAYMENT TRANSACTIONS (pmttx)*	COLUMN NAME	DATA TYPE
Date	pmtdate	date
Customer Identification	custid	
Amount	pmtamt	dollar

*the R:base 5000 table name

FIGURE 6.1   Database for Halliday's Retail Management System

The table definition form is drawn to look like an empty relational table. This form has seven columns with two rows delineated at the top. In the top row we insert the column names, and in the second row we specify the data types of the columns. The lines delineating the columns extend below the second row to visually suggest that data could be placed below these column definition rows. However, the space below the second delineated row is not used by EXPRESS.

```
Enter the name for this table


 ┌─────────┐
 │         │
 └─────────┘
 ┌─────────┬───────┬───────┬───────┬───────┬───────┬───────┐
 │         │       │       │       │       │       │       │
 ├─────────┼───────┼───────┼───────┼───────┼───────┼───────┤
 │         │       │       │       │       │       │       │
 │         │       │       │       │       │       │       │




[F1] Insert  [F2] Delete  [F3] Review  [F5] Reset value  [F10] Help
Database RETAIL
```

The first table we define is the inventory master table. We enter *invmast* into the box in the upper lefthand corner to identify this table to R:BASE. The cursor now moves to the box in the first row of the leftmost column. The first column in the inventory master table is the inventory identification column; thus we enter the name *invid* in the box, and the expanded cursor moves to the box immediately below it in the second row. At this point a menu is displayed immediately below the table definition form.

This menu lists the different data types available for defining the column. An expanded cursor highlights the first of these choices—TEXT. We may move this cursor until it rests on the data type we desire for this column. Since *invid* is to be a text column, we select the first choice on the menu. Text columns are of different widths, so EXPRESS prompts us for the width desired. We enter 3. Thus, the first column in the table is named *invid* and has a data type of TEXT 3.

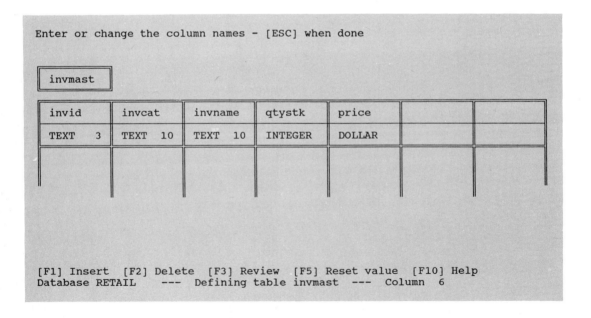

```
Enter or change the column names - [ESC] when done


 ┌─────────────┐
 │ invmast     │
 └─────────────┘
 ┌─────────────┬───────┬───────┬───────┬───────┬───────┬───────┐
 │ invid       │       │       │       │       │       │       │
 │ ▓▓▓▓▓▓▓      │       │       │       │       │       │       │
 ├─────────────┼───────┼───────┼───────┼───────┼───────┼───────┤
 │             │       │       │       │       │       │       │
 │             │       │       │       │       │       │       │
 └─────────────┴───────┴───────┴───────┴───────┴───────┴───────┘

 ╔══════════════Select column data type - [ENTER] to choose═══════════╗
 ║  ┌──────┐                                                           ║
 ║  │ TEXT │ DOLLAR  INTEGER  REAL  DATE  TIME                         ║
 ║  └──────┘                                                           ║
 ╚═════════════════════════════════════════════════════════════════════╝


 [F1] Insert  [F2] Delete  [F3] Review  [F5] Reset value  [F10] Help
 Database RETAIL    ---  Defining table invmast  ---   Column  1
```

The expanded cursor now moves to the first row of the second column. We repeat the column definition process by giving the second column the name of *invcat* and the data type of TEXT 10. We continue in this manner until we have defined all the columns of the table given in Figure 6.1.

```
Enter or change the column names - [ESC] when done


 ┌─────────────┐
 │ invmast     │
 └─────────────┘
 ┌───────────┬───────────┬───────────┬───────────┬───────────┬──────┬──────┐
 │ invid     │ invcat    │ invname   │ qtystk    │ price     │      │      │
 │ TEXT    3 │ TEXT   10 │ TEXT   10 │ INTEGER   │ DOLLAR    │      │      │
 ├───────────┼───────────┼───────────┼───────────┼───────────┼──────┼──────┤
 │           │           │           │           │           │      │      │
 │           │           │           │           │           │      │      │
 └───────────┴───────────┴───────────┴───────────┴───────────┴──────┴──────┘



 [F1] Insert  [F2] Delete  [F3] Review  [F5] Reset value  [F10] Help
 Database RETAIL    ---  Defining table invmast  ---   Column  6
```

At this point it is worthwhile to note what is happening behind the scenes in Application EXPRESS. We have not only defined a table (*invmast*) for our database, but we have also defined a set of columns which may be used in other tables as well. Each of these columns has a name and a data type. Application EXPRESS keeps a list of columns already defined for the database. We may display this list at any time by pressing function key [F3] (Review). The list of columns and tables we have defined to this point is displayed.

```
Tables
------
invmast

Column names
------------
invid      TEXT     3
invcat     TEXT     10
invname    TEXT     10
qtystk     INTEGER
price      DOLLAR
```

The other four tables in the database are defined in a similar manner with two variations:

■ Column names used in one table may be used in defining subsequent tables.

■ Tables may be defined having more than 7 columns.

Both points can be illustrated in defining the sales transactions table (*saltx*). The sixth column of this table (*invid*) was previously defined as the first column of the inventory master table. When we enter *invid* as the name of the sixth column of table *saltx,* EXPRESS consults its list of columns previously defined for this database. It locates *invid* and its data type. EXPRESS then fills in the data type for *invid* and moves the expanded cursor to the next column.

If a table, such as *saltx,* already has more than seven columns defined, EXPRESS simply shifts the previously defined columns to the left, causing the leftmost column to disappear and making room for a new column on the right.

The database definition process of Application EXPRESS illustrates principles of visual and interactive programming. The programmer "sees" the table definition, is given a menu of data types, and has data types for previously defined columns automatically inserted.

Defining Halliday's Retail Management System

Our goal is to use Application EXPRESS to develop a system which will perform the following functions:

1. Provide a menu structure for end-user access to system functions.
2. Support on-line maintenance of the 3 master tables (Inventory, Salesperson, Customer). This means we need the capability to add, change, delete, and view master records.
3. Provide input screens for transactions (Sales and Payment).
4. Generate a monthly commission statement for all salespeople, and generate an inventory report.
5. Respond to a variety of management queries relative to the content of the database.
6. Provide a batch processing program that updates the inventory master with the contents of the sales transactions.

R:BASE 5000 provides facilities to accomplish all of the above. Management queries and batch processing will be covered in the next chapter. Menus, on-line maintenance functions, and input forms can be defined in the Application EXPRESS. Report generation will be covered in the next section on the rbase Report Generator.

To incorporate functions 2–6 listed above, we designed the overall menu structure as shown in Figure 6.2. As we proceed, you will see that specification of the menu structure leads directly to implementation of the application objectives.

To develop the application system for Halliday's, we choose option 3 ("Define a new application") from the Application EXPRESS Main menu. The system will then prompt us to identify the database for which we are developing the application (RETAIL) and to name the application system itself. We name the application RETMGT (for retail management).

The EXPRESS presumes that the underlying structure of all applications can be expressed via a menu. Thus, the next group of EXPRESS prompts are directed toward the creation of the Main menu and subsequent menus. Since most applications, including the present one, can be viewed as a set of functions whose organization and execution can be controlled by a menu, this structure is appropriate for most systems.

Defining the Menu Structure

Each time we define a menu, EXPRESS will ask us to:

1. Name the menu
2. Identify its type as Vertical or Horizontal
3. Enter its title and options
4. Define exit and *help* information for the menu
5. Define the actions for each option on the menu

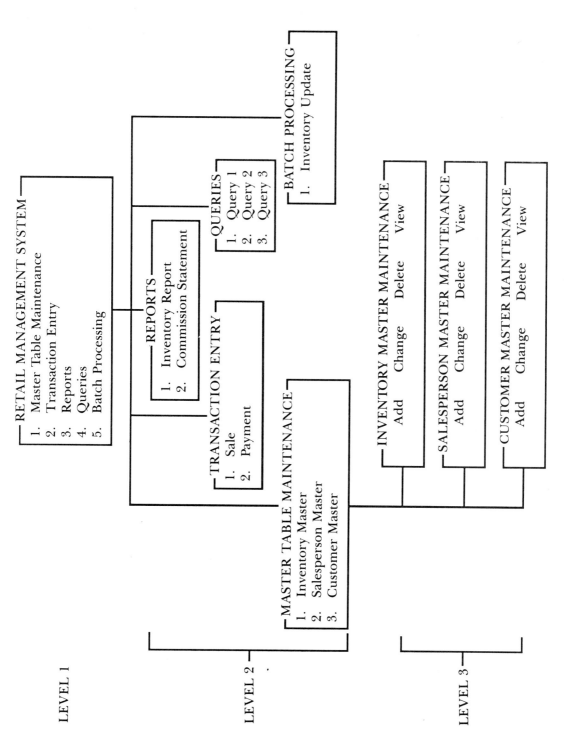

FIGURE 6.2   Menu Structure for Halliday's Retail Management System

A vertical menu lists options vertically, while a horizontal menu lists options horizontally. The advantage of using a vertical menu is that each option can be described in more detail. Horizontal menus, on the other hand, allow a larger number of options. In our example application system the only horizontal menus are the three submenus of the master table maintenance menu.

We will now demonstrate how the menu structure for this application can be implemented using the Application EXPRESS. We name the first menu MAIN and identify its type as vertical. EXPRESS then displays a vertical menu skeleton and prompts for the menu title. After we enter RETAIL MANAGEMENT SYSTEM, the menu title is centered.

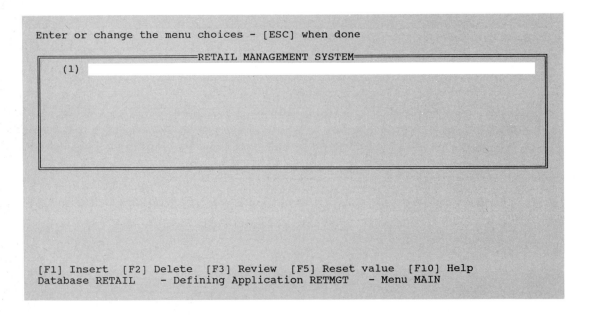

```
Enter or change the menu choices - [ESC] when done
╔══════════════════════RETAIL MANAGEMENT SYSTEM══════════════════════╗
║ (1)                                                                 ║
║                                                                     ║
║                                                                     ║
║                                                                     ║
║                                                                     ║
║                                                                     ║
╚═════════════════════════════════════════════════════════════════════╝




[F1] Insert   [F2] Delete   [F3] Review   [F5] Reset value   [F10] Help
Database RETAIL    - Defining Application RETMGT   - Menu MAIN
```

Note that EXPRESS automatically numbers the menu options. As we enter the description of each option, EXPRESS increments the number and prompts us for the next menu option. After we have entered all 5 options, we have the screen shown at the top of the next page.

We next press the escape key [ESC], and we are ready to define menu exit and help information. When a menu is displayed in a running application system, the user must have some means of leaving the menu, either to exit from the system or to return to the previous menu. Application EXPRESS allows us to adopt the convention that the user will always exit by pressing the escape key. In this application we assume that the escape key will be the user's means of exit from any menu. Thus, when EXPRESS prompts us as to whether ESC is to be used to exit the menu, we always answer yes.

```
Enter or change the menu choices - [ESC] when done

╔══════════════════════════════RETAIL MANAGEMENT SYSTEM══════════════════════════╗
║  (1)   Master Table Maintenance                                                 ║
║  (2)   Transaction Entry                                                         ║
║  (3)   Reports                                                                   ║
║  (4)   Queries                                                                   ║
║  (5)   Batch Processing                                                          ║
║  (6)                                                                             ║
║                                                                                  ║
║                                                                                  ║
╚══════════════════════════════════════════════════════════════════════════════════╝
```

After we define the means of exiting, EXPRESS asks whether a help screen is to be defined for the menu. If we answer yes, EXPRESS allows us to develop a customized screen of user documentation to explain the meanings of the menu options. To obtain this help screen while viewing the menu, the user need only strike the appropriate function key and our customized help screen will be displayed.

```
Enter/edit the help text for this menu                  < 16, 77>  [ESC] to exit
The items on this menu represent the major functions performed by the RETAIL
MANAGEMENT SYSTEM.

(1)  Master Table Maintenance makes changes to the master tables: the Inventory
Master, the Salesperson Master, and the Customer Master.  The user may add
records, change records, delete records, or view records in any of these tables.

(2)  Transaction Entry allows the user to enter Sales transactions and Payment
transactions.

(3)  The system generates a number of reports, any of which can be selected by
the user.

(4)  The system also provides the user with the capability of making any of
a number of different queries.  The user selects the query desired and the
system processes the database in a manner appropriate to the query selected.

(5)  The system processes a transaction table in order to update a master
table.
```

We are now ready for the last step in defining the Main menu: We must define the actions for each menu option. To assist us, EXPRESS provides its action menu shown at the top of the next page.

Note that EXPRESS continues to display the Main menu for the application that we are in the process of defining. It also indicates that we are now defining the actions for menu selection 1. At the bottom of the screen, EXPRESS notes that we are working with database RETAIL, defining application RETMGT, and working on the menu named MAIN. By interactively providing such visual assistance, the EXPRESS makes it easier for the developer to avoid losing the current position in the application.

```
===============================RETAIL MANAGEMENT SYSTEM=================
|                    (1)  Master Table Maintenance                     |
|                    (2)  Transaction Processing                       |
|                    (3)  Reports                                      |
|                    (4)  Queries                                      |
|                    (5)  Batch Processing                             |
=======================================================================


The actions for menu selection  1 will be defined

================Select action for this menu selection==================
| Load   Edit   Delete   Browse   Select   Print   Custom   Macro   Menu   Exit |
=======================================================================




[F3] Review   [F5] Reset value   [F10] Help
Database RETAIL    - Defining Application RETMGT    - Menu MAIN
```

Application EXPRESS provides ten choices on its action menu. For this application we shall be using six of these choices: Load, Edit, Delete, Select, Custom, and Menu.

Before we define actions for any of the menu selections, let us review the overall menu structure for our application as was shown in Figure 6.2. You will note that the menu structure is three levels deep. At the top level is the Main menu. Beneath the Main menu, on the second level, are five submenus. Beneath one of these second level submenus is a third level consisting of three more submenus. The Main menu has 5 selections. Each of these selections leads to a submenu. One of these submenus (Master Table Maintenance) has 3 selections, each of which leads to yet another submenu. Whenever a menu selection leads to a submenu we will indicate to Application EXPRESS that the action for this menu selection is Menu.

In the action menu shown above, EXPRESS is prompting us to define the action for Main menu selection 1 by choosing one of the options on its action menu. We choose Menu from the EXPRESS action menu so that, when the user chooses selection 1 (Master Table Maintenance) from Halliday's Main menu, the system will display the Master Table Maintenance submenu (which we are about to define). Now that we selected Menu, EXPRESS prompts for the name, type, title, and options of this submenu. We name the submenu *masmaint*, designate it as a vertical menu, and define its title and options.

```
Enter or change the menu choices - [ESC] when done
                          ═════MASTER TABLE MAINTENANCE══════════════════════
 ┌──────────────────────────────────────────────────────────────────────────┐
 │  (1)   Inventory Master                                                    │
 │  (2)   Salesperson Master                                                  │
 │  (3)   Customer Master                                                     │
 │                                                                            │
 │                                                                            │
 │                                                                            │
 │                                                                            │
 │                                                                            │
 │                                                                            │
 │                                                                            │
 │                                                                            │
 └──────────────────────────────────────────────────────────────────────────┘



 [F1] Insert  [F2] Delete  [F3] Review  [F5] Reset value  [F10] Help
 Database RETAIL    - Defining Application RETMGT    - Menu masmaint
```

The actions corresponding to the three options of the Master Table Maintenance menu are not defined at this time. Instead, EXPRESS moves to the second selection of the Main menu and asks us to define its action. We define the action of Main menu selections 2, 3, 4, and 5 as submenus in the same manner as we defined the action for selection 1 as a submenu.

We have now completely defined the Main menu of our application. We have also completed the first three steps in the definition of each of the five level 2 submenus. To complete the menu structure of our application we need only define the submenus below the Master Table Maintenance menu. We do this in the same manner as we have previously done with the higher level menus.

Defining Maintenance Actions

We will assume that the menu structure outlined in Figure 6.2 is now complete. However, our application consists of more than just menus and submenus. Menus and submenus are created to lead the user to specific actions that do the work of the application system. Thus, for example, the Inventory Master Maintenance menu indicates that the system provides the capability to add, change, delete, or view an inventory master record. We must still define actions that will actually accomplish each of these functions. Similarly, the maintenance actions for the other master tables must be defined. We must also define the actions for the Transaction Entry, Reports, Queries, and Batch Processing menus.

Since the three master maintenance menus are identical in format, the definition of actions for each of these menus will be essentially the same. We will only describe the action definition for the first of these menus (Inventory Master Maintenance) in detail.

Load.   We must provide actions to add, change, delete, and view records in the inventory master table. EXPRESS prompts us to define the action for "Add", the first of these functions shown in our application menu. The selection from the action menu which most appropriately fits the function of adding records to a table is Load. Therefore, we select Load from the action menu.

```
┌──────────────────────INVENTORY MASTER MAINTENANCE────────────────────────┐
│ ┌─────────────────────────────────────────────────────────────────────┐ │
│ │ Add   Change   Delete   View                                         │ │
│ └─────────────────────────────────────────────────────────────────────┘ │
│                                                                           │
│                                                                           │
│ The actions for menu selection  1 will be defined                         │
│ ┌───────────────────────Select action for this menu selection──────────┐ │
│ │ Load   Edit   Delete   Browse   Select   Print   Custom   Macro   Exit│ │
│ └───────────────────────────────────────────────────────────────────────┘ │
│                                                                           │
│                                                                           │
│                                                                           │
│                                                                           │
│                                                                           │
│                                                                           │
│                                                                           │
│                                                                           │
│ [F3] Review   [F5] Reset value   [F10] Help                               │
│ Database RETAIL    - Defining Application RETMGT    - Menu masmaint       │
└───────────────────────────────────────────────────────────────────────────┘
```

Load means to allow the user to add records to a table. The EXPRESS will now take us through a step-by-step process to establish the means for the user to add records to the inventory master table. There are four steps involved in defining the Load action:

1. Identify the database table into which records are to be loaded.
2. Identify the name of the data entry screen (or "form") through which the user will enter data.
3. Identify the columns into which data will be entered.
4. Generate the format of the data entry form.

In response to EXPRESS prompts we supply the name of the table to be loaded (*invmast*) and the name of the form that will be used for loading (*invmast*). Since we want to enter data for all of the columns, we select (ALL) when EXPRESS prompts us to identify the columns.

```
====================INVENTORY MASTER MAINTENANCE====================
  Add   Change   Delete   View


======Select columns to load - [ENTER] to choose - [ESC] when done======
   invid        invcat      invname     qtystk      price       (ALL)
```

We are now given a sample data entry form to which we give the title "INVENTORY MASTER MAINTENANCE". Note that the system names for the columns of the inventory master table are listed on the form. If we make no changes to the form, it will be displayed to the user precisely as shown.

```
Enter the form title - [ENTER] when done

INVENTORY MASTER MAINTENANCE

              invid:
             invcat:
            invname:
             qtystk:
              price:
```

However, we would prefer to use data labels that are more descriptive than the system's column names. Therefore, we change the labels for each column name. This completes the fourth and final step in the definition of the Load action.

```
Enter the prompt for column: invid     - [ESC] when done

INVENTORY MASTER MAINTENANCE

Inventory Identification:
      Inventory Category:
          Inventory Name:
        Quantity in Stock:
                   Price:
```

Edit.   The second menu item in our Inventory Master Maintenance menu is "Change". The EXPRESS action corresponding to "Change" is Edit. The Edit action will provide the user with the facility to display an inventory master record on the screen, make changes to it, and then rewrite it to the inventory master table.

```
                          ═INVENTORY MASTER MAINTENANCE═
    Add   Change   Delete   View
```

The actions for menu selection 2 will be defined

```
                    ═Select action for this menu selection═
    Load   Edit   Delete   Browse   Select   Print   Custom   Macro   Exit
```

In specifying the steps of the Edit action, we must specify the four steps required for the Load action and several additional steps. For Steps 1 and 2 we specify the table name *invmast* and the form name *invmast*. Since we specified a form which has already been defined, Steps 3 and 4 are unnecessary—they were completed when we designed the form for the Load action. Therefore, EXPRESS skips these steps and moves to the additional steps required for Edit. These steps are:

5. Identify the order in which rows are to be edited. This step is optional.
6. Identify the column by which a row will be selected for editing; identify the type of comparison to be made with the column's value; and define the prompt message to be displayed when the user is prompted for the data value of the column.

The underlying idea of Step 6 is that the user will want to change selected records in the table, and that these records will be selected based on their relationship to a value that the user will enter when the application system is running. Suppose, for example, that the user desires to change the price of inventory item A15. Naturally, we would expect that: the user should enter *A15,* the system will fetch the record with *invid* equal to *A15,* the user will make the change, and the system will rewrite the record. Thus, we first want to identify *invid* as the column by which the desired record is identified. Second, we want to specify that the *invid* of the record should be *equal* to a value entered by the user. And finally, we want to provide a means for prompting the user to enter the comparison value. These three steps correspond to the three parts of Step 6 above.

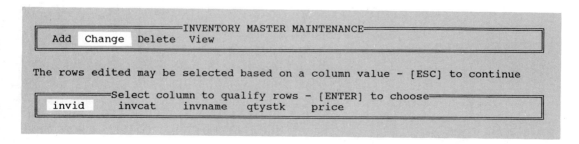

```
                          ═INVENTORY MASTER MAINTENANCE═
    Add   Change   Delete   View
```

The rows edited may be selected based on a column value - [ESC] to continue

```
                    ═Select column to qualify rows - [ENTER] to choose═
    invid     invcat     invname     qtystk      price
```

```
╔══════════════════INVENTORY MASTER MAINTENANCE═══════════════════╗
║ Add   Change   Delete   View                                     ║
╚══════════════════════════════════════════════════════════════════╝

The rows edited may be selected based on a column value - [ESC] to continue

╔═══════════════Select condition - [ENTER] to choose═══════════════╗
║  EQ    NE   GT   GE   LT   LE   CONTAINS   EXISTS   FAILS         ║
╚══════════════════════════════════════════════════════════════════╝
```

```
╔══════════════════INVENTORY MASTER MAINTENANCE═══════════════════╗
║ Add   Change   Delete   View                                     ║
╚══════════════════════════════════════════════════════════════════╝

The rows edited may be selected based on a column value - [ESC] to continue

Enter the prompt message   Inventory Id of item to be changed:
```

Delete.   In our descriptions of the Load and the Edit actions we identified six definition steps used by Application EXPRESS. The Delete action (corresponding to our third menu option) uses Steps 1 (identify the table) and 6. As before, we identify the table as *invmast* and the selection column as *invid*. We indicate that the value entered by the user must be *equal* to the record's *invid*. The last step is to define the prompt message:

```
╔══════════════════INVENTORY MASTER MAINTENANCE═══════════════════╗
║ Add   Change   Delete   View                                     ║
╚══════════════════════════════════════════════════════════════════╝

The rows deleted may be selected based on a column value

Enter the prompt message   Inventory Id of item to be deleted:
```

Select.   The last option on our Inventory Master Maintenance menu is "View". With this option we allow the user to retrieve the contents of records in the table and display them on the screen. The action most appropriate to this function is Select. As before, we must identify the table from which data is to be selected (*invmast*). EXPRESS next prompts us to identify the columns to be displayed.

```
╔══════════════════INVENTORY MASTER MAINTENANCE═══════════════════╗
║ Add   Change   Delete   View                                     ║
╚══════════════════════════════════════════════════════════════════╝

╔══Select columns to display - [ENTER] to choose - [ESC] when done══╗
║ invid      invcat     invname     qtystk     price      (ALL)    ║
╚══════════════════════════════════════════════════════════════════╝
```

Because the rows are displayed horizontally, there may not be adequate room to display all columns. Therefore, we only identify those columns which we feel are most important. For this example, we identify all of the columns except *invcat.* We identify the columns one at a time, and they are removed from and displayed below the box where they were originally listed. Four columns have been selected for display. Note that the box now only contains the single, unselected column *invcat,* as well as the option (RESET). If we had made an error in selecting a column, we could choose (RESET) and again see all the columns listed.

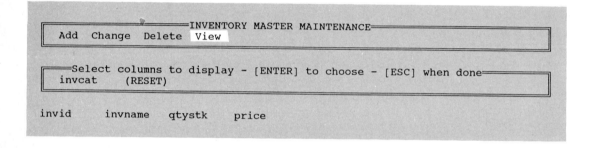

We must also identify the column by which records will be selected for display. For the Edit and Delete actions we selected the *invid* column. However, for this action we shall select *invname* instead.

Defining Other Actions.   The actions for the maintenance menus of the other master tables are defined in a manner corresponding to that shown above for the inventory master table. In addition, we complete the definition of the Transaction Entry menu by defining Load actions for both of its options.

Custom.   The remaining menu options require more complex processing than we can define directly in Application EXPRESS. For the time being we shall merely identify the names of files which will contain the commands needed to carry out this processing. The file names will be identified by using the Custom action. The files themselves will be created later.

To illustrate the process that will be used for all of the remaining undefined menu options, we will consider the process for the Batch Processing menu option "Inventory Update". When prompted for the action, we select Custom. This means that we want to write our own file of R:BASE commands which will be processed every time this menu option is selected. EXPRESS then prompts us for the name of this custom file. For this example we enter the name *iuproc*—for *inventory update procedure.* We are now given a blank screen on which we can write as many R:BASE commands as we wish. In this case we simply write the single command *run iumacro.*

We now press the escape [ESC] key, and our single command file is stored under the name *iuproc*. When the user selects this menu option, *iuproc* will be run, which will in turn cause *iumacro* to be run. This last file, *iumacro*, has not yet been created. We shall create it in the next chapter.

You are probably wondering why it was necessary to create two files (*iuproc* and *iumacro*), rather than just one. It is advantageous to create two files for the following reasons:

1. If we use only one file, we must define the contents of the file while we are in Application EXPRESS. This approach allows us to formulate our command file at a later time.

2. After we finish defining the application system, EXPRESS creates the system by generating a large file of commands. If we wish to change one of our Custom processing files we must go back into Application EXPRESS, work our way through the menu structure, and make the change. By using two files, we can easily make the change by using a standard text editor and working directly on the command file (*iumacro* in our example).

REPORT GENERATION

In the introductory paragraphs of this chapter we mentioned that all of the facilities which we shall cover in Chapters 6 and 7 are included in the two R:BASE 5000 programs known as *express* and *rbase*. The remainder of this chapter and all of Chapter 7 will be devoted to discussion of the facilities of the *rbase* program.

The *rbase* program is an interactive program which contains most of the facilities of the R:BASE 5000 command language. R:BASE displays a prompt *R>* to notify the user that it is ready to receive a command. The user then has the opportunity to enter any of a large number of commands to manipulate data, run programs, generate reports, etc. We shall study only one of these commands—the REPORTS command—in detail in this chapter. The next chapter will be devoted to a discussion of other R:BASE commands.

We shall illustrate the usage of the REPORTS command by building two report generation programs in our application system. One generates commission statements and the other an inventory report. Commission statements for two salespeople are shown in Figure 6.3.

The Commission Report

A salesperson's commission statement provides a detailed list of all of the sales transactions for that salesperson during the month. It calculates the commission due on each sale and provides totals of sales and commissions for all transactions. The report program which we develop will generate a statement for each salesperson who completed one or more sales transactions during the month.

```
                    HALLIDAY'S DEPARTMENT STORE

                    COMMISSION STATEMENT          07/01/--

Identification: 101
          Name: Smith
Commission Rate: .10

                         RECORD OF SALES

     Date        Inventory Id    Quantity    Sale Price   Commission
   ----------    ------------    --------    ----------   ----------

   06/02/--          A53            1            75.00          7.50
   06/10/--          F88            1           750.00         75.00
   06/23/--          F84            1           450.00         45.00
                                             ==========     ==========
                                  TOTALS:      1275.00        127.50
```

```
                    HALLIDAY'S DEPARTMENT STORE

                    COMMISSION STATEMENT          07/01/--

Identification: 105
          Name: Jones
Commission Rate: .15

                         RECORD OF SALES

     Date        Inventory Id    Quantity    Sale Price   Commission
   ----------    ------------    --------    ----------   ----------

   06/13/--          F30            1           150.00         15.00
   06/15/--          A61            1           250.00         25.00
                                             ==========     ==========
                                  TOTALS:       400.00         40.00
```

FIGURE 6.3   Commission Statements for Halliday's Salespeople

We create the program to generate these commission statements by using the REPORTS command of the R:BASE 5000 command language. For this particular report we must complete the following steps:

1. Name the report.

2. Identify the primary table from which the report data will be taken.

3. Place the constant data (headings, footers, data labels) on the report layout. This function is called *editing* the report.

4. Define variables containing calculated data and data retrieved from tables other than the primary table.

5. Place (*locate*) the variable data on the report layout. This variable data will come from the primary table or will be from variables defined in Step 4.

6. Indicate which lines on the report layout are to be printed as headers, which as footers, and which as detail lines. This is called *marking* the report.

The REPORTS command provides the means for carrying out these six steps. On completion of these steps, a report program is generated which can be run by issuing the PRINT command at the R> prompt. The PRINT command will cause the actual report, which we have defined with the REPORTS command, to be generated and printed.

Getting Started.   Before we can define a report we must identify the database which we will be using. Thus, the first step is to open the database by entering *open retail* at the R> prompt. R:BASE accesses the disk containing our definition of the RETAIL database created by the steps already described, and if it is able to open the database successfully, it displays the message "Database exists".

We now issue the REPORTS command at the R> prompt. R:BASE then prompts us for the name of the report (*commrpt*) and the name of the primary table (*saltx*). We have completed the first two steps of the report definition process, and R:BASE displays the Reports menu which contains the functions needed to carry out the remaining four steps. The first four items on this menu correspond respectively to Steps 3–6 listed above. "Quit" is used when we are through defining the report. We shall not use the other functions listed on this menu.

```
——Edit report—Define—Locate—Mark—Set—Help—Quit——————————————————
```

Placement of Data.   When we select "Edit report", R:BASE displays a (nearly) blank screen and allows us to place constant data wherever we wish. Using this "open screen", all of the report's constant data can be entered by moving the cursor to the desired locations and keying the appropriate information. The escape key is pressed to save this information when we are done.

```
                                      < 15, 39>  [F3] to list, [ESC] to exit
                         HALLIDAY'S DEPARTMENT STORE

                            COMMISSION STATEMENT

  Identification:
            Name:
  Commission Rate:


                            RECORD OF SALES

    Date           Inventory Id      Quantity     Sale Price     Commission
  ------------     ------------      --------     ----------     ----------

                                                 ==========     ==========
                          TOTALS:
```

Definition of Variables. We must now define all variable data that is *not* in the primary table (*saltx*). By examining the sample report in Figure 6.3 we can identify six such data elements. They are: Statement Date, Salesperson Name, Salesperson Commission Rate, Sale Commission Amount, Total of Sales for the Month, and Total Commission for the Month.

To define these data items we select "Define", and R:BASE displays another nearly blank screen with the prompt "Expression:". In response to this prompt, we enter each variable name, the equals sign, and the definition of the variable. For example, we want Statement Date to be equal to the computer system's date; thus we enter: *rptdate = #DATE*. Rptdate is the variable name we have chosen for the Statement Date. #DATE is an R:BASE reserved word for the system date. After we define *rptdate*, R:BASE calculates the data type of *rptdate* and places it together with our definition into a list of variables. We can then define the remaining five variables.

```
                                            [F3] to list, [ESC] to exit
  Expression:

  1:DATE     : rptdate  = #DATE
  2:TEXT     : name     = spname   IN spmast   WHERE spid = spid
  3:REAL     : rate     = commrate IN spmast   WHERE spid = spid
  4:DOLLAR   : cmsn     = salprice x rate
  5:DOLLAR   : totprice = SUM      OF salprice
  6:DOLLAR   : totcmsn  = SUM      OF cmsn
```

As can be seen, the variables are numbered and their calculated data types (e.g., DATE, TEXT, etc.) are given in each case prior to the definition which we entered. These definitions implicitly assume several report processing concepts which we should explain before proceeding further. After the report definition is completed and the report is run (via execution of the PRINT command), each record in the *saltx* table will be read and processed. The order of record access is stated in the PRINT statement and we assume in defining this report that the order of access will be by salesperson identification (*spid*). Thus, all sales records for one salesperson will be read and processed before any records are read for another salesperson.

Each time a *saltx* record is read, all six calculations shown above are performed, *using the contents of the current saltx record.* To illustrate, we will explain the calculation of variables 3, 4, and 6, assuming *spid* equals 101 and *salprice* = 200.

```
3: rate = commrate IN spmast WHERE spid = spid
```

This statement defines the variable name *rate* as equal to the field *commrate* in a particular record of the *spmast* table. The statement "WHERE spid = spid" is shorthand for: "WHERE spid of spmast = spid of saltx."

In other words, the system searches the *spmast* table for a record having the same value in the *spid* field as the current *saltx* record has in its *spid* field. When this record is found, then the variable named *rate* is given the value of the *commrate* field (.10) in this *spmast* record. This is an example of a table look-up function which is performed automatically by the report generator.

```
4: cmsn = salprice × rate
```

Now that we have looked up the commission rate (.10), we can calculate the commission (*cmsn*) on this sale. Since the value of *salprice* in the *saltx* record is 200.00, the value of *cmsn* is 20.00. Note that we used the variable *rate* in this calculcation, and that this variable was calculated immediately before the present calculation. In other words, the order of the definition of the variables is important. The order in which the variables are listed will be the order in which the calculations are performed.

```
6: totcmsn = SUM OFcmsn
```

This definition instructs R:BASE to add the calculated value of *cmsn* to the previously calculated value of *totcmsn*. Thus, *totcmsn* keeps a running total of commission earned by the salesperson. Later, we shall see how *totcmsn* can be reset to zero each time we begin processing data for a new salesperson.

Placement of Variables. We have now completed Step 4 in the report definition process. For Step 5 we select "Locate" from the Reports menu, and the report we earlier began is displayed, with the prompt to enter the name of a column or variable.

```
Name of column or variable: spid                    [F3] to list, [ESC] to exit
                             HALLIDAY'S DEPARTMENT STORE

                             COMMISSION STATEMENT

       Identification:
                 Name:
       Commission Rate:

                              RECORD OF SALES

      Date           Inventory Id   Quantity    Sale Price   Commission
   ------------     ------------    --------    ----------   ----------

                                                ==========   ==========
                              TOTALS:
```

We illustrate the process using the column *spid*. We enter *spid* and move
the cursor to the point where we would like the salesperson identification
field to begin. We strike the S key, and R:BASE displays an S (for start) at
that point. We move the cursor to the point where we want the field to end
and strike E. We repeat this process until all variable data has been located.

```
Name of column or variable:                         [F3] to list, [ESC] to exit
                      HALLIDAY'S DEPARTMENT STORE

                        COMMISSION STATEMENT        S          E

       Identification: S E
                 Name: S        E
       Commission Rate: S  E
                          RECORD OF SALES

      Date           Inventory Id   Quantity    Sale Price   Commission
   ------------     ------------    --------    ----------   ----------
   S           E        S E           SE       S        E   S        E
                                               ==========   ==========
                              TOTALS:  S        E   S        E
```

It is sometimes difficult to remember the names we have given to columns
or defined variables. R:BASE will give us a list of all variables and columns
in the primary table if we press the F3 function key, as noted in the upper-
right corner of the display.

Marking and Control Breaks.   We are now ready for the last step in report
definition, that of marking the report, by identifying when each line should
be printed. Since this concept is an outgrowth of the manner in which
records in the primary table are processed, we now extend our earlier
discussion of report processing.

We previously mentioned that the PRINT statement, used for printing this report, will specify that records in the *saltx* table are to be processed in order by salesperson id (*spid*). Thus, we can think of the *saltx* table as being sorted by *spid,* and then being read and processed sequentially. Each time a *saltx* record is read, the system must determine whether it has the same *spid* as the previous record (and therefore represents just another detail line on the commission statement currently being printed), or whether the *spid* value is new (and therefore represents a different salesperson). In the latter case, the system must print totals of sales and commissions for the previous salesperson, and then must print header information for the commission statement of the new salesperson on the next page.

From the above discussion we can identify three types of lines to be printed on each commission statement:

- Header lines, which are printed each time a new *spid* is encountered.
- Detail lines, which are printed for each *saltx* record.
- Footer lines (for totals), which are printed at the end of the salesperson's statement whenever a *saltx* record for the *next* salesperson is encountered.

Marking the report consists of identifying which of these three categories each line on the report falls into. When we select "Mark" from the Reports menu, the system displays a menu which includes four marking options: Report, Page, Detail, and Break.

```
——Report——Page——Detail——Break——List——Help——Quit———————————————————————————
```

The relationship between these four selections and the three categories of report lines (header, detail, footer) is simple. "Detail" on the menu is used to mark detail lines on the report. "Report", "Page", and "Break" on the menu each are used to mark both header and footer lines. On the commission statement, for example, all header and footer lines are printed whenever the value of *spid* changes. Whenever a control variable like *spid* changes its value we say that a *control break* occurs. Thus, to identify header and footer lines on our commission statement, we select "Break" from the menu and specify which lines are header lines and which are footer lines. An example of selecting the "Report" and "Page" options to identify report headers and footers and page headers and footers is discussed with the inventory report later in this chapter.

To mark the header and footer lines of the commission statement, then, we select "Break" from the menu. The system responds by asking a series of preliminary questions:

1. *What is the break column?* This question asks us to identify the column whose value will indicate that a new set of records is starting and therefore that footers should be printed for the previous set and headers should be printed for the new set. Since the *saltx* table is in order by *spid*, we are grouping records by the value of *spid*. Thus, *spid* is the break column.

2. *Page eject before break heading?* Every time we encounter a new salesperson id (*spid*) we want to start a new commission statement. Since these statements will be distributed individually to the salespeople, we want to be able to separate them on the page perforation. Thus, we *do* want a page eject before the break heading.

3. *Which variables should be reset after break?* Every time we start processing records for a new salesperson we want to reset our running totals to zero. These running totals are kept in the variables *totprice* and *totcmsn*. Consequently, we indicate that these two variables should be reset.

We are next prompted to indicate, in succession, which lines should be header, footer, and detail lines. The lines marked "H1" will print every time a header prints, the lines marked "F1" will print every time a footer prints, and the line marked "D" will print every time a detail line prints. Note that header and footer lines print only when a break occurs—that is, when the value of *spid* in a *saltx* record is different from its value in the previously processed *saltx* record. The detail line, however, will print every time a *saltx* record is processed.

```
Press [D] to mark detail                14                    [ESC] to exit
H1                         HALLIDAY'S DEPARTMENT STORE
H1
H1                            COMMISSION STATEMENT        S        E
H1
H1      Identification: S E
H1               Name: S          E
H1    Commission Rate: S   E
H1
H1                               RECORD OF SALES
H1
H1      Date          Inventory Id    Quantity    Sale Price    Commission
H1    ------------    ------------    --------    ----------    ----------
D     S         E         S E           SE        S        E    S        E
F1                                                ==========    ==========
F1                                    TOTALS:     S        E    S        E
```

We have now completed all of the steps required to generate the report program. To produce the report, we simply run the program by entering the following at the R> prompt:

```
PRINT commrpt SORTED BY spid
```

The Inventory Report

Suppose we wish to produce an inventory report in the format given in Figure 6.4. This report displays the contents of the inventory master file

```
                        HALLIDAY'S DEPARTMENT STORE

PAGE    1                    INVENTORY REPORT      07/01/--

 Category          Name        Ident    Qty   Price          Ext
Appliance       Television      A53       5    75.00       $375.00
                                A54       7   320.00      2,240.00
                                                          --------
                SUBTOTAL                                  2,615.00

                Washer          A61      10   250.00      2,500.00
                                A62       1   275.00        275.00
                                A63       3   300.00        900.00
                                                          --------
                SUBTOTAL                                  3,675.00

                CATEGORY TOTAL                            6,290.00

Furniture       Chair           F30      20   150.00      3,000.00
                                F33      15   100.00      1,500.00
                                                          --------
                SUBTOTAL                                  4,500.00

                Sofa            F84       6   450.00      2,700.00
                                F88       3   750.00      2,250.00
                                                          --------
                SUBTOTAL                                  4,950.00

                CATEGORY TOTAL                            9,450.00

                GRAND TOTAL                              15740.00
                                                         ========
```

FIGURE 6.4   Halliday's Inventory Master File Report

in order by inventory identification within inventory name within inventory category. It calculates the extended price (quantity × price) of every item, and calculates subtotals by name and by category. Finally, a grand total of extended price is given at the end of the report.

Using the REPORTS command, we define the report name (*invrpt*), the primary table (*invmast*), and the report variables. The system's display of this information and the edited report format (with located variables and marked report lines) are shown on the next page.

```
                                    [ESC] to return to variable definition
Report: invrpt      Table: invmast

Variables:

   1:INTEGER : pagenum  = #PAGE
   2:DATE    : rptdate  = #DATE
   3:DOLLAR  : extprice = qtystk    x price
   4:DOLLAR  : subtotal = SUM       OF extprice
   5:DOLLAR  : cattotal = SUM       OF extprice
   6:DOLLAR  : grdtotal = SUM       OF extprice

Columns:

     # Name       Type      Length

     1 invid      TEXT        3 characters
     2 invcat     TEXT       10 characters
     3 invname    TEXT       10 characters
     4 qtystk     INTEGER     1 value(s)
     5 price      DOLLAR      1 value(s)
```

```
Press [F] to mark break footing        12                  [ESC] to exit
HR                    HALLIDAY'S DEPARTMENT STORE
HP
HPPAGE S  E                   INVENTORY REPORT              S         E
HP
HP Category            Name          Ident    Qty   Price      Ext
HP----------        ----------      -----    ---   ------   --------
H1S        E
H2                  S       E
D                                   S E      S E   S     E   S       E
F2                                                                  --------
F2                  SUBTOTAL                              S       E
F1
F1                  CATEGORY TOTAL                        S       E
FR
FR                  GRAND TOTAL                           S       E
FR                                                               ========
```

The "markings" down the column on the left side of this report require some explanation. As previously mentioned, we can categorize the headers and footers as either "Report," "Page," or "Break."

Report headers and footers.   These are the lines marked "HR" and "FR", respectively. Each of these lines is printed only once—the "HR" line at the beginning of the report, and the "FR" lines at the end of the report. We mark these lines by choosing "Report" from the Mark menu.

Page headers and footers.   These lines are marked "HP" and "FP". (In this example there are no page footers. However, we could have formatted the report with page footers if we had chosen.) Page headers and footers are printed every time the printer ejects to a new page. We mark these lines by choosing "Page" from the Mark menu.

Break headers and footers.   These lines are marked "H1", "H2", and "F1", "F2". The lines marked "H1" and "F1" identify the header and footer lines that are printed whenever "break 1" occurs. Break 1 is defined to occur whenever the value of inventory category (*invcat*) changes. Similarly, "H2" and "F2" lines are printed whenever break 2 occurs. Break 2 is defined to occur whenever inventory name (*invname*) changes. Whenever break 2 occurs the value of the variable *subtotal* is reset to zero. Whenever break 1 occurs the variables *subtotal* and *cattotal* are reset. We mark these break headers and footers by selecting "Break" on the Mark menu twice. Each time we select "Break" we are asked to identify the number of the break.

Detail lines.   We mark detail lines by choosing "Detail" from the Mark menu. Our detail line on this report is marked "D".

In order to properly set the control breaks on this report, the PRINT statement must specify three column names on which to sort. The order of the column names is significant. It indicates that the inventory master file should be accessed in order by *invid* within *invname* within *invcat*. That is, *invcat* is the primary sort key, followed by *invname*, followed by *invid*.

```
PRINT invrpt SORTED BY invcat  invname  invid
```

The printed copy of this report is shown in Figure 6.5. Note the difference between this report and our report specification of Figure 6.4. For example, "Appliance", "Television", and "A53" all appear on the same line in Figure 6.4. They are on three separate lines in Figure 6.5. The reason for this is that the inventory category (Appliance) and the inventory name (Television) are printed as header information, while the inventory identification is part of the detail line. Since the report generator does not allow us to designate part of the information on a line as header and part as detail, we had no choice but to place these three items on separate lines.

Integrating Reports into the Menu Structure

The commission statement report program and the inventory report program may now be integrated into the RETMGT system quite easily. Recall that many of the actions for the menu structure of Figure 6.2 were one-line procedures of the form: *run iumacro*. Suppose that the actions for the Reports menu were the one-line procedures: *run irmacro* and *run csmacro*. We now create the command files *irmacro* and *csmacro* as follows:

irmacro

```
        PRINT invrpt SORTED BY invcat  invname  invid
```

csmacro

```
        PRINT commrpt SORTED BY spid
```

When the user selects either of the report options shown on the Reports menu, these statements will cause the appropriate report to be generated.

```
                    HALLIDAY'S DEPARTMENT STORE

PAGE    1                INVENTORY REPORT      07/01/--

Category         Name         Ident   Qty   Price        Ext
----------       ----------   -----   ---   ------     --------
Appliance
                 Television
                              A53       5    75.00     $375.00
                              A54       7   320.00    2,240.00
                                                      --------
                 SUBTOTAL                             2,615.00

                 Washer
                              A61      10   250.00    2,500.00
                              A62       1   275.00     $275.00
                              A63       3   300.00     $900.00
                                                      --------
                 SUBTOTAL                             3,675.00

                 CATEGORY  TOTAL                      6,290.00

Furniture
                 Chair
                              F30      20   150.00    3,000.00
                              F33      15   100.00    1,500.00
                                                      --------
                 SUBTOTAL                             4,500.00

                 Sofa
                              F84       6   450.00    2,700.00
                              F88       3   750.00    2,250.00
                                                      --------
                 SUBTOTAL                             4,950.00

                 CATEGORY  TOTAL                      9,450.00

                 GRAND  TOTAL                        15740.00
                                                     ========
```

FIGURE 6.5   R:BASE Version of Inventory Master File Report

REVIEW QUESTIONS

6.1. List some features of the R:BASE 5000 development environment. List the features of both the Application EXPRESS and the report generator. What is the difference in approach between the Application EXPRESS and the report generator?

6.2. Based on the information in this chapter, what are some limitations of the Application EXPRESS? What are its strengths?

6.3. Suppose you wished to generate a report that required the processing of two tables sequentially. Could you generate such a report with the report generator? Discuss some of the limitations of the report generator.

6.4. In what sense does the report generator use visual programming? How does it combine visual and non-visual programming elements?

6.5. How can the features of the R:BASE 5000 system be related to our definition of 4GLs?

6.6. In general, what does the Application EXPRESS generate?

6.7. Discuss the database definition process provided by Application EXPRESS. In what sense is this process visual?

6.8. In what way does Application EXPRESS support the concept of a centralized data dictionary?

6.9. How are user-defined help screens supported by EXPRESS?

6.10. What is a weakness in the way EXPRESS handles the Delete function? In the way EXPRESS handles the View function?

6.11. Why is it desirable to create a Custom file consisting of only one command (a RUN command, referring to another file), rather than creating the entire command file while using EXPRESS?

6.12. What is the difference between the REPORTS command and the PRINT command?

6.13. What does it mean to "edit," "mark," and "locate" variables on a report?

6.14. What is the difference between "report," "page," and "break" headers and footers?

6.15. How is a table look-up carried out?

EXERCISES

The following exercises assume that the student has access to R:BASE 5000 on a microcomputer system.

6.1. Following the database definition given in Figure 6.1, use Application EXPRESS to define the five tables shown there and to implement the menu structure shown in Figure 6.2. Modify the menu structure of Figure 6.2 to include Add, Change, Delete, and View submenus for the two transaction entry items. Use "run command-file-name" Custom entries for the Reports, Queries, and Batch Processing menus. Implement the commission statement and inventory reports as shown in the text.

6.2. Add a customer purchases report to the Reports menu in the system implemented in Exercise 6.1. Use the REPORTS command of R:BASE to create the program which generates this report. The customer purchases program should print a separate statement for each customer for whom there is a transaction in the *saltx* table. The statement should show the customer's id, name, and address, and should list all sales to that customer. A total of sales should also be shown. Additionally, a grand total of all sales to all customers should be shown at the end of the report.

6.3. Add a payment summary report to the Reports menu. This report should show the identification, name, and total amount paid (for all payment transactions) for each customer who has made a payment. Note that this report has no detail lines.

CHAPTER 7

R:BASE 5000: THE COMMAND LANGUAGE

■ ■

The command language of R:BASE 5000 is a significantly enhanced version of relational algebra. It includes versions of all the relational algebra operations described in Chapter 3 except division and product, and it includes many other powerful capabilities as well. Because of the size of the language, it is not possible to cover all of the commands in this book. We shall concentrate on data manipulation capabilities, focusing on approximately one-fourth of the commands in the language.

R:BASE 5000 commands are executed by the interactive program called r:base. To notify the user that it is ready to receive a command, r:base displays the prompt R>. After the user enters a command, the program executes the command and redisplays the R> prompt.

In the previous chapter we discussed three R:BASE commands: REPORTS, PRINT, and RUN. The last of these is of particular interest in the present chapter. Suppose we entered the command *RUN cmdfile* at the R> prompt. R:BASE would search the default disk directory for a file named "cmdfile" and would execute the contents of this file as if they were commands entered by the user from the keyboard. That is, we can build a set of commands, place them in a file, and use the RUN command to execute the entire file of commands without further intervention from the keyboard. Any command that can be executed interactively can be placed in a command file.

Additionally, R:BASE provides control commands (IF, WHILE, etc.) which allow conditional and repeated execution of commands. Thus, the R:BASE program provides not only an interactive command language, but it provides a full-powered programming language as well.

The commands we shall consider can be logically divided into three groups: (1) data manipulation commands, (2) program control commands, and (3) user/computer interaction commands. The present chapter is devoted to discussion and illustration of the application of these commands. To provide continuity with the previous chapter we shall continue using Halliday's retail database, with sample data shown in Figure 7.1.

DATA MANIPULATION COMMANDS

This chapter concentrates on the following commands for data manipulation: INTERSECT, UNION, SUBTRACT, WHERE clause, PROJECT, COMPUTE, and JOIN. Other commands and clauses are introduced as needed to demonstrate usage of those listed.

INTERSECT

The INTERSECT command is nothing more than the natural join of relational algebra, possibly combined with a projection.

GENERAL SYNTAX

```
INTERSECT table1 WITH table2 FORMING table3 +
     [USING collist]
```

The plus sign (+) indicates the continuation of the statement to the next line. In executing this command, the system naturally joins table1 to table2 on all columns which are common to the two tables. The resulting table is table3. Why is this operation called an intersection? The operation becomes a relational algebra intersection whenever the two tables have *all* of their columns in common. In this case the tables are union compatible, and relational algebra intersection is defined. But when that happens, intersection and natural join have the same result.

The last part of the statement (in square brackets) is called the USING clause. The square brackets indicate that this part of the statement is optional. If the USING clause is included, then only those columns listed in the clause (the "collist") are included in the new table (table3).

EXAMPLE: Create a table of customer names and their payment amounts.

```
INTERSECT custmast WITH pmttx FORMING new1 +
                   USING custname pmtamt
```

Result: **Table new1**

custname	pmtamt
C. Brown	100.00
C. White	300.00
C. Brown	110.00

RETAIL MANAGEMENT DATABASE

INVENTORY MASTER (invmast)

invid	invcat	invname	qtystk	price
A53	Appliance	Television	5	75.00
A54	Appliance	Television	7	320.00
A61	Appliance	Washer	10	250.00
A62	Appliance	Washer	1	275.00
A63	Appliance	Washer	3	300.00
F30	Furniture	Chair	20	150.00
F33	Furniture	Chair	15	100.00
F84	Furniture	Sofa	6	450.00
F88	Furniture	Sofa	3	750.00

SALESPERSON MASTER (spmast)

spid	spname	commrate
101	Smith	.10
105	Jones	.15

CUSTOMER MASTER (custmast)

custid	custname	custaddr	custbal
200	C. Brown	111 Any St.	250.00
202	C. Green	4091 Main	100.00
205	C. White	255 B St.	400.00

SALES TRANSACTIONS (saltx)

saldate	saltime	spid	custid	cashchg	invid	salqty	salprice
6/02/--	14:00	101	202	A	A53	1	75.00
6/10/--	9:30	101	200	H	F88	1	750.00
6/13/--	10:15	105	200	H	F30	1	150.00
6/15/--	15:27	105	205	A	A61	1	250.00
6/23/--	9:45	101	202	H	F84	1	450.00

PAYMENT TRANSACTIONS (pmttx)

pmtdate	custid	pmtamt
6/12/--	200	100.00
6/14/--	205	300.00
6/20/--	200	110.00

FIGURE 7.1   Database for Halliday's Retail Management System

The natural join of this operation takes place on *custid,* since this is the column that the tables *custmast* and *pmttx* have in common. However, *custid* does not appear in the final result since it was not listed in the USING clause.

UNION

The syntax of UNION is nearly identical to that of INTERSECTION:

GENERAL SYNTAX

```
UNION table1 WITH table2 FORMING table3 +
     [USING collist]
```

The UNION operation is the *outer join* of relational algebra. The outer join works as follows: records in the two tables are matched on their common columns as in the natural join. If they match, then a new record is created containing the values of all of the columns of the two records. If a record in either table matches *no* record in the other table, a new record is created by adding the additional columns from the other table. These new columns contain null values.

EXAMPLE: Create the union of table *custmast* and *pmttx.*

```
UNION custmast WITH pmttx FORMING new2
```

Result: Table new2

custid	custname	custaddr	custbal	pmtdate	pmtamt
200	C. Brown	111 Any St.	250.00	6/12/--	100.00
202	C. Green	4091 Main	100.00	-0-	-0-
205	C. White	255 B St.	400.00	6/14/--	300.00
200	C. Brown	111 Any St.	250.00	6/20/--	110.00

Since C. Green has not submitted a payment, that record is filled with nulls (-0-) in the payment columns.

SUBTRACT

GENERAL SYNTAX

```
SUBTRACT table1 FROM table2 FORMING table3 +
     [USING collist]
```

The SUBTRACT operation is a generalization of the relational algebra subtraction. Records in two tables are matched on common columns. If a record in table2 matches no record in table1, then that record is included in table3. As before, the USING clause identifies those columns which are to be included in the new table.

EXAMPLE: Identify customers who have made no payment.

```
SUBTRACT pmttx FROM custmast FORMING new3
```

Result: Table new3

custid	custname	custaddr	custbal
202	C. Green	4091 Main	100.00

C. Green is the only customer who has not submitted a payment. Note that if there is no USING clause, then the columns of the new table are the same as those of table2.

The WHERE Clause

A clause is not a command, but rather a logically identifiable portion of a command. Some clauses appear in many different commands, as, for example, the USING clause seen above. The WHERE clause also appears in several commands, and because of its importance and complexity we will discuss it separately.

The WHERE clause is used within a command in the same way that the selection operation is used in relational algebra. That is, the WHERE clause is used to identify those rows in a previously specified table upon which the larger command will operate.

GENERAL SYNTAX

```
WHERE condition-list
```

The condition list is a set of simple conditions connected by Boolean *ANDs* and *ORs*. Parentheses are *not* allowed. Possible simple conditions are given in Figure 7.2.

Several of the terms in Figure 7.2 require explanation. *Column-name* means the name of a column in a table. For example, *invcat* is a column-name in the table *invmast*.

Value can be either a literal value (e.g., 45, 23.05, Smith) or the value of a variable. A variable is not a column-name, but rather a name of a work area value previously defined by the user. In order to distinguish the value of a variable from a string literal (like "Smith"), the user must precede the variable name with a period, as shown in the examples on page 160.

CONDITION	MEANING
column-name EXISTS	True if column-name is not null
column-name FAILS	True if column-name is null
column-name OP value	OP may be EQ, NE, GT, GE, LT, LE
column-name1 OP column-name2	OP may be EQA, NEA, GTA, GEA, LTA, LEA
column-name CONTAINS string	True if column-name contains the specified string
LIMIT OP value	OP may be EQ, GE
COUNT OP value	OP may be EQ, GE
COUNT OP LAST	OP may be EQ, GE; and LAST means the last row in the table

FIGURE 7.2   Simple Condition Formats

"Column-name1 OP column-name2" compares two different columns in the same row of the same table. Note that for comparison of two columns, the relational operators (OP) require a trailing "A".

The following are examples of the use of the WHERE clause:

```
WHERE pmtamt EXISTS
WHERE pmtamt FAILS
```

Using table new2, previously created, the WHERE clause with FAILS will be true for the second row while the clause with EXISTS will be true for all the other rows.

```
WHERE invcat EQ Appliance
```

Use of a string literal causes selection of only the rows containing the literal value in the specified column. In this case, the only rows selected are those where the inventory category is Appliance.

```
WHERE qtystk GE 10
```

This clause will cause items A61, F30, and F33 to be selected from *invmast*.

```
WHERE qtystk EQ .stock
```

This WHERE clause assumes that a variable named *stock* has been previously defined. Rows in *invmast* will be selected if their *qtystk* column is equal to the current value of the variable *stock*.

```
WHERE custaddr CONTAINS Main
```

This clause will cause all customer rows to be selected where the customer lives on Main Street. In fact, if "Main" appears anywhere in the address, the row will be selected.

```
WHERE LIMIT EQ 20
```

LIMIT is an R:BASE reserved word. The LIMIT operator above tells the system to process no more than 20 rows.

```
WHERE COUNT EQ 30
```

COUNT is also an R:BASE reserved word. In this case, the system will select only the 30th row in the table.

```
WHERE COUNT EQ LAST
```

In this case, the system will select only the (physically and chronologically) last row in the table. It is sometimes useful to be able to identify the row most recently added to a table, in order to perform some special processing on that row.

Remember that the WHERE clause is not an operation or command, but rather a clause used by several different operations and commands to identify which rows will be used. The next two commands will provide examples of the use of the WHERE clause.

PROJECT

The PROJECT command combines the selection and projection operations of relational algebra.

GENERAL SYNTAX

```
PROJECT table2 FROM table1 USING +
     {ALL|collist} [SORTED BY collist] +
     [WHERE condition-list]
```

The columns to be included in the new table (table2) are identified in the USING clause, which is required. The syntax "{ALL|collist}" means that one of the choices separated by "|" must be chosen. The WHERE clause is optional. If ALL (meaning "all columns") appears in the USING clause, and a WHERE clause is included, then the PROJECT command is simply a relational algebra selection. The SORTED BY clause can be used to place the rows in order for display.

EXAMPLE: Create a table containing the inventory id, name, and price of furniture priced below $200.

```
PROJECT new4 FROM invmast USING invid invname price +
     WHERE invcat EQ Furniture AND price LT 200
```

Result: **Table new4**

invid	invname	price
F30	Chair	150.00
F33	Chair	100.00

COMPUTE

The COMPUTE command is used to calculate values for groups of rows. Its general syntax may take any of the following three forms:

GENERAL SYNTAX

```
COMPUTE [variable-name AS] function +
    column-name FROM table +
    [WHERE condition-list]
```

```
COMPUTE [variable-name AS] ROWS FROM table
```

```
COMPUTE ALL column-name FROM table +
    [WHERE condition-list]
```

In the first format, the function operator is from the set: AVE, COUNT, MAX, MIN, and SUM. The second COMPUTE format merely counts the number of rows in the designated table. The third calculates and displays all five functions for a designated column and table. In the first or second formats, the result may be displayed on the screen or, optionally, may be placed in a user-designated variable. In the third, the results are displayed on the screen. The examples below illustrate the first format.

QUERY: What is the highest priced washer?

```
COMPUTE MAX price FROM invmast WHERE invname = Washer
```

QUERY: What is the total of sales to customer 202?

```
COMPUTE SUM salprice FROM saltx WHERE custid = 202
```

QUERY: What is the inventory name that comes earliest in alphabetical order?

```
COMPUTE MIN invname FROM invmast
```

QUERY: Count the number of sales exceeding $200 and place the result in the variable "hisales".

```
COMPUTE hisales AS COUNT salprice WHERE salprice GT 200
```

QUERY: What is the average sale for salesperson 101?

```
COMPUTE ave101 AS AVE salprice FROM saltx +
        WHERE spid = 101
```

JOIN

Since the natural join and the outer join are available in the INTER-SECTION and UNION commands, the more general JOIN command is not used frequently. However, to illustrate the extent of R:BASE 5000's support of relational algebra, we will give the JOIN syntax.

GENERAL SYNTAX

```
JOIN table1 USING column-name1 WITH table2 +
     USING column-name2 FORMING table3 +
     [WHERE op]
```

"Op" in the WHERE clause is one of the six operators: EQ, NE, GT, GE, LT, LE. If the WHERE clause is omitted, the system assumes that EQ has been specified. Records in table3, which are created by this JOIN, consist of a record from table1 and a record from table2 such that the relationship "op" holds between the designated columns. Thus, except for syntax, this JOIN is identical to the join of relational algebra described in Chapter 3.

Sample Queries

We now illustrate the practical application of these commands by developing two simple "canned" queries which could be implemented in an applications system. These queries will consist of a set of data manipulation commands which could be placed in a command file and executed via the RUN command. Such queries could also be integrated into an applications system as shown in the previous chapter.

QUERY: Calculate the largest sale for a given salesperson and display it on the screen. The user should be prompted for the salesperson's name and, using the name entered, that salesperson's maximum sale will be calculated.

```
FILLIN vspname USING "Enter salesperson name: "
INTERSECT spmast WITH saltx FORMING new5
COMPUTE MAX salprice FROM new5 +
        WHERE spname EQ .vspname
```

The first line in this query introduces the FILLIN command, which prompts the user for data by displaying a message on the screen. In this case, the message is "Enter salesperson name: ". The system then pauses while the user enters the name. The entered name is stored in the variable *vspname,* which is created by the system if it did not already exist. The system then performs the INTERSECT command, which creates the table "new5" as the natural join of *spmast* and *saltx.* This new table is used to compute the maximum sale price of all sales made by the salesperson whose name is stored in *vspname.* Since we did not specify a variable into which the result of the COMPUTE statement should be placed, the result will be displayed on the screen.

Note that the WHERE clause in the COMPUTE statement reads *WHERE spname EQ .vspname* rather than *WHERE spname EQ vspname.* If the latter form had been used, then *vspname* would have been interpreted as a string literal rather than a variable name.

QUERY: List all items in a user-specified category for which there is no sales transaction. In other words, we want to know which items have not been sold in the period covered by these transactions.

We shall illustrate two different approaches to this query, one using UNION, the other using SUBTRACT.

```
FILLIN vinvcat USING "Enter inventory category:  "
PROJECT new6 FROM invmast USING invid invname +
     WHERE invcat EQ .vinvcat
UNION new6 WITH saltx FORMING new7
SELECT invid invname FROM new7 WHERE saldate FAILS
```

The PROJECT command produces a table containing only the id numbers and names of items in the user-selected category. The UNION command creates the outer join of this table and the *saltx* table. Items which have not been sold will have null values in the *sales* columns. Thus, for example, if an item has not been sold, then its value for *saldate* in the *new7* table will be null. The last command, SELECT, is nearly identical in function to the PROJECT command. The only difference between them is that the PROJECT command creates a new table, while the SELECT command displays its result on the screen. In this example of UNION, SELECT tells the system to display the *invid* and *invname* of every row in *new7* which has a null value for *saldate.*

This next approach shows how the SUBTRACT command can be used. The first two commands of this query are identical to the previous query. The third command removes all items from *new6* for which there is a sales transaction, creating a table (*new7*) containing only those items which have not been sold. The SELECT command simply displays the contents of *new7.*

```
FILLIN vinvcat USING "Enter inventory category:  "
PROJECT new6 FROM invmast USING invid invname +
    WHERE invcat EQ .vinvcat
SUBTRACT saltx FROM new6 FORMING new7
SELECT ALL FROM new7
```

GENERAL SYNTAX

```
SELECT {ALL|column-list} FROM table +
    [SORTED BY column-list] +
    [WHERE condition-list]
```

To illustrate the SORTED BY clause, suppose we want the result of the last query to be displayed in order by inventory identification. Then we would have written the last command:

```
SELECT ALL FROM new7 SORTED BY invid
```

Result: Table new 7

invid	invname
A54	Television
A62	Washer
A63	Washer
F33	Chair

PROGRAM CONTROL COMMANDS

In this section we demonstrate how to use the programming language facility to create a batch program which uses the records from the sales transactions table (*saltx*) to update the inventory master table (*invmast*). We shall call this program the Inventory Master Update program. This program constitutes the last remaining piece of the applications system which we partially developed in the previous chapter.

In order to appreciate what the R:BASE programming language can and cannot do, it is useful to examine the requirements of this program in more depth. Whenever an item is sold, a transaction is recorded in the *saltx* table. The sale of the item should cause the quantity in stock to be reduced by the quantity sold. Thus, the Inventory Master Update program should apply these transactions to their respective inventory master records, and reduce the quantity in stock by the quantity sold.

Ideally, it is most desirable to update the inventory master immediately after the item is sold, but for various reasons this approach is not always practical. Since the need for inventory master update provides an excellent example of the R:BASE batch processing capability, we shall assume that the inventory master is updated on a periodic basis using a table of batched sales transactions.

If we were to write this program using a 3GL such as COBOL, we could sort both tables in order by inventory id, and then use sequential processing to process the two tables together. Since there are likely to be multiple sales transactions for any given inventory item, we would hold an inventory master record in memory while we apply transactions (one at a time) to that record. When we finally read a transaction for a different inventory master record, we would write the updated inventory master record and then read another. The process of updating would then start over with this new inventory master record.

The relational data manipulation approach of processing multiple records at a time will help us avoid the single record processing which is characteristic of 3GLs. We will not be able to avoid single record processing altogether, but R:BASE does provide support for multiple record processing which we shall find helpful in this problem. In particular, instead of applying the transactions one at a time to a given inventory master record, we shall apply all of the transactions at once.

Our approach will be simple. We read a master record. Then we set up a loop to first, apply all of the transactions to the master record and, second, to read the next master record. To accomplish this, we need commands to read records sequentially, change the contents of those records, and control the repeated execution of commands. We now introduce the commands to perform these functions.

SET POINTER

The SET POINTER command accomplishes several functions.

1. It identifies a table to be processed.
2. It specifies the order in which records are to be processed via its SORTED BY clause.
3. It restricts processing, via the WHERE clause, to records satisfying specified conditions.
4. It uses a number to identify the first record satisfying the criteria established by the first three functions; that is, the first record in the named table, which is in the order given in the SORTED BY clause, and which satisfies the conditions of the WHERE clause.
5. It defines a variable whose value indicates whether there is a record satisfying the first three criteria. This variable can be used as an end of file indicator.

The general syntax is shown at the top of the next page, with "n" in this format being an integer.

GENERAL SYNTAX

```
SET POINTER #n [variable-name] FOR table +
    [SORTED BY collist] +
    [WHERE condition-list]
```

EXAMPLE: SET POINTER #1 eof FOR invmast SORTED BY invid

This statement (1) identifies the table as *invmast*, (2) indicates (via the SORTED BY clause) that the records are to be processed in order by the value of *invid*, (3) indicates that all records in the table are to be processed (by the absence of the WHERE clause), (4) indicates that the expression "#1" will be used in subsequent commands to identify the record in *invmast* which is first in order by the value of *invid*, and (5) defines a variable (*eof*) which will indicate by its value whether or not there is a record pointed to by "#1".

NEXT

The SET POINTER command carries out the five functions we have identified above. The first three functions apply to the processing of the table in general, not to the processing of any particular record. Functions 4 and 5 apply only to the first record to be processed. In order to process the second and all subsequent records in the table, we need another command: the NEXT command.

GENERAL SYNTAX

```
NEXT #n [variable-name]
```

EXAMPLE: SET POINTER #1 eof FOR invmast SORTED BY invid
(commands to process the record retrieved)
NEXT #1 eof

Using the database of Figure 7.1, this set of commands first retrieves and processes the record with *invid* = A53. The NEXT command would then retrieve the record with *invid* = A54.

Note that the NEXT command assumes the table, SORT order, and WHERE conditions established by the previously executed SET POINTER command. By using the same number (#1 in this example) in the NEXT command as was used in the SET POINTER command, we inform the system that these two commands are related to each other.

SET VARIABLE

Our goal is to reduce the quantity in stock by the quantity sold. We will obtain the quantity sold by using the COMPUTE command on the *saltx* table. However, before we can use the COMPUTE command, we must store the value of *invid* from the inventory master record in a variable. Only then can this value be used in the COMPUTE command. To store a column value in a variable we use SET VARIABLE.

GENERAL SYNTAX

```
SET VARIABLE variable-name TO value
"value" can be any of the following:
■ a literal value
■ .variable-name2
■ column-name IN table
        [WHERE condition-list]
■ column-name IN #n (n defined by
        SET POINTER command)
■ arithmetic or string expression
```

An expression contains values combined by operators such as +, −, ×, /, % for arithmetic (numeric) variables and +, & for string variables. The plus and ampersand (+, &) concatenate string values. The ampersand causes a space to be placed between the values, while the plus causes concatenation with no space between the values.

We now are ready to show the commands needed to compute the quantity sold for the first inventory master record.

```
SET POINTER #1 eof FOR invmast SORTED BY invid
SET VARIABLE vinvid TO invid IN #1
COMPUTE vqtysold AS SUM salqty FROM saltx +
        WHERE invid = .vinvid
```

The variable *vqtysold* now contains the quantity sold of item *invid*.

ASSIGN

We are now ready to reduce the quantity in stock in the *invmast* record by the quantity sold as contained in *vqtysold*. To change this data record, we use the ASSIGN command.

GENERAL SYNTAX

```
ASSIGN column-name TO expression IN +
        {#n | table [WHERE condition-list]}
```

The ASSIGN syntax is slightly misleading. The column-name field, not the expression, is being changed. The column in the designated record(s) is changed to the calculated value of the expression. The expression may take any of the following forms:

```
column-name1 OP column-name2
column-name  OP value
value        OP column-name
value        OP value
```

In this format, OP is $+$, $-$, $\times$, $/$, %, or &. The plus sign can be used to add numbers or to concatenate string values. The ampersand is used only with string values and causes them to be concatenated with a space between them. The other operators are used only with numbers.

We shall use the ASSIGN command to change the value of the column *qtystk* in *invmast*. As a result of the SET POINTER command, the record we wish to change is identified by the pointer #1. Adding the appropriate ASSIGN command to our previously developed statements, we have:

```
SET POINTER #1 eof FOR invmast SORTED BY invid
SET VARIABLE vinvid TO invid IN #1
COMPUTE vqtysold AS SUM salqty FROM saltx +
        WHERE invid = .vinvid
ASSIGN qtystk TO qtystk - .vqtysold IN #1
```

The use of "#1" in the ASSIGN command refers to a specific record, whose *qtystk* column we are changing. This is the way such pointers are typically used. Note that the column being changed can be referenced in the expression. The column's value as used in the expression is its value *prior* to being changed by the ASSIGN command.

WHILE

We have written the commands needed to update one inventory master record. In fact we have demonstrated all of the commands needed for our program except for one to control the repeated execution of the updating commands. For this we need the WHILE statement.

GENERAL SYNTAX

```
WHILE condition-list THEN
     while-block (one or more statements)
ENDWHILE
```

The condition-list is one or more simple conditions connected by Boolean *AND*s and *OR*s. Parentheses are not allowed. Allowable formats for simple conditions are given in Figure 7.3. Note that the ENDWHILE is an essential

variable-name EXISTS
variable-name FAILS
variable-name CONTAINS string
variable-name OP value

OP is EQ, NE, GT, GE, LT, or LE
"value" is a literal or a variable name preceded by a period

FIGURE 7.3   Formats For WHILE and IF Condition Lists

part of the WHILE statement; it appears on a separate line from WHILE
and is not a continuation.

The R:BASE WHILE statement is used in the same manner as it is used
in other programming languages. The statements in the while-block are
executed repeatedly, each time if and only if the condition-list, considered
as a single condition, is true. If the condition-list is found to be false prior
to an execution of the while-block, then the while-block is not executed
and control passes to the statement immediately after ENDWHILE. WHILE
statements can be nested within other WHILE statements.

We now give the completed version of our Inventory Master Update
program:

```
SET POINTER #1 eof FOR invmast SORTED BY invid
WHILE eof = 0 THEN
     SET VARIABLE vinvid TO invid IN #1
     COMPUTE vqtysold AS SUM salqty FROM saltx +
          WHERE invid = .vinvid
     ASSIGN qtystk TO qtystk - .vqtysold IN #1
     NEXT #1 eof
ENDWHILE
```

To this point we have ignored the specific meaning of the variable *eof* in
the SET POINTER and NEXT commands. If a record is successfully found
as a result of either of these commands, *eof* is set to 0. If a record is not
successfully found—such as when all records have been processed, and we
have, therefore, come to an end of file—*eof* is set to a non-zero value. Thus,
we are using *eof* to process the *invmast* table sequentially and to detect end
of file. At that point the WHILE loop terminates.

This program follows the outline of the program we gave at the beginning
of the section: Read a master record (SET POINTER), then set up a loop
to process the record and read the next master record (NEXT).

IF

One of the most basic building blocks of computer applications systems is the statement whose execution is conditional. In most languages, such statements are controlled by IF constructions.

GENERAL SYNTAX

```
IF condition-list THEN
      then-block (one or more statements)
[ELSE
      else-block] (one or more statements)
ENDIF
```

The condition-list format for IF is identical to that for WHILE. Simple condition formats were shown in Figure 7.3. Note that ELSE and its associated else-block of statements are optional. IF works in R:BASE in the same manner as it does in other languages: If the condition-list is true, the then-block is executed. If not, the else-block (if any) is executed. Control then proceeds to the statement following ENDIF.

We illustrate the IF statement by enhancing our program. Suppose we wish to identify those inventory items for which there has been no sale during the period covered by the *saltx* table. In that case the quantity sold should be 0. We will use the IF statement to test the value of *vqtysold*. If it is 0, we will display a message. Otherwise, we will update the inventory master record (and, of course, *not* display a message). The following code gives the new version of the program:

```
SET POINTER #1 eof FOR invmast SORTED BY invid
WHILE eof = 0 THEN
      SET VARIABLE vinvid TO invid IN #1
      COMPUTE vqtysold AS SUM salqty FROM saltx +
            WHERE invid = .vinvid
      If vqtysold EQ 0 THEN
            SET VARIABLE soldmsg TO .vinvid & "NOT SOLD"
            WRITE .soldmsg
      ELSE
            ASSIGN qtystk TO qtystk - .vqtysold IN #1
      ENDIF
      NEXT #1 eof
ENDWHILE
```

The SET VARIABLE command is used to develop a message for display by concatenating the literal "NOT SOLD" to the value of the string variable *vinvid*. This creates a value which states that "inventory id such-and-such has not been sold during this period." The WRITE command that appears in the program code is discussed below.

WRITE

The WRITE command is used to display a message on the screen.

GENERAL SYNTAX

```
WRITE message [AT screen-row screen-column]
```

"Message" is a string value, either a literal (with or without quotation marks) or a string variable name preceded by a period. Note that, optionally, the location on the screen where the message is to begin can be specified.

ADDITIONAL COMMANDS

In the previous two sections we have covered the principal data manipulation and program control commands in detail. R:BASE supports many other commands which are useful in applications systems. In this section we shall give brief descriptions of a number of these, presented in alphabetical order.

APPEND

GENERAL SYNTAX

```
APPEND table1 TO table2 +
       [WHERE condition-list]
```

APPEND adds the rows of table1 to the end of table2. If there is a WHERE clause, it qualifies those rows of table1 which are to be added to table2. If table1 contains duplicates of rows in table2, there will be duplicate rows in table2 after the APPEND operation is completed. To eliminate these duplicates, use the DELETE DUPLICATES version of the DELETE command (see page 173).

BREAK

The BREAK command is used only within WHILE loops. When executed, it terminates the WHILE loop. Control passes to the first statement after ENDWHILE. Normally, BREAK is part of an IF statement, and causes the remaining statements in the WHILE loop to be skipped.

GENERAL SYNTAX

```
BREAK
```

CHANGE

CHANGE can be used to change the value of a column in one table or in all tables of the database. The rows containing the value to be changed can be defined by a pointer or by a WHERE clause. If the pointer is not used, the WHERE clause is required. To change the value of the column in every row of the table, the WHERE clause should be structured to be true about every row (e.g., WHERE column-name EXISTS).

GENERAL SYNTAX

```
CHANGE column-name TO value +
     {IN #n | [IN table] +
     WHERE condition-list}
```

EXAMPLE: Change every occurrence of *invid* A54 to A58.

```
CHANGE invid TO A58 WHERE invid = A54
```

This changes *invid* A54 to A58 in every table in the database containing *invid*.

DELETE

GENERAL SYNTAX

```
DELETE ROWS FROM {#n | table +
     WHERE condition-list}
```

```
DELETE DUPLICATES FROM table
```

The first format can be used to delete a single row (identified with a pointer number) or a set of rows (satisfying a WHERE clause) from a table. The second format is used to eliminate duplicate rows from a table, as in the result of an APPEND.

LIST

This command is valuable in system development. It provides means for accessing the R:BASE documentation of an applications system.

GENERAL SYNTAX

```
LIST list-type
where list-type is one of:
COLUMN NAMES - lists all column definitions in the open
               database
DATABASES - lists all available databases
FORMS - lists form names defined for the open database
REPORTS - lists names of reports defined for the open
         database
TABLES - lists tables in the open database
table - lists information about the specified table
```

NEWPAGE

This command causes the output device (printer or screen) to start a new page. The printer will eject to the next page. If the output device is the screen, then a blank screen will be displayed with the cursor at the top.

GENERAL SYNTAX

```
NEWPAGE
```

OPEN

This command is necessary to make the database accessible for updating and for screen and report definition.

GENERAL SYNTAX

```
OPEN database-name
```

OUTPUT

GENERAL SYNTAX

```
OUTPUT {PRINTER | SCREEN | file-name} +
       [WITH device-id]
```

"Device-id" is one of: SCREEN, PRINTER, BOTH, or file-name. Before the OUTPUT command is executed, all messages resulting from a WRITE or PRINT statement are sent to the screen. After the OUTPUT command is executed, they are sent to the device indicated. The WITH clause may be used to indicate that a second (or possibly third) device should also receive output.

EXAMPLE: Cause all output to be printed, to be displayed on the screen, and to be saved on a file named "optext".

```
OUTPUT optext WITH BOTH
```

PACK

The DELETE and REMOVE commands cause data to be inaccessible, but the space formerly occupied by the data is not made available for system use. PACK is used to recover that space. If the database-name is not specified, the PACK will be performed on the open database. If the system goes down while the PACK is in progress, the database can be lost. Therefore, the database should be backed up before PACK is executed.

GENERAL SYNTAX

```
PACK [database-name]
```

PAUSE

This command causes the system to suspend execution until the user strikes a key on the keyboard. It does *not* send a message to the screen. Therefore, some other command (e.g., WRITE) must be executed to notify the user to strike a key when ready to proceed.

GENERAL SYNTAX

```
PAUSE
```

PRINT

Examples of the PRINT statement were given in the previous chapter. PRINT may contain a WHERE clause. Thus, if the data from the primary table is to be restricted to rows satisfying certain criteria, these criteria can be specified in the WHERE clause.

GENERAL SYNTAX

```
PRINT report [SORTED BY column-list] +
      [WHERE condition-list]
```

REMOVE

Most of the data manipulation commands (INTERSECT, UNION, PROJECT, etc.) cause new tables to be created. To keep the database uncluttered and utilize space in the most economical way, it is necessary to remove these tables after they have been used. The REMOVE command deletes the indicated table from the database. However, the space formerly occupied by the table is not available for system use until a PACK command is executed.

GENERAL SYNTAX

```
REMOVE table
```

RETURN

GENERAL SYNTAX

```
RETURN
```

It is possible to develop a modular program structure by combining RUN and RETURN commands. For example, assume we have created two files named "file1" and "file2" containing the following commands:

file1
```
WRITE "file 1 is executing"
RUN file2
WRITE "file 1 is executing again"
```

file2
```
WRITE "file 2 is executing"
RETURN
```

If the command *RUN file1* is entered at the R> prompt, the following sequence of messages will be displayed:

file 1 is executing
file 2 is executing
file 1 is executing again

When the RUN statement in file1 is encountered, the system suspends execution of file1 and begins executing statements in file2. When the RETURN statement in file2 is encountered, the system leaves file2 and returns to file1, beginning execution at the statement immediately after the RUN statement. This technique follows the standard practice of most programming languages.

RUN

The RUN command causes a file of commands to be executed, just as if they had been entered from the keyboard.

GENERAL SYNTAX

```
RUN command-file
```

SUMMARY

R:BASE supports many more commands and functions than we can cover in this text. For instance, commands are supported for forms development and use, database definition modification, data security and integrity, data loading, operating system interaction, and system debugging. Clearly, there is substantial power in the R:BASE system for automating important business applications.

REVIEW QUESTIONS

7.1. Under what circumstances is the UNION operation of R:BASE the same as the union of relational algebra?

7.2. When is the SUBTRACT operation of R:BASE the same as the subtract of relational algebra?

7.3. How is the relational algebra project operation incorporated into R:BASE operations? Which R:BASE operations include a relational algebra project?

7.4. How is the relational algebra select operation incorporated into R:BASE operations? Which R:BASE operations include a relational algebra select? Is there an R:BASE operation which is essentially a relational algebra select and project?

7.5. How is the relational algebra assignment operation implemented in R:BASE commands?

7.6. How does the R:BASE prohibition of parentheses in the WHERE clause present difficulties in formulating commands? Can you develop a condition with parentheses that would be difficult or impossible to express without parentheses?

7.7. Compare the R:BASE COMPUTE command with the built-in functions of SQL and the aggregate operators of QUEL.

7.8. Which R:BASE commands give the R:BASE language the full capability of structured programming?

7.9. What are some practical reasons for preferring batch update processing to on-line update processing? (Consider the problems of response time, system failure, multiple users, etc.)

EXERCISES

For the following exercises it is assumed that the student has access to R:BASE 5000 on a microcomputer system. We further assume the database of Figure 7.1.

QUERIES

Create R:BASE command files to carry out the following queries. These may be integrated into the system developed in Chapter 6.

7.1. List all salespeople who have sold more than a selected dollar amount of a selected inventory name. The user should be prompted for both the dollar amount and the inventory name.

7.2. List all inventory items sold by salespeople receiving more than a user-specified commission rate.

7.3. Calculate the total sales amount of inventory items in a user-specified category.

7.4. List all salespeople who have not sold any inventory items with a price over a user-specified amount. Use *price* in the inventory master relation.

UPDATE and REPORT PROGRAMS

7.5. Create a program to update the customer master balance field (*cust-bal*). Assume that a purchase increases the customer's balance and a payment reduces the balance. Write the program as a batch program which uses the entire customer master, sales transactions, and payment transactions tables.

7.6. Create a program integrated into the program of exercise 7.5 (or a standalone program) to generate a customer statement report. A separate statement should be printed for each customer. The statement should include the customer's id, name, address, and beginning balance in the header, and should list all purchases and payments. Totals of purchases and payments should be calculated and printed. Also, an end-of-statement balance should be printed.

CHAPTER 8

THE ENVIRONMENT
OF
dBASE III PLUS

▪ ▪

dBASE III Plus, a product of Ashton-Tate, is a microcomputer-based database management system which provides a powerful multifaceted environment for application development. Among its features are a database definition and manipulation language; a procedural programming language; program, report, and screen generators; and a file interface for communication with other systems. dBASE III Plus supports interactive and batch command execution, and it uses visual programming concepts in several programs.

The philosophy represented in the structure of dBASE III Plus presents an interesting contrast to that of R:BASE 5000. With the exception of the CLOUT natural language interface, R:BASE 5000 is oriented to the system developer. The R:BASE Application EXPRESS and the report generator discussed in Chapter 6 are powerful tools for developing relatively complex applications. dBASE, on the other hand, provides more tools that benefit the novice user. These tools make it easier to use the system interactively and to develop simple applications. However, because these dBASE tools are oriented toward the novice user, they are less suited to the development of more complex applications. We shall study these tools in this chapter.

The present chapter will be concerned with those aspects of the dBASE environment found in the Applications Generator, the dBASE Assistant, and the dBASE report generation facility. Chapter 9 will cover the dBASE command and programming languages. The principal facilities of dBASE III Plus are contained in the program whose execution name is "dbase". When "dbase" is executed, the "dot" prompt (".") tells the user that a dBASE command is expected.

THE APPLICATIONS GENERATOR

The Applications Generator generates files of dBASE commands as a result of interactive instructions from the programmer. These command files can then be executed as application programs by the dBASE system. The Applications Generator is itself a dBASE program which is executed from the dBASE dot (.) prompt. From the dot prompt, the user simply enters *DO appsgen,* and the Applications Generator begins execution.

Throughout this chapter and the next, we shall continue to use the Halliday's database as redefined in Figure 8.1. As indicated, this database provides the basis for a retail management system which we shall build through the facilities of dBASE III Plus. This system will provide processing services for Halliday's, a fictitious department store. The system's services include maintenance of database files, generation of a simple inventory report, batch update of the inventory master, and a variety of database queries in support of management functions.

The database in Figure 8.1 is essentially the same as that defined in Chapter 6 (Figure 6.1) for R:BASE 5000. The system we develop using the Applications Generator of dBASE III Plus will have many of the same functions as the system developed in Chapter 6.

The Applications Generator provides support both in defining the database and in generating the database file maintenance capability. The extent of this support will be illustrated in the following pages as we define Halliday's database and build portions of the retail management system.

As a final note, before we begin our discussion of system development in dBASE, we indicate a difference in terminology between R:BASE and dBASE. R:BASE tends to follow Codd's relational terminology of *table, row,* and *column,* whereas dBASE tends to use the more traditional terminology of *file, record,* and *field* respectively. In this chapter we shall use these terms interchangeably.

Defining Halliday's Database

The database of Figure 8.1 consists of 5 tables (or files), each of which has a number of columns. To develop an application system using this database, we must first define the database files. Each database file is defined separately, using a simple, straightforward procedure, which begins with the Applications Generator Main menu shown at the top of page 182.

We begin database definition by selecting choice 1 from this menu. The Generator then prompts us for a database file name, and for this example we respond by entering *invmast.* The Generator now displays a table definition form with two columns for field descriptions. The upper part of the screen displays cursor movement instructions. An empty, expanded cursor, immediately below "Field Name" in the left-hand column, indicates where to enter the first field definition as illustrated on page 182.

RETAIL MANAGEMENT DATABASE

INVENTORY MASTER (*invmast*)*	COLUMN NAME	DATA TYPE
Inventory Identification	invid	character 3
Inventory Category	invcat	character 10
Inventory Name	invname	character 10
Quantity in Stock	qtystk	numeric 3,0
Price	price	numeric 7,2

SALESPERSON MASTER (*spmast*)*	COLUMN NAME	DATA TYPE
Salesperson Identification	spid	character 3
Salesperson Name	spname	character 8
Commission Rate	commrate	numeric 5,3

CUSTOMER MASTER (*custmast*)*	COLUMN NAME	DATA TYPE
Customer Identification	custid	character 6
Customer Name	custname	character 15
Customer Address	custaddr	character 30
Customer Balance	custbal	numeric 8,2

SALES TRANSACTIONS (*saltx*)*	COLUMN NAME	DATA TYPE
Date	saldate	date
Time	saltime	character 8
Salesperson Identification	spid	character 3
Customer Identification	custid	character 3
Cash	cash	logical
Inventory Identification	invid	character 3
Quantity	salqty	numeric 3,0
Sale Price	salprice	numeric 8,2

PAYMENT TRANSACTIONS (*pmttx*)*	COLUMN NAME	DATA TYPE
Date	pmtdate	date
Customer Identification	custid	character 3
Amount	pmtamt	numeric 8,2

*the dBASE III Plus database file name

FIGURE 8.1   Database for Halliday's Retail Management System

```
                          d B A S E   I I I   P L U S
             A P P L I C A T I O N S   G E N E R A T O R   M E N U

                    1. CREATE DATABASE
                    2. CREATE SCREEN FCRM
                    3. CREATE REPORT FORM
                    4. CREATE LABEL FORM
                    5. SET AUTOMATIC COLOR
                    6. AUTOMATIC APPLICATIONS GENERATOR
                    7. RUN APPLICATION
                    8. ADVANCED APPLICATIONS GENERATOR
                    9. MODIFY APPLICATION CODE

                    0. EXIT

                              select   0

Command          |<B:>|                        |              |        |
```

```
                                        Bytes remaining:    4000

  CURSOR  <-- -->     INSERT         DELETE        Up a field:      ↑
    Char:    ←    →     Char:  Ins     Char:   Del   Down a field:    ↓
    Word: Home End     Field:  ^N     Word:   ^Y    Exit/Save:      ^End
    Pan:    ^←  ^→      Help:   F1     Field:  ^U    Abort:          Esc

       Field Name   Type     Width  Dec         Field Name   Type      Width  Dec

  1                 Character

  CREATE           |<B:>| INVMAST                |Field 1/1         |        |
                          Enter the field name.
  Field names begin with a letter and may contain letters, digits and underscores
```

Since we are defining the inventory master table, we enter "INVID" as the name of the first column (or field). Note that dBASE automatically enters our field names as uppercase. After we strike the Enter key, the cursor moves to the "Type" position where the system has already entered CHARACTER as the default for field type. Since the type of this field is

CHARACTER, we merely strike Enter again, and then the cursor will be positioned to allow entry of the field width (3). We then move to the definition of the next field. Each of the first three fields are of type CHARACTER. However, the fourth field, qtystk, is numeric. Consequently, after we have entered "QTYSTK", we must change the type from the default (CHARACTER) to NUMERIC. To do this we press the space bar as indicated on the second line from the bottom of the screen.

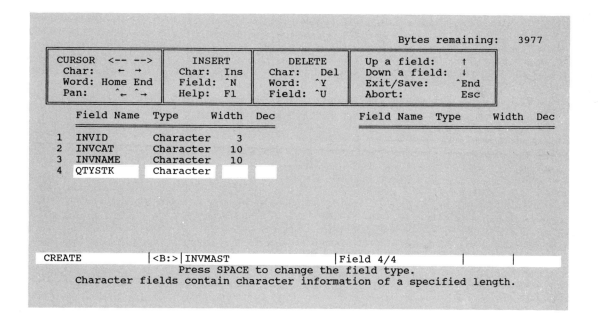

```
                                                  Bytes remaining:    3977

  CURSOR    <-- -->       INSERT          DELETE      Up a field:      ↑
  Char:      ←   →     Char:   Ins     Char:   Del    Down a field:    ↓
  Word: Home End       Field:  ^N      Word:   ^Y     Exit/Save:      ^End
  Pan:      ^← ^→      Help:   F1      Field:  ^U     Abort:          Esc


      Field Name   Type      Width  Dec        Field Name   Type    Width  Dec

  1   INVID        Character    3
  2   INVCAT       Character   10
  3   INVNAME      Character   10
  4   QTYSTK       Character




 CREATE          |<B:>|INVMAST               |Field 4/4        |       |
              Press SPACE to change the field type.
    Character fields contain character information of a specified length.
```

If we were to continue pressing the space bar we would see the other possible field types displayed: DATE, LOGICAL, and MEMO. Since we wish this field to be numeric, we press the space bar only once and strike the Enter key. We then define the width of the field (3) and the number of positions to the right of the decimal point (0). In this manner we define the remaining fields in the table as shown at the top of page 184.

Note that the last field, price, has width 7 with 2 positions to the right of the decimal point. The 7 positions in the width include the decimal point as well as the two positions to the right of the decimal. Thus, by implication, the price field has 4 positions to the left of the decimal point.

The other four tables in the database are defined in a similar manner. You should note that a column used in more than one table must be defined in each table in which the column is used. dBASE does not keep a centralized dictionary of column definitions.

```
                                                 Bytes remaining:      3967

  CURSOR   <-- -->        INSERT          DELETE      Up a field:      ↑
    Char:    ←  →       Char:   Ins    Char:   Del    Down a field:    ↓
    Word: Home End      Field:  ^N     Word:   ^Y     Exit/Save:      ^End
    Pan:      ^← ^→     Help:   F1     Field:  ^U     Abort:           Esc

        Field Name   Type    Width  Dec        Field Name   Type    Width  Dec

   1   INVID         Character    3
   2   INVCAT        Character   10
   3   INVNAME       Character   10
   4   QTYSTK        Numeric      3    0
   5   PRICE         Numeric      7    2
   6                 Character

  CREATE          |<B:>|INVMAST                   |Field 6/6         |        |
                          Enter the field name.
  Field names begin with a letter and may contain letters, digits and underscores
```

As can be seen from the database definition process, dBASE defines a series of individual database files, whereas R:BASE defines a database, including all of the columns and tables in the database. In general, most dBASE commands deal with a single database file, which corresponds to a single R:BASE table, while R:BASE commands may apply to several tables at once. dBASE makes working with a single file much easier, while R:BASE is stronger for multiple table manipulation. Of course, dBASE provides additional commands for working with multiple files, but overall, its orientation is toward single file commands.

Defining Halliday's Retail Management System

We are interested in using the Applications Generator to develop a system which will perform the following functions:

1. Maintain the 3 master files (inventory, salesperson, customer) in the database. This means we need the capability to add, change, delete, or view master records.

2. Provide input screens for transactions (sales and payment).

3. Generate a simple inventory report.

4. Respond to a variety of management queries relative to the content of the database.

5. Provide a batch processing program that updates the inventory master with the contents of the sales transactions.

dBASE III Plus provides facilities to accomplish all of the above. The first three functions will be covered in this chapter, and functions 4 and 5 will be covered in the next chapter. Functions 1 and 2 can be handled by the Applications Generator. The report generator provides most of the capability needed for function 3.

In addition to the functions listed, a means is needed for defining an overall framework or menu structure for the system. In Chapter 6 we saw that the Application EXPRESS of R:BASE 5000 provided this capability. The Applications Generator of dBASE III Plus is more modest in its capabilities, so we will not be demonstrating the building of a menu structure at this point in our discussion of dBASE. However, dBASE does provide a simple yet powerful means of building menu structures which we shall discuss thoroughly in the next chapter. For the present chapter, however, we shall limit our discussion to the building of functions 1, 2, and 3.

Automatic Applications Generator.   Assume we choose option 6 ("Automatic Applications Generator") from the Applications Generator Main menu. The system will then prompt us, in the sequence shown below, to name the application, identify the database file to be used, and identify an index file for the database file.

```
A U T O M A T I C    A P P L I C A T I O N S    G E N E R A T O R         / /
═══════════════════════════════════════════════════════════════════════════════

   ┌─────────────────────────────────────────────────────────────────┐
   │                                                                   │
   │   The application needs a name.  You can use up to eight          │
   │   characters.   A file identifier of ".prg" will be added         │
   │   by the program.   If you use the same name as an existing       │
   │   application you will be allowed to abort the process or         │
   │   overwrite the existing application.   If you choose to          │
   │   overwrite the existing application, you will be given the       │
   │   option to edit the old menu entries if they are available.      │
   │   Enter a "?" for a list of existing applications.                │
   │                                                                   │
   └─────────────────────────────────────────────────────────────────┘


Enter APPLICATION filename :INVMNT
```

```
A U T O M A T I C    A P P L I C A T I O N S    G E N E R A T O R         / /
═══════════════════════════════════════════════════════════════════════════════

   ┌─────────────────────────────────────────────────────────────────┐
   │                                                                   │
   │   A database must be identified to generate an application.       │
   │   The program will check to see if the database exists.   If      │
   │   you do not enter a database file name or the database           │
   │   does not exist, you will return to the Application              │
   │   Generator Menu without creating an application.                 │
   │   Enter a "?" for a list of available databases.                  │
   │                                                                   │
   └─────────────────────────────────────────────────────────────────┘


Enter DATABASE filename :INVMAST
```

```
AUTOMATIC   APPLICATIONS   GENERATOR        / /

    ┌─────────────────────────────────────────────────┐
    │ A database may use an index file to keep it       │
    │ sorted.  When                                     │
    │ viewed, the information will stay in order         │
    │ regardless of                                     │
    │ how it was originally inserted.  If you wish to    │
    │ use an                                            │
    │ index provide an index name.  If the index does   │
    │ not exist,                                         │
    │ you will be asked to give a keyfield name to       │
    │ index on.                                          │
    │ Enter a "?" for a list of available index files.  │
    └─────────────────────────────────────────────────┘

Enter INDEX filename :INVIND
Enter index keyfield :INVID
```

Index files are used by dBASE to keep database file records in order by a user-designated key. Since we had not previously created an index file for *invmast*, the Applications Generator will create one for us; but we must indicate the field on which the file is to be indexed. We will indicate *invid* as the field on which *invmast* is to be ordered. If the index file is used, the records will always be listed in order by the value of *invid*, no matter what order records are entered into *invmast*.

The Automatic Generator next prompts for the name of a special screen format to be used for the file, for the name of a report form that may be used to display the contents of the file, and for the name of a label form which can be used to develop mailing labels. All of these are optional, and we shall not be using any of them.

At this point, the Generator generates dBASE program code for the application system and creates a dBASE program name. The name consists of the application filename followed by the extension .PRG. In this example, the generated dBASE program will be named INVMNT.PRG. When the Generator completes this task, it once more displays its Main menu.

We can run the application from either the dBASE dot prompt or the Applications Generator Main menu. At the dot prompt we simply enter *DO invmnt*. From the Applications Generator Main menu we select option 7, "Run Application." Either of these actions causes the menu screen of our application to be displayed as shown at the top of page 187.

Note that the choices on this menu correspond to the choices which are typically used for master file maintenance: "Add," "Change," "Remove" (or "Delete"), and "Review." An "Exit" option is also provided. All of these options, as well as the language used to describe them on the menu, are automatically provided by the Applications Generator. Since these facilities are needed for virtually all master files, dBASE has appropriately provided a means of automatically generating programs for these basic tasks.

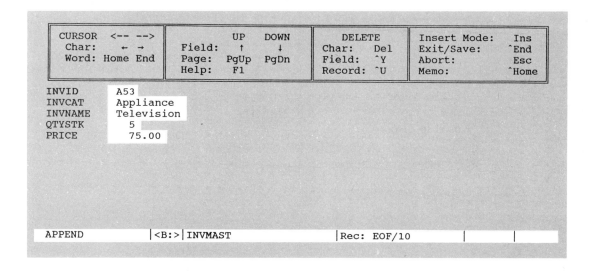

```
   I N V E N T O R Y   M A S T E R   M A I N T E N A N C E


                    1. ADD INFORMATION
                    2. CHANGE INFORMATION
                    3. REMOVE INFORMATION
                    4. REVIEW INFORMATION

                    0. EXIT

                         select   0
```

When the "Add" option is selected, a data entry screen is displayed containing the defined field names. The user can then enter the data for each field.

```
 CURSOR   <-- -->              UP   DOWN      DELETE        Insert Mode:    Ins
   Char:    ←  →    Field:     ↑     ↓     Char:    Del     Exit/Save:    ^End
   Word: Home End   Page:    PgUp  PgDn    Field:   ^Y      Abort:        Esc
                    Help:     F1           Record:  ^U      Memo:        ^Home

 INVID      A53
 INVCAT     Appliance
 INVNAME    Television
 QTYSTK     5
 PRICE      75.00






 APPEND           |<B:>| INVMAST            |Rec: EOF/10        |        |
```

The option information at the top of this and other application screens indicates that records can be deleted by striking Control-U. dBASE does not physically remove records when they are deleted in this way. Rather, it marks them for deletion. Menu option 3 in our application ("Remove Information") physically removes records from the file.

When the "Change" option is selected, the system displays the first record (by value of *invid*) in the file, in a format similar to the "Add" data entry screen. The user may then change one or more fields or may step through the file by striking the [Pg Dn] key. The "Review" option displays the entire inventory master file of our example.

```
INVID INVCAT----  INVNAME--- QTYSTK PRICE--
A53   Appliance   Television       5   75.00
A54   Appliance   Television       7  320.00
A61   Appliance   Washer          10  250.00
A62   Appliance   Washer           1  275.00
A63   Appliance   Washer           3  300.00
F30   Furniture   Chair           20  150.00
F33   Furniture   Chair           15  100.00
F84   Furniture   Sofa             6  450.00
F88   Furniture   Sofa             3  750.00
```

File maintenance systems can be developed in a similar manner for all of the master and transaction files in our system. The mechanism for tying these databases together into a single multi-file system will be discussed later.

Comparing the dBASE method of application development with the R:BASE method, we conclude that the R:BASE method is much more powerful, but at the same time it is more complex. This illustrates the philosophical difference between the two systems.

Advanced Applications Generator.   The application described above was generated by the Automatic Applications Generator. This generator requires a minimum of effort on the part of the user, and it causes standard applications to be generated. More sophisticated applications can be generated using the Advanced Applications Generator. We select the Advanced Generator from the Applications Generator Main menu, which then displays the working screen for the Advanced Applications Generator. In this example, we have also entered text for four menu options, along with the dBASE command that will perform the selected function.

```
A D V A N C E D    A P P L I C A T I O N S    G E N E R A T O R         /  /

      MENU OPTION TEXT            EXECUTABLE dBASE COMMAND    SCREEN FORMAT

 1. MASTER FILE MAINTENANCE       DO INVMNT                        N
 2. LIST EXPENSIVE ITEMS          LIST FOR Price > 1000            N
 3. PRINT INVENTORY SUMMARY       DO SUMMRPT                       N
 4. QUERY BY CATEGORY             DO CATQUERY                      N
 5.                                                                N
 6.                                                                N
 7.                                                                N
 8.                                                                N
 9.                                                                N
 0. EXIT                          RETURN
```

When the finished application is run, the custom menu just created will be displayed. If the user selects the first option, then the inventory maintenance system, which we developed above, is run. The second menu option causes the dBASE LIST command to be executed (see the next chapter for an explanation of this command), and the other menu options cause other dBASE command files (named SUMMRPT and CATQUERY) to be executed.

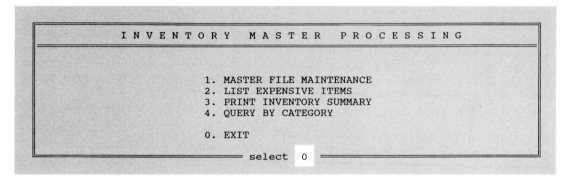

```
 I N V E N T O R Y   M A S T E R   P R O C E S S I N G


              1. MASTER FILE MAINTENANCE
              2. LIST EXPENSIVE ITEMS
              3. PRINT INVENTORY SUMMARY
              4. QUERY BY CATEGORY

              0. EXIT
                        select   0
```

The Advanced Applications Generator, like the Applications Generator, assumes a single database file to which the commands apply. We can manipulate other database files by including appropriate commands in command files which are executed by the DO command, but the basic assumption of the Advanced Applications Generator is that we are using a single database file.

THE dBASE ASSISTANT

dBASE III Plus is an interactive database management system which can be used by both programmers and end-users to manipulate data. For convenience we shall identify two primary ways in which dBASE can be used: (1) command mode, and (2) system-prompt mode.

The Applications Generator, discussed in the previous section, provides an example of the *system-prompt mode*. The user is given a menu followed by specific, fill-in-the-blank prompts which provide a step-by-step method of defining database files or developing applications. Other system-prompt facilities will be discussed shortly.

The *command mode* is also called *dot prompt mode*. The dot prompt (.) indicates that the system is ready to receive a command from the user. The user may then enter any commands needed to accomplish desired goals. Some of these commands are used directly for data manipulation, while others are used for application development. Some commands, particularly those used for application development, will initiate a temporary switch to system-prompt mode. ASSIST is one such command.

When "ASSIST" is entered at the dot prompt, dBASE enters a sophisticated system-prompt mode known as "The Assistant," and displays the following opening screen:

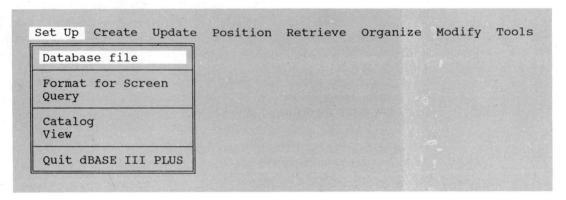

The Assistant is actually a menu-driven helper for executing dBASE commands which could otherwise be executed directly from the dot prompt. It is easier, particularly for the dBASE novice, to use the Assistant than to learn the complex syntax of a large number of commands. The Assistant may be used both for data manipulation and for application development. We shall illustrate both uses with examples of on-line retrieval and report generation, respectively.

The top of the screen contains the Assistant's menu bar, consisting of the eight options: "Set Up," "Create," "Update," "Position," "Retrieve," "Organize," "Modify," and "Tools." Each option has a number of sub-options. When the highlight (currently shown on "Set Up") is placed on any of these options, a menu of sub-options is displayed immediately below it. For example, in the above screen, the menu of "Set Up" sub-options is shown ("Database file," "Format for Screen," and so on). Since this menu is displayed vertically and immediately below the option to which it applies, it is referred to as a *pull-down menu.* The other seven options in the menu bar have pull-down menus as well. When we move the highlight to any of these menu bar options, we "pull down" its submenu.

These submenus illustrate the single file orientation of dBASE. None of the four middle options ("Update," "Position," "Retrieve," "Organize") can be used until a particular, single database file is identified for use. To illustrate the data manipulation capabilities provided by the Assistant, we shall identify a database file and execute several of the commands via the Assistant's pull-down menus.

Data Manipulation

Suppose we wish to manipulate data in the inventory master database file. For this example we shall show how to view the first record in the file.

First, we must indicate which file we wish to use. The Set Up menu is provided for this purpose. When the screen appears as shown above, we say that the Set Up menu is "open." "Database file" is highlighted, so we select it by pressing the Enter key. The system will now display a series of pull-down menus, allowing us in each case to make a choice before it proceeds to the next menu. After we select from a list of disk directories, the Assistant lists database files currently residing on the selected directory.

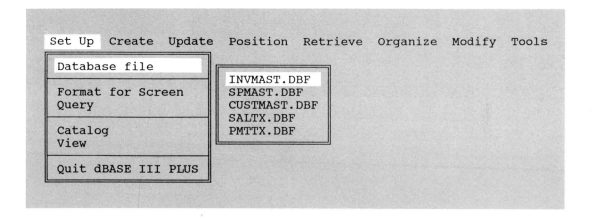

We select INVMAST.DBF by highlighting it and striking Enter. The Assistant then asks whether this file is indexed and if we respond "Yes," the list of index files created for this file will be displayed. We select INVIND.NDX, which was created earlier, as the file's index.

We have now designated the file we wish to use (together with its index), and so have completed our work with the "Set Up" command. We are now in a position to perform data manipulation on the inventory master file, using the many dBASE commands that are available for that purpose. Since we would like to view the first record in the file, we select the "Retrieve" command. The Retrieve submenu opens and we select the "Display" option.

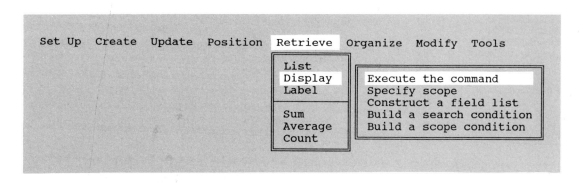

We shall not take the time now to explain all of the options of this submenu. For our purposes, the appropriate choice is "Execute the command." When this choice is selected, the system displays the first record in the file on the bottom of the screen.

```
Record#   INVID   INVCAT      INVNAME     QTYSTK    PRICE
      1   A53     Appliance   Television       5    75.00
```

This is just one example of the use of the Assistant for data manipulation. The use of this powerful tool for system development will be illustrated in the remainder of this chapter, as well as in the next chapter.

Report Generation

We saw in the first section of this chapter that the Applications Generator, though similar in concept to the R:BASE Application EXPRESS, is more easily and quickly used, yet is limited to the generation of simpler systems. Similarly, the dBASE Assistant report generation facility is also easier to use, but less powerful than the corresponding R:BASE facility. In this section we shall illustrate the dBASE report generator by developing an inventory master file report program.

Generating the Inventory Master File Report.   We are interested in generating the report illustrated in Figure 8.2. In Chapter 6 we saw that we could generate a report nearly conforming to this format using the R:BASE report generator. The final version of our R:BASE report was given in Figure 6.5. The dBASE format of this report will be adequate for our purpose, but it will also be somewhat diferent from the desired format shown in Figure 8.2.

Extended price, in the right-most column of Figure 8.2, is a calculated value. It is derived by multiplying the quantity in stock by the price. Before we use the dBASE report generator, we will calculate this value for all records in the inventory master file. For simplicity, we shall assume a database file, *newinv*, which has the same definition as *invmast* except that it has a column containing the result of this calculation. The definition of this file is shown in Figure 8.3. This file will be the data file we use to generate our report.

```
                   HALLIDAY'S DEPARTMENT STORE

              INVENTORY REPORT          07/01/--

  Category          Name        Ident   Qty    Price        Ext
  Appliance      Television      A53      5     75.00      $375.00
                                 A54      7    320.00     2,240.00
                                                          ---------
                 SUBTOTAL                                 2,615.00

                 Washer          A61     10    250.00     2,500.00
                                 A62      1    275.00      $275.00
                                 A63      3    300.00      $900.00
                                                          ---------
                 SUBTOTAL                                 3,675.00

                 CATEGORY  TOTAL                          6,290.00

  Furniture      Chair           F30     20    150.00     3,000.00
                                 F33     15    100.00     1,500.00
                                                          ---------
                 SUBTOTAL                                 4,500.00

                 Sofa            F84      6    450.00     2,700.00
                                 F88      3    750.00     2,250.00
                                                          ---------
                 SUBTOTAL                                 4,950.00

                 CATEGORY  TOTAL                          9,450.00

                 GRAND  TOTAL                            15740.00
                                                          ========
```

FIGURE 8.2   Inventory Master File Report

INVENTORY MASTER (*newinv*)	COLUMN NAME	DATA TYPE
Inventory Identification	invid	character 3
Inventory Category	invcat	character 10
Inventory Name	invname	character 10
Quantity in Stock	qtystk	numeric 3,0
Price	price	numeric 7,2
Extended Price	extprice	numeric 8,2

FIGURE 8.3   Database Definition for NEWINV

As shown earlier, we indicate our use of the *newinv* database file by using the Set Up menu. We then move to the Create menu to create the report, selecting the "Report" option.

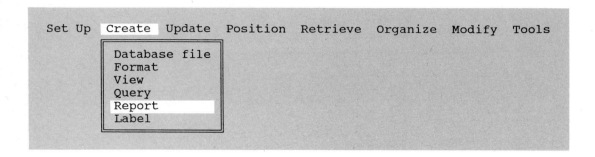

```
Set Up  Create  Update  Position  Retrieve  Organize  Modify  Tools
        ┌─────────────────────┐
        │ Database file       │
        │ Format              │
        │ View                │
        │ Query               │
        │ Report              │
        │ Label               │
        └─────────────────────┘
```

The Assistant prompts us for the disk drive and report command file name. The Assistant will store the report commands it generates on this disk drive under the file name that we enter. The file name we specify is "INVRPT". The screen is next cleared and the report generator's menu bar is displayed. We shall deal with the first three options ("Options," "Groups," "Columns") to create the report. The Options pull-down menu is initially displayed.

```
 Options              Groups          Columns          Locate        Exit
┌──────────────────────────────────────┐
│ Page title                           │
│ Page width (positions)     80        │
│ Left margin                 8        │
│ Right margin                0        │
│ Lines per page             58        │
│ Double space report        No        │
│ Page eject before printing Yes       │
│ Page eject after printing  No        │
│ Plain page                 No        │
└──────────────────────────────────────┘
```

Options.   The Options submenu assists us in setting parameters associated with the report as a whole such as: report title, format on the page, and page eject information. The last choice, "Plain page", refers to whether or not page numbers and the system date should be printed on each page of the report. The default, "No", indicates that the page should *not* be plain, and that this information should be printed on each page. For our report, we shall not alter the default values shown on the Options menu. We shall only specify the page title.

When we select "Page title" from the Options menu, a four-line work area is displayed next to the menu. We enter the report title (INVENTORY REPORT) into this work area. This causes the title to appear, automatically centered, on every page of the report.

Groups.   The Groups submenu allows us to indicate how the data in the *newinv* file should be grouped for subtotaling.

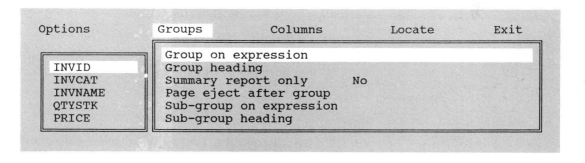

```
Options          Groups          Columns          Locate          Exit

               ┌────────────────────────────────────────────────────────┐
               │ Group on expression                                     │
               │ Group heading                                           │
               │ Summary report only        No                          │
               │ Page eject after group                                  │
               │ Sub-group on expression                                 │
               │ Sub-group heading                                       │
               └────────────────────────────────────────────────────────┘
```

Referring again to Figure 8.2, we see that we want subtotals each time the inventory category changes; and within the inventory category, we want a subtotal each time the inventory name changes. Thus, our major group is *invcat* and our sub-group is *invname*. We designate the group by selecting "Group on expression" from the Groups menu. If we strike the F10 function key, a menu of the fields in *newinv* will be shown.

```
Options          Groups          Columns          Locate          Exit
               ┌────────────────────────────────────────────────────────┐
┌────────────┐ │ Group on expression                                     │
│ INVID      │ │ Group heading                                           │
│ INVCAT     │ │ Summary report only        No                          │
│ INVNAME    │ │ Page eject after group                                  │
│ QTYSTK     │ │ Sub-group on expression                                 │
│ PRICE      │ │ Sub-group heading                                       │
└────────────┘ └────────────────────────────────────────────────────────┘
```

We move the highlight down to the desired field (*invcat*) to select this field. We enter "Category" as the group heading. In a similar manner, we select *invname* as the sub-group and enter "Name" as its heading.

Columns.   We now move to the Columns submenu, where we will indicate which columns are to be printed on the report. The menu box at the top indicates the parameters controlling a single column. The bottom box shows the report format as the columns are indicated.

```
      Options          Groups        Columns          Locate          Exit
                                 ┌────────────────────────────────────────────┐
                                 │ Contents                                    │
                                 │ Heading                                     │
                                 │ Width                    0                  │
                                 │ Decimal places                             │
                                 │ Total this column                          │
                                 └────────────────────────────────────────────┘




      ┌─Report Format──────────────────────────────────────────────────────────┐
      │>>>>>>>>?------------------------------------------------------------------│
      │                                                                          │
      │                                                                          │
      ├──────────────────────────────────────────────────────────────────────────┤
      │                                                                          │
      └──────────────────────────────────────────────────────────────────────────┘
```

Our model report of Figure 8.2 shows all six columns of data. However, the first two columns are used for grouping subtotals, and we have previously identified them for this report. Thus, we need only indicate the inclusion of the other four columns.

After we have indicated *invid* as a column to be included on the report, the screen below is shown. The second line, "Heading," is encoded information used to indicate the four lines of column heading. The semicolons mean "move to the next heading line." Thus, the first two lines of the column heading will be blank, the third line will contain "Ident," and the last line will contain "-----". This report heading is shown in the Report Format box at the bottom. Below this heading, the value "XXX" indicates that the data will occupy three columns, and will be character data. The column width, as indicated in the table at the top of the screen, is 5, since the heading has width 5.

```
  Options          Groups          Columns          Locate          Exit
                  ┌─────────────────────────────────────────────────────┐
                  │ Contents               INVID                         │
                  │ Heading                ;;Ident;-----                  │
                  │ Width                    5                            │
                  │ Decimal places                                       │
                  │ Total this column                                    │
                  └─────────────────────────────────────────────────────┘




 ┌──Report Format──────────────────────────────────────────────────────────┐
 │>>>>>>>>?-----------------------------------------------------------------│
 │                                                                          │
 │        Ident                                                             │
 │        -----                                                             │
 ├──────────────────────────────────────────────────────────────────────────┤
 │        XXX                                                               │
 └──────────────────────────────────────────────────────────────────────────┘
```

After all columns are similarly specified, we arrive at the final version of the report format as shown below. Data formats designated by 9's indicate numeric non-totaled fields, while data formats designated by #'s indicate numeric totaled fields.

```
 ┌──Report Format──────────────────────────────────────────────────────────┐
 │>>>>>>>>?-----------------------------------------------------------------│
 │                                                                          │
 │        Ident Qty  Price    Ext                                           │
 │        ----- ---  ------  --------                                        │
 ├──────────────────────────────────────────────────────────────────────────┤
 │        XXX   999 999.99 #####.##                                         │
 └──────────────────────────────────────────────────────────────────────────┘
```

A printed sample of the report is shown in Figure 8.4. You will note a substantial difference in format between the report of Figure 8.4 and that of Figure 8.2. However, the *information* provided by the two reports is the same.

```
Page No.       1
07/01/--
                              HALLIDAY'S DEPARTMENT STORE

                                    INVENTORY REPORT


        Ident Qty    Price      Ext
        ----- ---    ------   --------


        ** Category Appliance

        * Name Television
          A53      5   75.00    375.00
          A54      7  320.00   2240.00
        * Subsubtotal *
                               2615.00


        * Name Washer
          A61     10  250.00   2500.00
          A62      1  275.00    275.00
          A63      3  300.00    900.00
        * Subsubtotal *
                               3675.00


        ** Subtotal **
                               6290.00


        ** Category Furniture

        * Name Chair
          F30     20  150.00   3000.00
          F33     15  100.00   1500.00

        * Subsubtotal          4500.00


        * Name Sofa
          F84      6  450.00   2700.00
          F88      3  750.00   2250.00
        * Subsubtotal *
                               4950.00
        ** Subtotal **
                               9450.00
        *** Total ***
                              15740.00
```

FIGURE 8.4   dBASE Version of Inventory Master Report

SUMMARY

In this chapter we have examined the dBASE Applications Generator, the Assistant, and the report generation facility, and we have contrasted them somewhat with similar facilities in R:BASE 5000. In the next chapter, when we cover the dBASE command and programming languages, we shall see how we can build on the capabilities discussed in this chapter to develop more powerful, full-featured systems.

REVIEW QUESTIONS

8. 1.   How well can the features of the dBASE III PLUS system be related to our definition of 4GLs?

8. 2.   In general, what does the Applications Generator generate?

8. 3.   Discuss the database definition process provided by the Applications Generator. Does it have visual elements? What interactive elements does it employ? Compare the database definition process of the Applications Generator with that of the Applications EXPRESS of R:BASE 5000.

8. 4.   Compare the support of the centralized data dictionary concept provided by Application EXPRESS with that provided by the Applications Generator.

8. 5.   Compare the Applications Generator's way of generating a file maintenance program with that of Application EXPRESS. What advantages does the Applications Generator offer? What advantages does Application EXPRESS offer?

8. 6.   Compared to the Automatic Applications Generator, what additional flexibility is provided by the Advanced Applications Generator? Compare the Advanced Applications Generator with Application EXPRESS.

8. 7.   Discuss the interactive nature of the Assistant in guiding the user through complex dBASE commands.

8. 8.   In the report generation facility of the dBASE Assistant, what is meant by the report "options?"

8. 9.   What is meant by "groups?" What do dBASE groups correspond to in the R:BASE 5000 REPORTS command?

8.10.   Compare report generation in dBASE with report generation in R:BASE. Which system is easier to use? Which system provides more flexibility in developing a large variety of report types? Compare the visual aspects of the two report generators.

EXERCISES

For the following exercises it is assumed that the student has access to dBASE III Plus on a microcomputer system.

8.1. Following the database definition given in Figure 8.1, use the Applications Generator to define the five database files shown there and to generate file maintenance programs for each of them. Implement the inventory report as shown in the text.

8.2. Implement a payment summary report. This report should show the customer identification and total amount paid (for all payment transactions) for each customer who has made a payment. Note that this report has no detail lines.

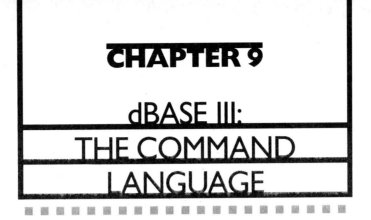

CHAPTER 9

dBASE III: THE COMMAND LANGUAGE

Unlike the other languages we have studied to this point, the command language of dBASE III Plus is not modeled after any of the theoretical relational languages. However, the data model used by dBASE is quasi-relational, and dBASE supports versions of the relational algebra operations of select, project, and join. In addition, many other commands are included in the language which give it significant power in business data processing applications.

Because of the size of the language it is not possible to cover all of the commands. Therefore, after presenting some basic concepts and key commands, we will concentrate on commands for queries, data update, and program control. We conclude the chapter with a brief look at other commands which support data management. To provide continuity with the previous chapter, we continue using Halliday's retail database. An example of this database is shown in Figure 9.1.

dBASE COMMAND FILES

As was discussed in Chapter 8, "dbase" is an interactive program. It displays a single dot as its command prompt to notify the user that it is ready to receive a command. After the user enters a command, dBASE executes the command and redisplays the dot prompt, notifying the user that it is ready to receive another command.

In addition to commands that can be executed interactively, dBASE provides (1) program control commands (IF, DO WHILE, etc.) that allow conditional and repeated execution of commands and (2) the ability to

RETAIL MANAGEMENT DATABASE

INVENTORY MASTER (*invmast*)

invid	invcat	invname	qtystk	price
A53	Appliance	Television	5	75.00
A54	Appliance	Television	7	320.00
A61	Appliance	Washer	10	250.00
A62	Appliance	Washer	1	275.00
A63	Appliance	Washer	3	300.00
F30	Furniture	Chair	20	150.00
F33	Furniture	Chair	15	100.00
F84	Furniture	Sofa	6	450.00
F88	Furniture	Sofa	3	750.00

SALESPERSON MASTER (*spmast*)

spid	spname	commrate
101	Smith	.10
105	Jones	.15

CUSTOMER MASTER (*custmast*)

custid	custname	custaddr	custbal
200	C. Brown	111 Any St.	250.00
202	C. Green	4091 Main	100.00
205	C. White	255 B St.	400.00

SALES TRANSACTIONS (*saltx*)

saldate	saltime	spid	custid	cash	invid	salqty	salprice
6/02/--	14:00	101	202	.T.	A53	1	75.00
6/10/--	9:30	101	200	.F.	F88	1	750.00
6/13/--	10:15	105	200	.F.	F30	1	150.00
6/15/--	15:27	105	205	.T.	A61	1	250.00
6/23/--	9:45	101	202	.F.	F84	1	450.00

PAYMENT TRANSACTIONS (*pmttx*)

pmtdate	custid	pmtamt
6/12/--	200	100.00
6/14/--	205	300.00
6/20/--	200	110.00

FIGURE 9.1   Database for Halliday's Retail Management System

build command files. In the previous chapter, we briefly discussed how a dBASE command file is built as a result of interactive instructions from the programmer. This command file can then be executed as a batch application program when the user enters the dBASE command DO and the name of the command file.

Thus, the dBASE program can be used not only as an interactive command language, but as a full-powered batch programming language as well. We can create many dBASE batch programs by using interactive commands, program control commands, and command files—that is, we can build a set of commands, place them in a file, and use the DO command to execute the file without further intervention from the user. The Applications Generator program introduced in Chapter 8 is an example of a command file written in the dBASE programming language. It is executed as a batch program when the user enters the command *DO appsgen* at the dBASE dot prompt.

THE FRAMEWORK OF THE dBASE COMMAND LANGUAGE

Before we can embark on our study of the dBASE command language, we must first understand its conceptual framework. In this section we shall discuss how dBASE employs file work areas and record pointers in order to process multiple files. In addition, we shall discuss how dBASE can be used to restrict data manipulation through the use of the scope option and the FOR and WHILE clauses.

Database File Work Areas

Although dBASE has a "single file" orientation, it nevertheless does provide means for working with multiple files. This is accomplished through file *work areas*. Each time a database file is opened for use, it resides in a file work area. For example, the command *USE spmast* opens the database file *spmast* for use. This USE statement causes *spmast* to be opened in the work area identified by the most recently executed SELECT statement as shown in the following example. If no SELECT statement has been executed, then the file is in work area 1 by default. The sequence of statements below would cause *saltx* to be opened in work area 2.

```
SELECT 2
USE saltx
```

Suppose we wish to use *spmast, saltx,* and *invmast* together. The sequence of statements below will accomplish our goal. After this sequence of statements has been executed, work area 3 is the currently selected work area and *invmast* is the "active file."

```
SELECT 1
USE spmast
SELECT 2
USE saltx
SELECT 3
USE invmast
```

If we desire *spmast* to be the active file we simply execute:

```
SELECT 1
```

Suppose area 1 is currently selected and we wish *custmast* to be the open file in area 3. We enter:

```
SELECT 3
USE custmast
```

If *invmast* were already open in area 3, dBASE would automatically close *invmast* and open *custmast*. If we want to close the database file in the current work area, and we do not want to open another file, we simply enter *USE* with no other parameters. To close all database files in all areas, we enter *CLOSE DATABASES*.

We mentioned in the previous chapter that a database file can be logically ordered by indexing it on one or more fields. Thus, we indexed *invmast* on the *invid* field. The index file containing the index information was named "invind". In order to use this ordering of *invmast* in a program, we must tell the system to open its index file. We can do this at the time we open *invmast* by modifying the USE statement to process the records of *invmast* in order by value of *invid*.

```
USE invmast INDEX invind
```

The Record Pointer

The system maintains a logical pointer for each open database file. This pointer indicates the next record to be processed. If all records in the file have been processed, the pointer points to end-of-file. If the file is opened without an index, the pointer will point to record number 1, that is, the first physical record in the file. If an index is named in the USE statement, then the pointer will point to the record with the lowest value for the key expression used in defining the index. After this record is processed, the pointer points to the record with the next higher key value.

If a SELECT statement is executed, causing the current work area to change, the pointer for the previously selected area remains fixed. Thus, when that area is again selected, the record which was being pointed to before execution of the two SELECT statements is still available for processing. The record being pointed to by the record pointer is called the *current record*.

Conditions on Records

In earlier chapters we saw numerous examples of restricting processing to records that satisfy a specified condition (for example, the selection operation of relational algebra and the WHERE clause of SQL, QUEL, and R:BASE 5000). dBASE expands this capability with the FOR clause, the WHILE clause, and the scope option. FOR and WHILE clauses are introduced by the keywords FOR and WHILE, whereas a scope option may consist of any of several keywords, possibly accompanied by a numeric parameter.

Scope.   The scope may be any of: (1) *NEXT n*, (2) *RECORD n*, (3) *ALL*, or (4) *REST*. In this syntax, "n" is an integer. "NEXT n" means that the scope is the span of the next n consecutive records beginning with the current record. "RECORD n" denotes a single record whose number is n. "ALL" means "all records in the file." "REST" means the remaining records in the file, starting with the current record.

If a scope is not specified in a dBASE command, the default is either the current record or ALL, depending on the command. If a FOR or WHILE clause is specified, the default scope is ALL.

FOR and WHILE Conditions.   A condition is a logical expression which, for any given record, evaluates to true or false.

GENERAL SYNTAX

```
Expression1 RelationalOperator Expression2
```

"RelationalOperator" is taken from the list shown in Figure 9.2. The "Expressions" on either side of RelationalOperator are constructed by taking some combination of fields, memory variables, constants, and arithmetic, string, or logical operators. A "memory variable" is a name of a work-area value in memory previously defined by the user. The arithmetic and string operators which may be used include addition, subtraction, multiplication, division, and exponentiation $(+, -, *, /, **)$ as well as string concatenation $(+)$. Logical operators are *.NOT., .AND.,* and *.OR.* Parentheses may be used for grouping.

GENERAL SYNTAX

```
FOR condition
```

```
WHILE condition
```

OPERATOR	MEANING
<	Less than
>	Greater than
=	Equal
<> or #	Not equal
<=	Less than or equal
>=	Greater than or equal
$	Is contained within (as a substring)

FIGURE 9.2   Relational Operators

The FOR clause is used as part of the syntax of several dBASE commands to search for records in a file. It is identical in meaning to the WHERE clause discussed previously for other languages (e.g., R:BASE). A command containing a FOR clause will act on a given record in the database file if the FOR condition evaluates to true for that record.

The WHILE clause is used to determine when to terminate execution of the command. The command will continue to execute as long as the WHILE condition evaluates to true. When for a given record the WHILE condition evaluates to false, the command will terminate execution.

The use of the FOR and WHILE clauses is most easily demonstrated with the LIST command. This command is used to display the contents of a database file. Note that brackets ([]) surrounding an item mean that the item is optional.

GENERAL SYNTAX

```
LIST [scope] [expression-list]
     [WHILE condition] [FOR  condition]
```

If *invmast* is the active file, the command LIST (with no parameters) will cause all of the *invmast* file to be displayed. If the current record is record number 2, the command LIST REST will cause all of *invmast* except record 1 to be displayed.

EXAMPLE: Assuming the current record is record 2, display the inventory items with more than 3 in stock.

```
LIST REST FOR qtystk > 3
```

Result:

Record #	invid	invcat	invname	qtystk	price
2	A54	Appliance	Television	7	320.00
3	A61	Appliance	Washer	10	250.00
6	F30	Furniture	Chair	20	150.00
7	F33	Furniture	Chair	15	100.00
8	F84	Furniture	Sofa	6	450.00

EXAMPLE: Assuming the current record is record 1, list up to the next 7 appliance entries.

```
LIST NEXT 7 WHILE invcat = 'Appliance'
```

Result:

Record #	invid	invcat	invname	qtystk	price
1	A53	Appliance	Television	5	75.00
2	A54	Appliance	Television	7	320.00
3	A61	Appliance	Washer	10	250.00
4	A62	Appliance	Washer	1	275.00
5	A63	Appliance	Washer	3	300.00

A condition may also consist of a single field name if the type of the field is logical. For example, the database file *saltx* contains a logical field, *cash*. If the value of this field is *.T.* (true), then the customer paid cash on this sale. If the value of this field is *.F.* (false), then the customer charged this sale. If we want to list all sales on which cash was paid, we enter the command *LIST FOR cash*. If we wish to identify credit sales, we enter *LIST FOR .NOT. cash*. "Cash" in these commands is a condition, since it evaluates to true or false. Logical fields are convenient for use in this manner.

QUERY COMMANDS

We shall now consider dBASE commands which can be used in the solution of queries. Although these commands may be classified in a variety of ways, for simplicity in our presentation we are classifying them as "query commands." The principal query commands are: (1) COPY, (2) JOIN, (3) TOTAL, (4) AVERAGE, (5) COUNT, and (6) SUM.

COPY

The COPY command combines the selection and the projection operations of relational algebra.

GENERAL SYNTAX

```
COPY TO file-name [scope] [FIELDS field-list]
        [FOR condition] [WHILE condition]
```

This command copies all or part of the active file to the file named in file-name. If the FIELDS clause is omitted, then all fields in the active file will appear in the copy. Otherwise, only those fields appearing in field-list will be in the new file. The equivalent of the relational algebra projection would be the form:

```
COPY TO file-name FIELDS field-list
```

Similarly, the equivalent of the relational algebra selection would be the form:

```
COPY TO file-name FOR condition
```

EXAMPLE: Create a file containing the inventory id, name, and price of furniture priced below $200.

```
USE invmast
COPY TO newl FIELDS invid,invname,price
     FOR invcat = 'Furniture' .AND. price < 200
```

Result: Table newl

invid	invname	price
F30	Chair	150.00
F33	Chair	100.00

JOIN

GENERAL SYNTAX

```
JOIN WITH file-name TO new-file-name
     FOR condition [FIELDS field-list]
```

"File-name" refers to an open file in a work area which is not currently selected. The effect of this command is to join records from the active file with records from "file-name". The condition of joining is determined by the FOR clause. As an example, suppose *invmast* is open in work area 1, *saltx* is open in work area 2, and work area 1 is currently selected. To execute a natural join of *invmast* and *saltx* we enter:

```
JOIN WITH saltx TO joinfile FOR invid = saltx->invid
```

The notation "saltx->invid" means "the value of *invid* in a given record of *saltx*". This JOIN command creates the new file named "joinfile". The system matches records in *invmast* (the active file) with records in *saltx*. If the values of *invid* in the two records are equal, then the records are joined. All fields from the *invmast* record are included in the new record. All fields from the *saltx* record *except invid,* are included in the new record. It is easy to see that the join in this example is a natural join. If we modify the query to include a FIELDS clause, the effect is a natural join followed by a projection:

```
JOIN WITH saltx TO joinfile FOR invid = saltx->invid
        FIELDS invname,spid, custid
```

Result: **Table joinfile**

invname	spid	custid
Television	101	202
Sofa	101	200
Chair	105	200
Washer	105	205
Sofa	101	202

Just as with the join of relational algebra, records in two files can be joined based on relationships other than equality of columns. Thus, if the FOR condition states a relationship such as "price > saltx->salprice", the dBASE join would be carried out just as in relational algebra.

Regardless of the FOR condition, dBASE will not include fields from the second file if they have the same names as fields from the active file. Thus, even in the case where the join is not a natural join, some fields may be automatically omitted from the joined file. In the previous example however, all fields from both files would have been included since *price* and *salprice* do not have the same name.

TOTAL

dBASE provides a command which creates a file of summary records, giving totals of selected numeric fields for the various values of a designated key. This is the TOTAL command.

GENERAL SYNTAX

```
TOTAL ON key-field TO file-name [scope]
        [FIELDS field-list]
        [FOR condition] [WHILE condition]
```

As an example of the usage of TOTAL, consider the *saltx* table. This table contains individual sales transactions. We can summarize the sales for each salesperson by using the TOTAL command. However, the *saltx* file must be indexed on *spid*. Assume that the index file *spindx* has been created for this purpose:

```
USE saltx INDEX spidndx
TOTAL ON spid TO salstots
```

Result: Table salstots

saldate	saltime	spid	custid	cash	invid	salqty	salprice
6/02/--	14:00	101	202	.T.	A53	3	1275.00
6/13/--	10:15	105	200	.F.	F30	2	400.00

If we only want the total of price and not quantity, the FIELDS clause is used:

```
TOTAL ON spid TO salstots FIELDS  salprice
```

Result: Table saltots

saldate	saltime	spid	custid	cash	invid	salqty	salprice
6/02/--	14:00	101	202	.T.	A53	1	1275.00
6/13/--	10:15	105	200	.F.	F30	1	400.00

We can use the FOR and WHILE clauses, as well as the scope option, to limit the records used in calculating the totals. For example, suppose we only want totals of credit sales:

```
TOTAL ON spid TO credsals FIELDS  salprice
        FOR .NOT. cash
```

Result: Table credsals

saldate	saltime	spid	custid	cash	invid	salqty	salprice
6/10/--	9:30	101	200	.F.	F88	1	1200.00
6/13/--	10:15	105	200	.F.	F30	1	150.00

AVERAGE, COUNT, and SUM

dBASE provides statistical functions for computing averages and sums of numeric fields in sets of records. It also provides a function for counting the number of records in a file. These commands also may contain FOR, WHILE, and the scope option.

GENERAL SYNTAX

```
AVERAGE [expression-list] [scope]
        [WHILE condition] [FOR condition]
        [TO memory-variable-list]
```

```
SUM [expression-list] [scope]
    [WHILE condition] [FOR condition]
    [TO memory-variable-list]
```

```
COUNT [scope] [WHILE condition]
      [FOR condition] [TO memory-variable]
```

In every case, the file used is the active database file. In the first two commands, "expression-list" indicates which fields are to be averaged or summed. If it is omitted, all numeric fields are averaged or summed. The "memory-variable-list" is used to indicate where the results of the operations are stored. In the case of COUNT, only one memory variable is named, since only a single answer is possible.

QUERY: What is the number, the sum, and the average of credit sales for salesperson 101?

```
COUNT FOR .NOT. cash .AND. spid = '101' TO  crcount
SUM salprice FOR .NOT. cash .AND. spid = '101' TO crsum
AVERAGE salprice FOR .NOT. cash .AND.
        spid = '101' TO cravg
```

Result: crcount = 2, crsum = 1200.00, cravg = 600.00

A Sample Interactive Query

We now illustrate the practical application of these commands by developing a simple "canned" query which could be implemented in an applications system. This query will consist of a set of data manipulation commands which could be placed in a command file and executed via the DO command. Such a query could also be integrated into an applications system and executed via menu selection.

Suppose we wish to calculate the average sale for a given salesperson. The user would be prompted for the salesperson's name and the system would then calculate that salesperson's average sale.

```
SELECT 1
USE spmast
SELECT 2
USE saltx
SELECT 1
INPUT 'Enter salesperson name: ' TO mspname
JOIN WITH saltx TO new2 FOR spid = saltx->spid
     .AND. spname = mspname
SELECT 3
USE new2
AVERAGE salprice
```

The first five lines in this query establish the database file environment needed for the JOIN command. The sixth line introduces a new command. The INPUT command prompts the user for data by displaying a message on the screen—in this case, "Enter salesperson name: ". The system then pauses while the user enters the name. The entered name is stored in the memory variable *mspname*, which is created by the system if it did not already exist.

The system next performs the JOIN command, which creates the table *new2* as the natural join of *spmast* and *saltx,* combined with a (relational algebra) select based on the input value of *mspname.* Note that these two operations, the natural join and the select, are combined into the single dBASE JOIN command. Using this newly created table (in file work area 3), we can now compute the average sale price of all sales made by the salesperson whose name is stored in *mspname.* Since we did not specify a variable into which the result of the AVERAGE statement should be placed, the result will be displayed on the screen.

Interactive Query Testing

Queries such as that given in the previous example are heavily dependent on the conditions used in selecting records. In the previous query a simple selection condition (*spname = mspname*) was included as part of the JOIN condition. Conditions are often considerably more complex, and forming them correctly may be difficult, particularly for the novice. dBASE provides an interactive facility for forming and testing selection conditions, which can prove valuable in developing queries. We illustrate its use by developing a query on the *invmast* file.

Suppose we wish to identify all furniture items for which the quantity in stock is above 10. We shall formulate a query for selecting records matching these criteria from the *invmast* file. We use the Assistant, set our database file to *invmast,* as was discussed in the previous chapter, and select "Query" from the Create menu.

```
  Set Filter                 Nest           Display              Exit
 ┌──────────────────────────────────────────────┐
 │ Field Name                                     │
 │ Operator                                       │
 │ Constant/Expression                            │
 │ Connect                                        │
 ├──────────────────────────────────────────────┤
 │ Line Number         1                          │
 └──────────────────────────────────────────────┘
```

Line	Field	Operator	Constant/Expression	Connect
1				
2				
3				
4				
5				
6				
7				

Note that this screen displays a menu bar across the top, containing four options: "Set Filter," "Nest," "Display," and "Exit." Building a selection condition (filter) consists of three steps:

1. Describing the simple conditions. Two examples of simple conditions are *invcat = 'Furniture'* and *qtystk > 10*.
2. Connecting the simple conditions with Boolean AND's and OR's.
3. Grouping conditions through the use of parentheses.

Steps 1 and 2 are accomplished via the "Set Filter" option. Step 3 is accomplished via the "Nest" option. The "Display" option is used to test the correctness of the selection condition by displaying records which satisfy it.

On the above screen, the highlight is located on Set Filter. The box across the bottom of the screen, which we shall call the "condition box," contains 7 lines which may be used for seven simple conditions. The Connect column at the far right will be used for the Boolean AND's and OR's.

The box immediately below Set Filter (the "option box") contains the options needed to specify one simple condition and its connection to the next simple condition. We select Field Name in this box, and dBASE displays a list of fields in the *invmast* file as shown at the top of page 214.

The first field in the list (INVID) is highlighted, and a description of the field overlays a portion of the condition box below. We move the highlight down one field and select INVCAT as the field to be used in our first simple condition.

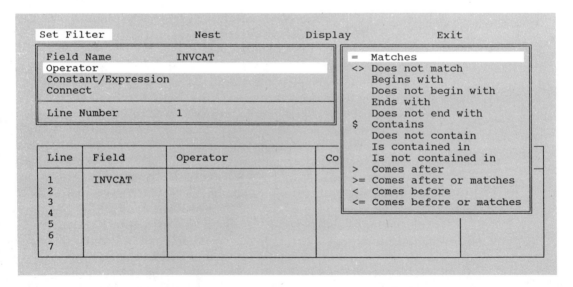

We now must select a relational operator for comparing our selected field with a value. Thus, we select Operator in the option box, opening a pull-down menu of relational operators that may be used with character fields. (Note that INVCAT, a character field, has previously been placed in the Field column on the first line of the condition box.)

We are interested in selecting records whose *invcat* field is equal to *Furniture,* so we select =*Matches* from the Operator menu. We finish the simple condition by selecting the next choice in the options box, "Constant/Expression," and specifying the constant string 'Furniture'.

```
┌─────────────────────────────────────────────────────────────────────────┐
│ Set Filter              Nest             Display              Exit         │
│ ┌──────────────────────────────────────────┐ ┌──────────────────────────┐│
│ │ Field Name            INVCAT              │ │┌─────────────────────────┐││
│ │ Operator              Matches            │ ││ No combination          │││
│ │ Constant/Expression   'Furniture'        │ │ Combine with .AND.       ││
│ │ Connect                                   │ │ Combine with .OR.        ││
│ │                                           │ │ Combine with .AND..NOT.  ││
│ │ Line Number           1                   │ │ Combine with .OR..NOT.   ││
│ └──────────────────────────────────────────┘ └──────────────────────────┘│
└───────────────────────────────────────────────────────────────────────────┘
```

Line	Field	Operator	Constant/Expression	Connect
1	INVCAT	Matches	'Furniture'	
2				
3				
4				
5				
6				
7				

When we select the Connect option, the pull-down menu of Boolean connectors is displayed. Our choice of .AND. from this menu will be displayed in the Connect field at the bottom of the screen.

We have now completed the first line of our condition. We repeat this process to form the second and final line of the condition (quantity in stock above ten). After entering the operator and the constant 10, we choose "No combination" from the Connect menu to indicate that the Set Filter portion of the condition is complete.

```
┌─────────────────────────────────────────────────────────────────────────┐
│ Set Filter              Nest             Display              Exit         │
│ ┌──────────────────────────────────────────┐                             │
│ │ Field Name            INVCAT              │                             │
│ │ Operator              Matches            │                             │
│ │ Constant/Expression   'Furniture'        │                             │
│ │ Connect                                   │                             │
│ │                                           │                             │
│ │ Line Number           2                   │                             │
│ └──────────────────────────────────────────┘                             │
└───────────────────────────────────────────────────────────────────────────┘
```

Line	Field	Operator	Constant/Expression	Connect
1	INVCAT	Matches	'Furniture'	.AND.
2	QTYSTK	More than	10	
3				
4				
5				
6				
7				

Since this condition does not require parentheses for grouping conditions, we shall not use the "Nest" option. Instead, we move to the "Display" option to test the condition we have developed. The first record in *invmast* which satisfies our condition will be displayed.

```
 Set Filter                 Nest            Display              Exit
 INVID      F30
 INVCAT     Furniture
 INVNAME    Chair
 QTYSTK     20
 PRICE      150.00
```

Line	Field	Operator	Constant/Expression	Connect
1	INVCAT	Matches	'Furniture'	.AND.
2	QTYSTK	More than	10	
3				
4				
5				
6				
7				

By striking PgDn, we can move to the next record satisfying the condition. By striking PgUp, we move to the previous record. In this way we can compare the system's results with our own understanding of which records should have been retrieved. If an appropriate record is omitted, or an inappropriate record is displayed, it is clear that an error has been made in the formulation of the condition. We can then revise the condition until the correct records are displayed.

The canned query we developed earlier to calculate the average sale for a given salesperson can also be tested using the mechanism which we just described. By entering specific values for *mspname* in the Constant/Expression column, we can display the appropriate records in the *new2* database file. It can be seen, then, that this feature of the Assistant has significant value in testing and debugging systems.

DATA UPDATE AND PROGRAM CONTROL COMMANDS

In this section we demonstrate several methods of using the programming language facility to create a batch program which uses the records from the sales transactions table (*saltx*) to update the inventory master table (*invmast*). We shall call this program the Inventory Master Update program. Except for the menu structure, which will be developed later in this chapter, this update program constitutes the last remaining piece of Halliday's Retail Management System.

In order to appreciate what the dBASE programming language can do, we shall review the requirements of this program in more depth. Whenever an item is sold, a transaction is recorded in the *saltx* table. The sale of the item will cause the quantity in stock to be reduced by the quantity sold. The Inventory Master Update program should therefore apply these transactions to their respective inventory master records, and reduce the quantity in stock by the quantity sold. This update could be carried out in either an on-line or a batch program. For our purposes, however, the need for inventory master update provides an excellent example of the use of the batch processing capability of the dBASE language. Thus, we shall assume that the inventory master is updated on a periodic basis using a table of batched sales transactions.

If we were to write this program using a 3GL such as COBOL, we could sort both tables in order by inventory id, and then use sequential processing to process the two tables together. Since there are likely to be multiple sales transactions for any given inventory item, we would hold an inventory master record in memory while we apply transactions one at a time to that record. When we finally read a transaction for a different inventory master record, we would write the updated inventory master record and then read another. The process of updating would then start over with this new inventory master record.

Several dBASE commands which support multiple record processing will help us avoid this single record processing which is characteristic of 3GLs. We shall illustrate two approaches: one which partially eliminates the need for single record processing, and one which altogether eliminates such processing.

Our first approach follows this outline: First we use the TOTAL command which will create a file of summary transactions, no more than one transaction for each value of *invid*. Next, we open this summary file and read the first summary transaction. Finally, we set up a loop of three steps which (1) randomly retrieves the master record corresponding to this summary record, (2) applies the summary record to the master record, and (3) reads the next summary record. To accomplish this, we need new commands to read records both sequentially and randomly, change the contents of records, and control the repeated execution of commands.

To perform these functions, we use the command sequence below. The first INDEX command creates the index file which orders *saltx* by *invid*. This index file is needed for the TOTAL command to operate properly. The TOTAL command creates a file named *qtytots* which contains summary records holding totals of *salqty* for *saltx* records having the same value of *invid*. We USE *qtytots* and create an index for it on *invid*. The *qtytots* file is now active in work area 1.

```
SELECT 1
USE saltx
INDEX ON invid TO saltxinv
TOTAL ON invid TO qtytots FIELDS salqty
USE qtytots
INDEX ON invid TO qtyinv
```

SEEK and REPLACE

The USE command in combination with the INDEX command opens *qtytots* for processing in order by *invid*. The record pointer points to the record with the lowest value of *invid*. We wish to apply this record and all *qtytots* records to their corresponding records in the *invmast* file. We start by specifying how to apply a single record from *qtytots* to a single record in *invmast*. The command sequence below opens *invmast* and its index in area 2.

```
SELECT 2
USE invmast INDEX invind
```

We can find the *invmast* record corresponding to the current *qtytots* record by using the SEEK command.

GENERAL SYNTAX

```
SEEK expression
```

This command provides us with a means of randomly accessing records in *invmast*. It uses the index file by matching keys of database file records with the value of "expression". It sets the record pointer to the first record whose key matches "expression". In this case we write an expression to locate the record in *invmast* corresponding to the current record in *qtytots*.

```
SEEK qtytots->invid
```

The pointer in *invmast* is now pointing to the correct record. To apply the summary record from *qtytots* to its corresponding *invmast* record, we use the REPLACE command.

GENERAL SYNTAX

```
REPLACE [scope] field WITH expression
        [, field2 WITH expression2, . . .]
        [WHILE condition] [FOR condition]
```

The scope, WHILE, and FOR clauses of this command indicate that it can be used on multiple records at one time. Also, more than one field can be changed at a time. However, we shall only change one field in one record in this example. In the absence of scope, WHILE, and FOR clauses, only the current record has its value altered.

```
REPLACE qtystk WITH qtystk - qtytots-> salqty
```

Program Control

We have shown how to locate and alter the *invmast* record corresponding to a given *qtytots* record. Now we develop the looping mechanism needed to apply all *qtytots* records to their corresponding *invmast* records.

DO WHILE.   We have written the commands needed to update one inventory master record. In fact we have demonstrated all of the commands needed for our program except two: We still need a loop to control the repeated execution of the updating commands and we need a command for reading the next sequential record. The first need is satisfied by the DO WHILE statement.

GENERAL SYNTAX

```
DO WHILE condition
     (one or more  commands)
ENDDO
```

The ENDDO is required to indicate the end of commands comprising the DO WHILE loop. The DO WHILE statement is used in the same manner as it is used in other programming languages. The commands within the loop are executed repeatedly, as long as the WHILE condition is true. If the condition is found to be false prior to an execution of the loop, then the loop is not executed and control passes to the statement immediately after ENDDO. DO WHILE statements can be nested within other DO WHILE statements.

SKIP.   The sequential read statement we need is the SKIP command.

GENERAL SYNTAX

```
SKIP [numeric-expression]
```

This command causes the record pointer in the active file to move the number of records corresponding to the value of "numeric-expression". If numeric-expression is positive, the pointer moves forward. If it is negative, the pointer moves backward. If it is omitted, the pointer moves forward one record. If an index is being used, SKIP causes the pointer to move in the order determined by the index. If SKIP causes the pointer to move past the last record in the file, the value of the function EOF() (end-of-file) is true. (We shall discuss this in more detail later.)

We now show the completed version of our Inventory Master Update program:

```
SELECT 1
USE saltx
INDEX ON invid TO saltxinv
TOTAL ON invid TO qtytots FIELDS salqty
USE qtytots
INDEX ON invid TO qtyinv

SELECT 2
USE invmast INDEX invind

DO WHILE .NOT. EOF()
     SELECT 2
     SEEK qtytots->invid
     REPLACE qtystk WITH qtystk - qtytots->salqty
     SELECT 1
     SKIP
ENDDO
CLOSE DATABASES
```

The command "SELECT 2" within the DO WHILE loop is redundant for the first *qtytots* record being processed. However, it is necessary for all subsequent records. "EOF()" is a system-supplied function which evaluates to false if the record pointer has not passed the last record in the active file. It becomes true after the last record is passed. Thus, it is ideal for controlling the processing in our DO WHILE loop.

Examine this code and compare it with the partially developed code shown earlier. This program follows the outline of the program we gave at the beginning of the section.

UPDATE.   The solution given above to the inventory master batch update problem is logically no different from an ISAM solution to the same problem in a 3GL. By using the TOTAL command, the solution may be easier to comprehend and the program may execute a little faster, but the *logic* we described would be usable without change in a single record processing environment (that is, *without* the TOTAL command).

We now demonstrate a second solution to the batch update problem, which is much simpler and which makes essential use of the power of the multi-record UPDATE command.

GENERAL SYNTAX

```
UPDATE ON key-field FROM file-name
       REPLACE field WITH expression
       [, field2 WITH expression, . . .]
       [RANDOM]
```

This command works as follows: The active database file is the master file which will be updated. The transaction file containing the transactions which are to be applied to master file records is active in another file work area. *Both* of these files have a field named "key-field", which is used by dBASE to match transaction file records against master file records. Fields in the master file record are altered according to the REPLACE and WITH clauses. The following code gives the altered version of the Inventory Master Update program using the UPDATE command:

```
SELECT 1
USE saltx
INDEX ON invid TO saltxinv

SELECT 2
USE invmast INDEX invind

UPDATE ON invid FROM saltx
     REPLACE qtystk WITH qtystk - saltx->salqty

CLOSE DATABASES
```

The power of this command in simplifying the logic of this program is obvious. The entire DO WHILE loop has been eliminated, including the complexity of switching back and forth between work areas. However, we should note that the UPDATE command requires the use of indexes on the "key-field" in both files. The index on the transaction file can be eliminated if we use the RANDOM option. In this case, the code is revised to:

```
SELECT 1
USE saltx

SELECT 2
USE invmast INDEX invind

UPDATE ON invid FROM saltx
     REPLACE qtystk WITH qtystk - saltx->salqty
     RANDOM

CLOSE DATABASES
```

The dBASE UPDATE command is a powerful multi-record command which provides a good example of the spirit of 4GL processing concepts.

IF.   One of the most basic building blocks of computer applications systems is the statement whose execution is conditional. In most languages such statements are controlled by IF constructions.

GENERAL SYNTAX

```
IF condition
    (one or more commands)
[ELSE
    (one or more commands)]
ENDIF
```

Note that ELSE and its associated commands are optional. IF functions in dBASE in the same manner as it does in other languages: If the condition is true, the set of commands following the condition is executed. If not, the commands following the ELSE (if it is present) are executed. Control then proceeds to the statement following ENDIF.

We illustrate the IF statement by enhancing our first update program. Suppose we wish to identify those inventory items whose quantity in stock has gone to zero as a result of applying sales transactions. We will use the IF statement to test the value of *qtystk*. If it is 0, we will display a reorder message. The following code gives the new version of the program (recall that a record in *qtytots* contains the total quantity sold for a given value of *invid*):

```
SELECT 1
USE qtytots INDEX qtyinv
SELECT 2
USE invmast INDEX invind

DO WHILE .NOT. EOF()
    SELECT 2
    SEEK qtytots->invid
    REPLACE qtystk WITH qtystk - qtytots->salqty
    IF qtystk = 0
        ? 'Re-order item ' + invid
    ENDIF
    SELECT 1
    SKIP
ENDDO
CLOSE DATABASES
```

You will note the use of a new command—the ? command—to cause a message to be displayed.

GENERAL SYNTAX

```
? expression-list
```

In the program above, "expression-list" was the single string expression consisting of the literal 'Re-order item ' concatenated with the value of *invid*.

DO CASE. A generalized version of the IF statement is the DO CASE statement.

GENERAL SYNTAX

```
DO CASE
      CASE condition1
            (condition1 commands)
      [CASE condition2
      (condition2 commands)]
  [ . . . ]
  [OTHERWISE
      (OTHERWISE commands)]
  ENDCASE
```

DO CASE executes as follows: Starting with condition1, each condition (condition1, condition2, etc.) is evaluated until a condition is found which evaluates to true. After this happens, all commands corresponding to this condition are executed, and control is passed to the first statement following ENDCASE. If none of the conditions are true, then the OTHERWISE commands (if any) are executed.

We illustrate the DO CASE statement by demonstrating how a menu can be built for controlling the execution of Halliday's Retail Management System. The following statements provide for display and execution of the Main menu:

```
DO WHILE .T.


      ?'*********************************************************'
      ?'*                                                      *'
      ?'*       HALLIDAY'S RETAIL MANAGEMENT SYSTEM            *'
      ?'*                                                      *'
      ?'*       1.  Master File Maintenance                   *'
      ?'*       2.  Transaction Processing                    *'
      ?'*       3.  Reports                                   *'
      ?'*       4.  Queries                                   *'
      ?'*       5.  Batch Processing                          *'
      ?'*       6.  Exit                                      *'
      ?'*                                                      *'
      ?'*********************************************************'
      ?

      INPUT 'Make Menu Selection: ' TO menusel
```

(continued on next page)

```
DO CASE
     CASE menusel = 1
          DO invmnt
     CASE menusel = 2
          DO txproc
     CASE menusel = 3
          DO repts
     CASE menusel = 4
          DO queries
     CASE menusel = 5
          DO batchprc
     CASE menusel = 6
          EXIT
     OTHERWISE
          ?'*** Error *** Invalid Menu Selection'
ENDCASE

ENDDO
```

This program causes a menu to be displayed through the use of ? statements. It then prompts the user to make a selection, and pauses while the user makes the selection. If the user keys a number between 1 and 6, the system causes the appropriate action to take place. Otherwise, it displays an error message, re-displays the menu, and waits for the user's entry.

The first line of the program—DO WHILE .T.—means "DO WHILE TRUE". You will recall that DO WHILE is followed by a condition which evaluates to true or false. As long as the condition is true, the DO WHILE loop will continue to execute. In this example, the condition is a constant, "true," so the loop will execute forever. Thus, after all processing associated with the user's selection has been completed, the loop begins again, the menu is displayed, and the user is asked to enter a selection. To escape from the DO WHILE loop, we use the EXIT statement.

The EXIT statement terminates the DO WHILE loop and passes control to the first statement after ENDDO. The syntax of EXIT is simply "EXIT".

This simple program illustrates the power of the DO CASE statement in knitting together the pieces of a larger system. Although dBASE's Applications Generator should be used primarily for small programs, the means of developing larger systems are available in other dBASE facilities such as those we have illustrated here.

In addition, the Applications Generator can be used to create parts of larger systems. For example, file maintenance programs, such as that developed for the inventory master in Chapter 8, can be integrated into a menu structure like that shown above. The command *DO invmnt* causes a program named INVMNT.PRG to be executed. The Applications Generator creates a program having this name when the user enters "INVMNT" as the application file name.

ADDITIONAL COMMANDS

In the previous three sections we covered the principal data manipulation and program control commands in detail. dBASE supports many other commands which are useful in applications systems. In this section we shall give brief descriptions of a number of these, presented in alphabetical order.

APPEND FROM

GENERAL SYNTAX

```
APPEND FROM file-name [FOR condition]
```

APPEND FROM adds the rows of file-name to the end of the active file. It copies only those fields of file-name which also exist in the active file. If a FOR clause is used, it may only refer to fields common to both files. FOR qualifies which rows of file-name are to be added to the active file. Records marked for deletion (see the DELETE command, below) in file-name are copied to the active file, if they meet the FOR condition. They are not marked for deletion in the active file.

CONTINUE

GENERAL SYNTAX

```
CONTINUE
```

This command identifies the next record in the active file satisfying the criteria stated in the most recently issued LOCATE command (described later). For example, if the active file were *saltx*, then the following sequence of commands will move the record pointer first to the *saltx* record dated 6/02-- and then to the record dated 6/23--.

```
LOCATE FOR custid = 202
CONTINUE
```

If no record is found after a CONTINUE command is issued, and if the last record in the file has been searched, then EOF() is true.

DELETE

GENERAL SYNTAX

```
DELETE [scope] [WHILE condition]
       [FOR condition]
```

The DELETE command marks records for deletion. In the absence of qualifying clauses (scope, WHILE, FOR), only the current record is marked for deletion. Otherwise, all records satisfying the qualifying conditions are marked. Records marked for deletion are not physically removed until a PACK command is executed. Records marked for deletion are shown with an asterisk (*) when displayed via LIST or DISPLAY. These records can be unmarked using the RECALL command.

DISPLAY

GENERAL SYNTAX

```
DISPLAY [scope] [expression-list]
    [WHILE condition] [FOR condition]
    [OFF] [TO PRINT]
```

DISPLAY causes all fields of the current record to be displayed, unless qualifying clauses (scope, expression-list, WHILE, FOR) are used. "Expression-list" can cause a variety of information, including calculations, to be displayed. The other clauses can cause multiple records to be displayed. The record number will be displayed unless OFF is specified. TO PRINT sends the displayed information to the printer.

In contrast to LIST, which shows the entire database file on the screen, DISPLAY focuses only on the current record. DISPLAY ALL is nearly identical to LIST, except that DISPLAY ALL pauses periodically (Ashton-Tate 1985).

DISPLAY STATUS and DISPLAY STRUCTURE

GENERAL SYNTAX

```
DISPLAY STATUS [TO PRINT]
```

```
DISPLAY STRUCTURE [TO PRINT]
```

DISPLAY STATUS displays information about the files and indexes currently open in the various work areas. DISPLAY STRUCTURE displays the field names, types, and lengths of the active file.

DO

GENERAL SYNTAX

```
DO command-file-name WITH parameter-list
```

The DO command causes a file of commands to be executed, just as if they had been entered from the keyboard. The parameter-list is a set of values being passed to command-file-name. These values are used in variables defined in command-file-name by the PARAMETER command.

GO or GOTO

GENERAL SYNTAX

```
GO expression | TOP | BOTTOM
```

```
GOTO expression | TOP | BOTTOM
```

The GO (or GOTO) command causes the record pointer to point to a specific record number, as calculated by some expression, to the first record in the file (TOP), or to the last record in the file (BOTTOM). If an index is being used, then TOP and BOTTOM refer, respectively, to the first and last records of the file as ordered by the index.

LOCATE

GENERAL SYNTAX

```
LOCATE [scope] [WHILE  condition]
[FOR condition]
```

LOCATE sets the record pointer to a record satisfying criteria specified in the scope, WHILE, and FOR clauses. It sets the record pointer to the first record in the file satisfying the criteria. If additional records satisfy these criteria, they may be identified by using the CONTINUE command. LOCATE is used whenever the file is not indexed on the fields being used in the criteria.

LOOP

GENERAL SYNTAX

```
LOOP
```

The LOOP command is used within a DO WHILE loop and causes control to return to the DO WHILE statement. Note that it is not the same as the EXIT command, which causes the termination of the loop. The LOOP command merely cuts short a single iteration of the loop. The DO WHILE loop then continues execution with a new iteration.

PACK

GENERAL SYNTAX

```
PACK
```

The DELETE command marks records for deletion, but does not physically remove them. In fact, these records can be unmarked through the RECALL command. The PACK command is used to physically remove records which have been marked for deletion.

PARAMETERS

GENERAL SYNTAX

```
PARAMETERS  parameter-list
```

This command is used at the beginning of a command file to identify the names of data variables in the command file which will receive data values. When the command file is called by another command file, the values of the parameters are passed by the calling command file. These values are then used in the called command file. See also the DO command.

RECALL

GENERAL SYNTAX

```
RECALL [scope] [WHILE  condition]
       [FOR  condition]
```

RECALL removes the deletion mark from previously marked records which satisfy the criteria stated in the scope option, WHILE, or FOR clauses.

SUMMARY

While there is not sufficient space to cover all dBASE facilities in these chapters, we have presented the core commands which make up the bulk of the database processing and application generation functions of the package. The number of dBASE systems installed guarantees that this product will remain an important microcomputer-based 4GL for some time to come.

REVIEW QUESTIONS

9. 1.   How does the SELECT statement in combination with the record pointer facilitate the use of multiple files in dBASE? What must the programmer do in order to work with more than one file?

9. 2.   How is the concept of an index file used in dBASE? What is the corresponding concept in R:BASE?

9. 3.   How does the record pointer of dBASE correspond to the SET POINTER command of R:BASE?

9. 4.   How is the relational algebra project operation incorporated into dBASE operations? Which dBASE operations include a relational algebra project?

9. 5.   How is the relational algebra select operation incorporated into dBASE operations? Which dBASE operations include a relational algebra select? Is there a dBASE operation which is essentially a relational algebra select and project? If not, how does it differ from a pure select and project?

9. 6.   How is the relational algebra assignment operation implemented in dBASE commands?

9. 7.   Compare the dBASE TOTAL, COUNT, SUM, and AVERAGE commands with: the COMPUTE command of R:BASE, the built-in functions of SQL, and the aggregate operators of QUEL.

9. 8.   Discuss the visual and interactive aspects of using the Assistant in developing and testing queries and their associated conditions.

9. 9.   Which dBASE commands give the dBASE language the full capability of structured programming?

9.10.   Compare the two versions of the Inventory Master Update program in this chapter with the R:BASE Inventory Master Update program in Chapter 7.

EXERCISES

For the following projects, it is assumed that the student has access to dBASE III Plus on a microcomputer system. We further assume the database of Figure 9.1.

9.1.   Create a menu-driven system which controls maintenance of the five files in the database. You may use the five programs created via the Applications Generator in the exercises of Chapter 8.

QUERIES

Create dBASE command files to carry out the following queries.

9.2. List all salespeople who have sold more than a selected dollar amount of a selected inventory name. The user should be prompted for both the dollar amount and the inventory name.

9.3. List all inventory items sold by salespeople receiving more than a user-specified commission rate.

9.4. Calculate the total sales amount of inventory items in a user-specified category.

9.5. List all salespeople who have not sold any inventory items with a price over a user-specified amount. (Use *price* in the inventory master file).

UPDATE and REPORT PROGRAMS

9.6. Create a batch program (which uses the entire customer master, sales transactions, and payment transactions files) to update the customer master balance field (custbal). Assume that a purchase increases the customer's balance and payment reduces the balance.

9.7. Create a program to generate a customer statement report. A separate statement should be printed for each customer. The statement should include the customer's id, name, address, and beginning balance in the header; and should list all purchases and payments. Totals of purchases and payments should be calculated and printed. Also, an end of statement balance should be printed. The program can stand alone or be integrated into the program of exercise 9.6.

MENU PROGRAM

9.8. Create a control program which displays menus controlling all the functions provided by the programs developed in exercises 9.1-9.7 above. The program should control a hierarchy of menus. That is, the Main menu should display only general categories of functions (e.g., file maintenance, queries, reports, update programs), while submenus should break down these categories into specific functions (e.g., inventory master maintenance, customer master maintenance, etc.).

CHAPTER 10

IDEAL/PDL

■ ■

IDEAL is a fourth generation application development and production execution environment developed by Applied Data Research (ADR). It is part of a larger environment that supports production, system development, and information center needs for large organizations. IDEAL itself includes editors, panel (screen) definition, report definition, and procedure definition facilities, as well as a compiler and various other batch and on-line services.

Besides IDEAL, components of the ADR environment include a database management system (DATACOM/DB), a centralized data dictionary (DATADICTIONARY), program development systems (ROSCOE and VOLLIE), an interactive end-user query system (DATAQUERY), and a decision support system (EMPIRE). Since many of the concepts on which this environment is based are covered elsewhere in this book, we shall only be concerned in this chapter with a detailed review of the language component of IDEAL: IDEAL/PDL (Procedure Definition Language).

IDEAL/PDL PROCESSING CONTROL STRUCTURES

In this chapter we shall again use the example of Halliday's Department Store. The structure of the database for Halliday's Department Store is shown in Figure 10.1. Note that *spmast* has a different structure from that used in Chapters 6–9, reflecting the scale of three commission rates. IDEAL naming conventions use a table name followed by a period and column name to identify a particular data item. Thus, the inventory name in the inventory master is identified by "invmast.invname".

RETAIL MANAGEMENT DATABASE

INVENTORY MASTER (*invmast*)	COLUMN NAME	DATA TYPE
Inventory Identification	invid	character 3
Inventory Category	invcat	character 10
Inventory Name	invname	character 10
Quantity in Stock	qtystk	numeric 3,0
Price	price	numeric 7,2

SALESPERSON MASTER (*spmast*)	COLUMN NAME	DATA TYPE
Salesperson Identification	spid	character 3
Salesperson Name	spname	character 8
Commission Rate 1	commrat1	numeric 5,3
Commission Rate 2	commrat2	numeric 5,3
Commission Rate 3	commrat3	numeric 5,3

CUSTOMER MASTER (*custmast*)	COLUMN NAME	DATA TYPE
Customer Identification	custid	character 3
Customer Name	custname	character 15
Customer Address	custaddr	character 30
Customer Balance	custbal	numeric 8,2

SALES TRANSACTIONS (*saltx*)	COLUMN NAME	DATA TYPE
Date	saldate	date
Time	saltime	character 8
Salesperson Identification	spid	character 3
Customer Identification	custid	character 3
Cash	cash	logical
Inventory Identification	invid	character 3
Quantity	salqty	numeric 3,0
Sale Price	salprice	numeric 8,2

PAYMENT TRANSACTIONS (*pmttx*)	COLUMN NAME	DATA TYPE
Date	pmtdate	date
Customer Identification	custid	character 3
Amount	pmtamt	numeric 8,2

FIGURE 10.1   Database for Halliday's Retail Management System

The strength of the IDEAL programming language lies principally in its processing control structures which provide a generalized looping mechanism, a generalized CASE statement, and an implicit looping structure which can be used in simulating several relational algebra operations. These three statements are called, respectively: LOOP, SELECT, and FOR. Together they constitute the focus of this chapter.

The LOOP Statement

The IDEAL LOOP statement may be used in three different formats, which we present in order of complexity.

WHILE and UNTIL.   In the loop format shown below, processing is controlled by conditions in WHILE and UNTIL clauses.

GENERAL SYNTAX

```
[label]
      LOOP
            zero or more processing statements
            [{WHILE | UNTIL} condition clauses]
            zero or more processing statements
      ENDLOOP
```

The optional label may be used by other statements to refer to the loop as a whole. WHILE and UNTIL condition clauses have their normal meaning: continue as long as the condition is true, or continue as long as the condition is false, respectively.

The format above provides for several common forms of loops.

```
LOOP...WHILE

LOOP
      WHILE condition
         statements
ENDLOOP

LOOP...UNTIL

LOOP
      statements
      UNTIL condition
ENDLOOP
```

In LOOP...WHILE, the WHILE condition is tested *before* any statements are executed. If the condition is found to be false, the loop terminates immediately. It is possible for the statements in a loop of this format never to be executed. In LOOP...UNTIL, the UNTIL condition is tested *after* the statements are executed. Thus, these statements will always be executed at least once.

Loops similar to the above, but with UNTIL and WHILE interchanged, are also permissible. A loop may have more than one WHILE or UNTIL clause. Thus, the following form is permissible:

```
WHILE and UNTIL Combined

LOOP
        statements1
        WHILE condition1
        statements2
        WHILE condition2
        statements3
        UNTIL condition3
        statements4
ENDLOOP
```

The logic of this code is illustrated in Figure 10.2. In this example, execution of the loop continues as long as condition1 and condition2 are true and condition3 is false. If, for example, condition2 were to become false during the execution of statements4, then statements1 and statements2 would be executed; condition2 would be tested, and assuming condition2 were still false, the loop would terminate; and the statement following ENDLOOP would be executed. Statements, including the WHILE and UNTIL clauses, are executed in the order in which they appear in the loop.

TIMES. The second format of the IDEAL loop structure is shown below.

GENERAL SYNTAX

```
[label]
    LOOP
        numeric-expression TIMES
            zero or more processing statements
        [{WHILE | UNTIL} condition clauses]
            zero or more processing statements
    ENDLOOP
```

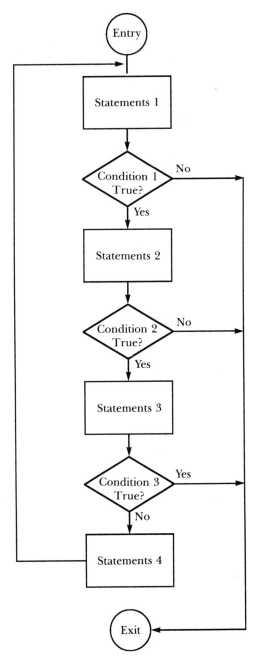

FIGURE 10.2   Loop Using WHILE and UNTIL

The logic of this code is illustrated in Figure 10.3. The only difference between this format and the WHILE or UNTIL format is "numeric-expression TIMES", which indicates that the statements in the loop are to be executed a number of times equal to the value of "numeric-expression". This is reminiscent of one of the forms of the COBOL PERFORM statement. However, in the case of the IDEAL LOOP structure, the loop can be terminated early, in accordance with the value of the condition in a WHILE or UNTIL clause.

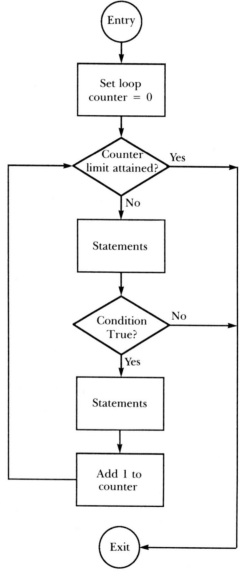

FIGURE 10.3   Loop Specifying TIMES

VARYING.   The third LOOP format utilizes the VARYING . . . FROM . . . BY . . . THRU loop control mechanism and is reminiscent of yet another form of the COBOL PERFORM.

GENERAL SYNTAX

```
[label]
      LOOP
            VARYING variable
              [FROM numeric-expression-1]
              [BY numeric-expression-2]
              [{UP | DOWN} THRU numeric-expression-3]
                  zero or more processing  statements
            [{WHILE | UNTIL} condition clauses]
                  zero or more processing statements
      ENDLOOP
```

This format causes "variable" to be set initially to the value of "numeric-expression-1". With each succeeding iteration of the loop, the variable is incremented by the value of "numeric-expression-2", until "variable" is larger than "numeric-expression-3". If "numeric-expression-2" is negative, then "variable" is decremented with each loop iteration, and the loop terminates when "variable" is less than "numeric-expression-3". (In this case, DOWN must also be coded.) As with the TIMES format, this format differs from the corresponding version of the COBOL PERFORM in that the loop can be terminated via a WHILE/UNTIL clause.

The SELECT Statement

We noted in Chapter 9 that the DO CASE statement of dBASE III PLUS is a generalized IF statement. IDEAL carries this notion a step further with the SELECT statement, which may be thought of as a generalized DO CASE statement. As with the LOOP statement, the SELECT statement has three formats.

In the *variable* format of the SELECT statement, processing is controlled by comparing the value in the variable against one or more WHEN expressions.

GENERAL SYNTAX

```
SELECT variable
       WHEN expression [OR expression ...]
              statements
       [WHEN expression [OR expression ...]
              statements ]

       ...


       [WHEN {OTHER | NONE}
              statements ]
       [WHEN ANY
              statements ]
ENDSELECT
```

This rather complex structure may best be explained by an example. Suppose we have built a system to allow a user to enter any of six types of transactions. We display a menu listing the six transactions and pause to wait for the user to enter a selection. After the user has chosen a transaction, we proceed with our program code as follows:

```
SELECT choice
       WHEN 1
              DO Trans-type-1
       WHEN 2
              DO Trans-type-2
       WHEN 3
              DO Trans-type-3
       WHEN 4
              DO  Trans-type-4
       WHEN 5
              DO Trans-type-5
       WHEN 6
              DO Trans-type-6
       WHEN NONE
              DO  Err-message
       WHEN ANY
              DO Log-trans
ENDSELECT
```

In this example, each WHEN is followed by a corresponding DO statement. The code may be read as: "When choice = 1, do trans-type-1 . . ." and so on, where trans-type-n is some other procedure within the program. The DO statement to be executed is the one which corresponds to the WHEN clause containing the current value of the variable "choice". After the DO statement causes another procedure (within the same program) to be executed, control returns to the SELECT procedure. We execute a different procedure for each transaction type. Thus, if the user selects transaction type 4, the SELECT statement causes the procedure "Trans-type-4" to be executed.

The WHEN NONE clause is executed if none of the numbers 1 through 6 is chosen. In other words, the user has struck an illegal key, and an error message should be displayed. Consequently, we execute the procedure named "Err-message".

The WHEN ANY clause is executed if any of the other WHEN clauses (except WHEN NONE) has been executed. For example, if the user enters a transaction, we want to execute "Log-trans", which presumably records the transaction on a log file. (A log file records all transactions for the day and can be used in auditing the system.)

This example follows a similar example given in the ADR/IDEAL reference manual (1983), which illustrates that this format of the SELECT statement has a natural application in menu-oriented systems.

The *FIRST ACTION* format of the SELECT statement is more general than the variable format.

GENERAL SYNTAX

```
SELECT [FIRST [ACTION]]
    WHEN  condition
            statements
    [WHEN condition
            statements ]

    ...


    [WHEN {OTHER | NONE}
            statements ]
    [WHEN ANY
            statements ]
ENDSELECT
```

The example we gave for the variable format could be expressed in the FIRST ACTION format as follows:

```
SELECT FIRST ACTION
    WHEN choice = 1
        DO Trans-type-1
    WHEN choice = 2
        DO Trans-type-2
    WHEN choice = 3
        DO Trans-type-3
    WHEN choice = 4
        DO Trans-type-4
    WHEN choice = 5
        DO Trans-type-5
```

```
      WHEN choice = 6
            DO Trans-type-6
      WHEN NONE
            DO Err-message
      WHEN ANY
            DO Log-trans
ENDSELECT
```

This format causes those statements to be executed which follow the first true condition. In this format, each condition is contained entirely in a WHEN clause, whereas in the variable format, the conditions were split between the SELECT clause and the individual WHEN clauses.

The variable format is more convenient for this menu example. For more general processing needs, however, the FIRST ACTION format is useful. Consider this example: Halliday's Department Store decides to pay sales commissions on a sliding scale. Items priced under $500 receive one rate, items priced between $500 and $1000 receive a second rate, and items priced over $1000 receive a third rate. The three commission rates that apply to a given salesperson are carried in that salesperson's record as *commrat1*, *commrat2*, and *commrat3*, respectively.

We now calculate the commission on a sales transaction—i.e., the commission on a record from the *saltx* table—using the FIRST ACTION format of the SELECT statement.

```
SELECT FIRST ACTION
      WHEN saltx.salprice < 500
            SET commission TO spmast.commrat1 * saltx.salprice
      WHEN saltx.salprice <= 1000
            SET commission TO spmast.commrat2 * saltx.salprice
      WHEN OTHER
            SET commission TO spmast.commrat3 * saltx.salprice
ENDSELECT
```

Suppose now that we must calculate the commission on an item whose sale price is $400. Since the first condition (*saltx.salprice* < 500) is true, then the statement following that condition will be executed. The next condition (*saltx.salprice* <= 1000) is also true. However, since the first condition was true, the second condition will not be examined. The system will execute only the statements following the *first* true WHEN clause and the true postscript (OTHER|NONE or ANY) clause. If this were not the case, it would be necessary to write the second WHEN clause as:

```
WHEN saltx.salprice >= 500 AND saltx.salprice <= 1000
```

The primary difference beween these formats is that the conditions in the variable format are restricted to specific values of the SELECT variable; in the FIRST ACTION format, entirely different conditions (which may refer to entirely different variables) may be used in each WHEN clause.

The *EVERY ACTION* format provides for any number of conditions, including *all* conditions, to trigger some processing activity.

GENERAL SYNTAX

```
SELECT EVERY [ACTION]
     WHEN condition
          statements
     [WHEN condition
          statements ]
     . . .

     [WHEN {OTHER | NONE}
          statements ]
     [WHEN ALL
          statements ]
     [WHEN ANY
          statements ]
ENDSELECT
```

In the FIRST ACTION format, only the action associated with the *first* true WHEN condition is executed. In the EVERY ACTION format, *every* true WHEN condition causes its associated action to be executed. Additionally, the EVERY ACTION format allows a WHEN ALL clause, which can define actions to be taken if every WHEN condition is true.

Suppose Halliday's initiates a sales incentive program with the following features:

- A bonus of $100 is paid on the sale of any item whose sale price is $2000 or above.
- An additional 10% commission is paid on the sale of any television.
- An additional $50 bonus is paid if both of the above are achieved.

We use the following code to implement these conditions, (assuming that the normal commission has previously been calculated and stored in a working variable named *commission*).

```
SELECT EVERY ACTION
     WHEN invmast.price >= 2000
          ADD 100 TO commission
     WHEN invmast.invname = 'Television'
          ADD .1 * invmast.price TO commission
     WHEN ALL
          ADD 50 TO commission
ENDSELECT
```

The logic of this code is illustrated in Figure 10.4. One attractive feature of this code is the degree to which it conforms to the statement of the conditions of the sales incentive program as described above. It is relatively

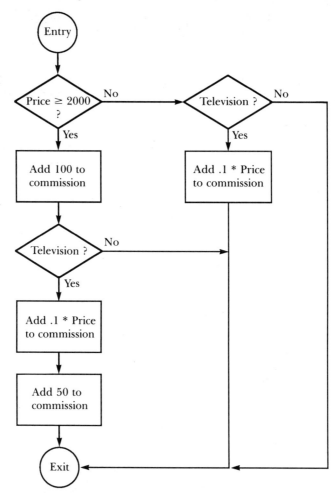

FIGURE 10.4   Logic of SELECT EVERY ACTION

easy to read the code and identify the features of the sales program. More-over, the logical requirements of the sales program are also captured in the structure of the SELECT statement's code.

The FOR Statement

The implicit loop structure provided by the FOR statement is one of the more advanced aspects of the IDEAL language.

For example, suppose we wish to initialize the quantity in stock of every record in the inventory master file to zero. The statement below is all that is required.

```
FOR EACH invmast
     SET invmast.qtystk TO 0
ENDFOR
```

If we wish to increase the price of television sets by 10%, we use the following:

```
FOR EACH invmast
     WHERE invmast.invname = 'Television'
             SET invmast.price TO invmast.price * 1.1
ENDFOR
```

Note that there is no explicit terminating condition for this loop. If this were an explicit loop, its terminating condition would be detection of end of file. Thus, it would also require two read statements (one prior to entering the loop, and one at the end of the loop). We further note that the FOR statement itself is very close to an English language statement of the problem. The point is that the FOR statement provides a programming construct that parallels the logical statement of the problem, and consequently has a very strong element of "naturalness" about it. It is a nonprocedural element which can be used as a powerful tool in a procedural programming language.

GENERAL SYNTAX

```
[label]
    FOR [{EACH | ALL | [THE] FIRST [num]}] table-name
         [WHERE condition]
              statements
         [WHEN NONE
              statements]
    ENDFOR
```

As shown in the previous example, the WHERE clause of the FOR statement can be used to perform a relational algebra selection operation on a table. The SET statement then performs processing operations on the selected records and places them back into their original table. Other IDEAL operations can be used with this relational algebra selection feature to display data or to transform it in other ways.

Instead of processing all of the records satisfying the WHERE clause we can designate that only the first record, or the first several ("num") records be processed. Thus, if we wish to display the commission rates of Smithart:

```
FOR THE FIRST spmast
  WHERE spmast.spname = 'Smithart'
    LIST spmast.commrat1, spmast.commrat2,
         spmast.commrat3
ENDFOR
```

If we desire to see the amounts of the first three sales transactions for salesperson 107:

```
FOR THE FIRST 3 saltx
    WHERE saltx.spid = '107'
            LIST saltx.salprice
ENDFOR
```

The relational algebra join operation is simulated by nesting FOR statements. Suppose, for example, that we wish to see the first three sales transactions for salesperson Smithart. This problem requires the joining of tables *spmast* and *saltx:*

```
FOR THE spmast
    WHERE spmast.spname = 'Smithart'
            FOR THE FIRST 3 saltx
                WHERE saltx.spid = spmast.spid
                        LIST saltx.salprice
            ENDFOR
ENDFOR
```

The outer FOR statement identifies the *spmast* record of Smithart. While this record remains fixed, the inner FOR statement causes the appropriate *saltx* records to be displayed. Note that this join only involves records applying to Smithart. Thus, the outer FOR can stop searching the *spmast* table once the first record for Smithart is identified. Similarly, the inner FOR need only identify three *saltx* records. Such a join uses considerably less processing time than a join which must examine all records in both tables.

A join which could involve all records in two tables is also handled with nested FOR statements. Suppose we wish to update the inventory master records by subtracting the quantity sold as reflected in the sales transaction records:

```
FOR EACH invmast
    FOR EACH saltx
        WHERE saltx.invid = invmast.invid
                SUBTRACT saltx.salqty FROM invmast.qtystk
    ENDFOR
ENDFOR
```

As with the previous example, the outer FOR statement identifies an inventory master record, which is fixed while the inner FOR statement executes. All of the sales transaction records which apply to this particular inventory master record are then processed via the inner FOR statement. The outer FOR statement then resumes execution by moving to the next inventory master record, and the process starts over again.

Suppose we wish to list the names of salespeople who have sold televisions. This requires the joining of three tables, and therefore the nesting of three FOR statements:

```
FOR EACH spmast
    FOR EACH saltx
        WHERE saltx.spid = spmast.spid
        FOR EACH invmast
            WHERE invmast.invname = 'Television' AND
                  invmast.invid = saltx.invid
            LIST spmast.spname
        ENDFOR
    ENDFOR
ENDFOR
```

You will note a similarity between the WHERE clause of this construction and that of a similar SQL statement. However, the syntax of IDEAL requires that the left side of any relational expression refer to the table identified in the FOR EACH clause. Thus, the following WHERE clause must occur after "FOR EACH saltx" rather than after "FOR EACH invmast".

```
WHERE saltx.spid = spmast.spid
```

Although this solution is straightforward and relatively easy to grasp, it executes somewhat inefficiently. A solution likely to be more efficient is as follows:

```
FOR EACH invmast
    WHERE invmast.invname = 'Television'
        FOR EACH saltx
            WHERE saltx.invid = invmast.invid
                FOR FIRST spmast
                    WHERE spmast.spid = saltx.spid
                    LIST spmast.spname
                ENDFOR
        ENDFOR
ENDFOR
```

This solution is more efficient because we select (in the relational algebra sense) the "Television" records before we join to the other files. Fewer records must be joined. We saw in Chapter 3 that a SELECT followed by a JOIN is more efficient than a JOIN followed by a SELECT. The same principle is operative in this example. A perfect system would note the equivalence between the two solutions and would process both solutions in the same way. As 4GLs continue to develop, it is to be hoped that such optimization will be built into the language processing systems.

SUMMARY

Only a small portion of IDEAL/PDL commands are presented here. With variations in the LOOP, SELECT, and FOR statements, however, you can see a portion of the power available to the user in this language and the ability to adapt the theoretical concepts of a 4GL to the processing realities of current computer systems.

EXERCISES

10. 1. Assume the existence of a READ command for reading a table in order by some key. For example, suppose we wish to process the payment transaction table in order by *custid*. We assume that a "READ pmttx" command will retrieve records sequentially in order by *custid*. Construct a loop which will process the entire table. How is the structure of the loop simplified by the IDEAL feature that the WHILE/UNTIL statement can be placed anywhere in the loop, rather than just at the beginning or at the end as in most conventional languages?

10. 2. A system consists of four functions executed respectively by statements1, statements2, statements3, and statements4. The user selects one of these by entering a number between 1 and 4 when a menu is displayed. Create an IDEAL structure to handle the user's response to the menu. Assume that the user enters "5" to exit from the system, and that an error procedure is executed if the user enters an invalid entry.

10. 3. Suppose the commission rate used to figure a salesperson's commission on sales exceeding $100 depends on quantity sold.

Quantity	Commission Rate
1 - 10	Rate 1
11 - 50	Rate 2
51 +	Rate 3

For sales of $100 or less, use Rate 1. Derive IDEAL code to handle this logic.

10. 4. Assume we calculate sale price by multiplying quantity by inventory master price. However, we want to give discounts. If the category is appliances, give a 10% discount. If the quantity is over 2, give a 20% discount. If the customer's balance is under $500, give a $100 discount. If all of these are true, give an additional $25 discount. However, do not let the final price be less than 50% of the original price.

10. 5. Set all salesperson commission rates to 10%, 15%, and 20%.

10. 6. Add 5% interest to all customer balances over $1000.

10. 7. List furniture (*invcat*) sales to customers with a balance under $500.

10. 8. List payments of customers with a balance over $1000.

10. 9. List the inventory names of items sold by salesperson 203.

10.10. Decrease the inventory price of all washers with more than 10 in stock by 25%.

PART FOUR

USER-ORIENTED INTERFACES

4GLs are particularly noted for increasing the ease and facility with which end users can access data in a database. In this last part, we examine two visual interfaces, Query-by-Example and Query-by-Forms. We also examine a natural language interface, CLOUT. These chapters illustrate two non-traditional approaches to programming and provide some insight to their strengths and weaknesses. In each case we shall relate the language discussed to concepts of the relational data model.

CHAPTER 11

QUERY-BY-EXAMPLE

■ ■

Query-by-Example (QBE) was originally developed by M. M. Zloof at IBM's Thomas J. Watson Research Center (Zloof 1975, Date 1986). Released as an IBM product in 1978 (Zloof 1981), QBE is one of two languages supported by IBM's Query Management Facility. The other language is SQL (Chapter 2).

QBE is a popular language which utilizes the concepts of visual programming. As we shall see in this chapter, it can be used not only to query a relational database, but also to make changes to the database. Throughout this chapter we shall use the database of Figure 11.1 to demonstrate the key features of QBE.

SIMPLE QUERIES

The Query Management Facility user of QBE develops queries interactively by making requests and receiving responses on a terminal screen. The system responses are often in the form of pictures—skeletons (i.e., descriptions without data) of database tables. The user then interacts with the system by making requests directly on the table skeletons themselves.

The user initiates a query by requesting an *example table*. If we wish to make a query on the appliances table, we first request the appliances table as an example table.

APPLIANCES	INVENTORY ID	DESCRIPTION	VENDOR	COST	PRICE

We indicate which information we desire by entering "P." beneath the appropriate column heading. Thus, if we wish to see the entire table, we enter the P. operator below APPLIANCES.

APPLIANCES	INVENTORY ID	DESCRIPTION	VENDOR	COST	PRICE
P.					

Result:

INVENTORY ID	DESCRIPTION	VENDOR	COST	PRICE
100	Refrigerator	22	150.00	250.00
150	Television	27	225.00	340.00
110	Refrigerator	20	175.00	300.00

APPLIANCE DATABASE

APPLIANCES

INVENTORY ID	DESCRIPTION	VENDOR	COST	PRICE
100	Refrigerator	22	150.00	250.00
150	Television	27	225.00	340.00
110	Refrigerator	20	175.00	300.00

VENDORS

VENDOR ID	CITY	STATE	RATING
22	Orem	Utah	8
20	Davis	Calif	6
27	Urbana	Illinois	9

SALESPEOPLE

NAME	ADDRESS	COMM RATE
Smith	301 E. Main	.20
Jones	11 W. First	.15

SALES

DATE	TIME	SP NAME	INV ID	QTY	SALE AMT
10/01	9:00	Jones	100	1	250.00
10/03	8:30	Smith	110	2	600.00
10/04	10:45	Smith	150	1	340.00

FIGURE 11.1   Appliance Database

If we desire to see only selected columns, we enter the P. operator below each column we want displayed.

APPLIANCES	INVENTORY ID	DESCRIPTION	VENDOR	COST	PRICE
		P.	P.		

Result:

DESCRIPTION	VENDOR
Refrigerator	22
Television	27
Refrigerator	20

The list above shows appliances and vendors who supply them, but it is not in any particular order. Suppose we desire a report showing all of the vendors of all of the appliances, but we want all appliances of a given type listed together. We can specify that the report be sorted alphabetically on the appliance description by merely entering "AO." in the description column.

APPLIANCES	INVENTORY ID	DESCRIPTION	VENDOR	COST	PRICE
		P. AO.	P.		

Result:

DESCRIPTION	VENDOR
Refrigerator	22
Refrigerator	20
Television	27

We may also want the report to be in order by vendor within description. We specify description as the primary sort key by entering "AO(1)." in the description column, and vendor as the secondary sort key by entering "AO(2)." in the vendor column.

APPLIANCES	INVENTORY ID	DESCRIPTION	VENDOR	COST	PRICE
		P. AO(1)	P. AO(2)		

Result:

DESCRIPTION	VENDOR
Refrigerator	20
Refrigerator	22
Television	27

"AO" stands for "ascending order." If we desire the report to be in descending order by a column value, we enter "DO" instead of "AO". If there is more than one sort key, we may mix "AO" and "DO", sorting in ascending order on one column and descending order on another.

Suppose we want only a list of all appliance types. If we were to specify only the description column, as in our previous queries, we would get an entry for every row, resulting in undesired repetition. To remove the repeated occurrences of the same type of appliance, we say that we want each row on our report to be "unique." This is done by placing the UNQ. operator beneath the name of the table.

APPLIANCES	INVENTORY ID	DESCRIPTION	VENDOR	COST	PRICE
UNQ.		P.			

Result: **DESCRIPTION**

Refrigerator
Television

SELECTING ROWS WITH CONDITIONS

If we do not want to look at the entire table, we set conditions to select rows for display. QBE will then display only those rows satisfying the conditions specified. QBE provides a rich variety of conditions. In this section, we shall cover conditions placed directly in example tables and conditions placed in condition boxes.

Specifying Conditions in Example Tables

In example tables, three types of operators may be used to select rows for display. The types are: comparison operators; Boolean AND and OR; and two string matching operators, IN and LIKE.

Comparison Operators.   Suppose we want a list of refrigerators only. We specify this condition by entering "Refrigerator" in the description column of the example table. Thus, we give QBE an example of the type of row to select. Hence arises the name "Query-by-Example".

APPLIANCES	INVENTORY ID	DESCRIPTION	VENDOR	COST	PRICE
P.		Refrigerator			

Result:

INVENTORY ID	DESCRIPTION	VENDOR	COST	PRICE
100	Refrigerator	22	150.00	250.00
110	Refrigerator	20	175.00	300.00

If we want a list of appliances priced over $275, we use the query shown on the next page. This query says "Print all information about appliances such that the price of the appliance is greater than $275." In general, we may specify that a column is equal to ($=$), not equal to ($\neg=$), greater than ($>$), greater than or equal to ($>=$), less than ($<$), or less than or equal to ($<=$) a given constant, merely by placing the comparison symbol and the constant in the column with which the constant is to be compared.

APPLIANCES	INVENTORY ID	DESCRIPTION	VENDOR	COST	PRICE
P.					>275.00

Result:

INVENTORY ID	DESCRIPTION	VENDOR	COST	PRICE
110	Refrigerator	20	175.00	300.00
150	Television	27	225.00	340.00

Boolean AND and OR. We can obtain a list of refrigerators priced above $275 by entering values in the two appropriate columns. If two or more columns contain such comparison formulas, QBE interprets the query as if both conditions must hold for each row selected. Thus, the condition states: "Select all rows where the description = refrigerator *AND* the price > 275.00."

APPLIANCES	INVENTORY ID	DESCRIPTION	VENDOR	COST	PRICE
P.		Refrigerator			>275.00

Result:

INVENTORY ID	DESCRIPTION	VENDOR	COST	PRICE
110	Refrigerator	20	175.00	300.00

Suppose we want an answer to the query: "Select all rows where the description = Refrigerator *OR* the price > 275.00." In this case, we use two lines in the example table.

APPLIANCES	INVENTORY ID	DESCRIPTION	VENDOR	COST	PRICE
P.					>275.00
P.		Refrigerator			

Result:

INVENTORY ID	DESCRIPTION	VENDOR	COST	PRICE
100	Refrigerator	22	150.00	250.00
150	Television	27	225.00	340.00
110	Refrigerator	20	175.00	300.00

The Boolean connective AND is specified by placing multiple conditions on the same line of an example table. The Boolean connective OR is specified by placing multiple conditions on different lines of the example table.

IN and LIKE Operators.   For a given query we may be interested in all appliances from selected vendors. Thus, suppose we want a list of appliances supplied by vendors 20 and 27. Then we say: "Select appliances where the vendor number is in the set (20, 27)."

APPLIANCES	INVENTORY ID	DESCRIPTION	VENDOR	COST	PRICE
P.			IN(20,27)		

Result:

INVENTORY ID	DESCRIPTION	VENDOR	COST	PRICE
150	Television	27	225.00	340.00
110	Refrigerator	20	175.00	300.00

If a column's data consists of character strings (such as the state column in the vendors table), we can select rows from the table even if we know only a portion of the character string. For example, if we want all vendors in California but do not know how the state name may have been abbreviated, we construct a query using wildcard characters as shown below. This query will print all the rows of the vendors table whose state column begins with the letters "Ca". The percent sign (%) is a wildcard character which stands for any combination of characters (including none). The underscore (_) character is a wildcard representing any single character; one underscore stands for one character, two underscores for two characters, and so on.

VENDORS	VENDOR ID	CITY	STATE	RATING
P.			LIKE 'CA%'	

Specifying Conditions in Condition Boxes

Some conditions are difficult or even impossible to express by placing values and symbols in example tables. At the user's request, QBE will provide *condition boxes* to give increased power and flexibility in formulating queries. Condition boxes, used together with example tables, provide visual and verbal programming features. A condition box contains verbal information which sets conditions on and clarifies the meaning of the visual information in example tables.

The example below shows an example table qualified by a condition box. The variables "_X" and "_Y" are called *example elements*. They represent price and description respectively in this example. By placing __X in the price column, we define __X as representing price. Similarly, __Y is defined as representing description. The condition box then states that rows should be selected if price (__X) is over $275 or if description (__Y) is refrigerator. This is exactly the same query as an earlier query, but specified in a different manner.

APPLIANCES	INVENTORY ID	DESCRIPTION	VENDOR	COST	PRICE
P.		_Y			_X

CONDITIONS
_X > 275.00 OR _Y = Refrigerator

An example element always consists of the underscore character, followed by up to 17 letters and digits. Thus, __PRICE and __DESCRIPTION would both be acceptable example elements.

An example of a more complex query would be to create a list of appliances whose cost is between $100 and $200 and whose price is between $250 and $350.

APPLIANCES	INVENTORY ID	DESCRIPTION	VENDOR	COST	PRICE
P.				_C	_P

CONDITIONS
_C >= 100 AND _C <= 200 AND _P >= 250 AND _P <= 350

The NOT Operator. Sometimes a condition is expressed most easily by negating a simple condition. This may be accomplished by applying the NOT operator. For example, if we desire a list of appliances supplied by vendors other than vendors 25 and 20, we use a NOT operator in a condition box to reverse the sense of the condition VENDOR IN (25, 20). It should be noted that the NOT operator may be used only in a condition box. Thus, the statement in the condition box below cannot be placed directly into an example table.

APPLIANCES	INVENTORY ID	DESCRIPTION	VENDOR	COST	PRICE
P.			_VEND		

CONDITIONS
NOT (_VEND IN (25,20))

Calculated Expressions.   An expression involving a calculated value may be used as part of a condition in a condition box. Suppose for example that a 5% sales tax is added to the price of every appliance at time of sale. If we wish to list all appliances with a price (including tax) that is under $300, we can use a calculated expression in the condition box.

APPLIANCES	INVENTORY ID	DESCRIPTION	VENDOR	COST	PRICE
P.					_PRICE

CONDITIONS
1.05 * _PRICE < 300.00

Similarly, suppose we want a list of appliances whose price is at least 50% higher than their cost.

APPLIANCES	INVENTORY ID	DESCRIPTION	VENDOR	COST	PRICE
P.				_COST	_PRICE

CONDITIONS
_PRICE >= 1.5 * _COST

In general, calculated expressions involving addition (+), subtraction (−), multiplication (∗), and division (/) may be used in condition boxes. They may also be used for other purposes as we shall see below.

CALCULATIONS, GROUPING, AND MULTIPLE TABLE MANIPULATION

So far our examples have been confined to the printing of data as it already exists in the database. We now explore some features of QBE which allow more flexible manipulation and display of data than we have seen to this point.

Target Tables

We showed in the previous section that conditions could be defined in terms of calculations. It is also possible to display the results of calculations. When the user enters the appropriate command, QBE sets up *target tables* to define columns of data for display. A target table is just an example table without column headings. By filling in information in the lower part of the target table, the user instructs QBE as to the kind of information that should be displayed.

An example of the use of a target table is shown below. The upper table is an example table. Note that the P. operator does not appear in the example table in this case. The example table is used to define example elements and conditions. The target table (the lower table) is used to specify what should be printed. Therefore, the P. operator appears in its first column. This target table specifies that inventory id, price, and cost should be printed in the first three columns of the report. The difference between price and cost (the profit on the item) should then be printed in the fourth column. Since the system did not have a natural name for the fourth column of the report (the column containing the calculated value), it used the default name of "Col 1."

APPLIANCES	INVENTORY ID	DESCRIPTION	VENDOR	COST	PRICE
	_ID	Refrigerator		_COST	_PRICE

P.	_ID	_PRICE	_COST	_PRICE - _COST

Result:

INVENTORY ID	PRICE	COST	COL 1
100	250.00	150.00	100.00
110	300.00	175.00	125.00

Built-in Functions

QBE supports the built-in functions of COUNT, SUM, AVERAGE, MAX, and MIN. They operate on the set of values for a given column in the specified rows of a table, as shown in the following example.

APPLIANCES	INVENTORY ID	DESCRIPTION	VENDOR	COST	PRICE
					_P

P.	CNT._P	SUM._P	AVG._P	MAX._P	MIN._P

Result:

COL 1	COL 2	COL 3	COL 4	COL 5
3	890.00	296.67	340.00	250.00

This example illustrates the meaning of each of these functions. COUNT (abbreviated CNT) gives the number of entries in the set of values (including duplicates). SUM adds them together. AVG determines their average value. MAX finds the largest value in the set, and MIN finds the smallest value. SUM and AVG are meaningful only if the column from which the values are taken is numeric. COUNT, MAX, and MIN may be applied to columns containing character or numeric values.

In the first section, we saw how to use the UNQ. (unique) operator to give a list, without duplicates, of all the different types of appliances. Suppose that, instead of a complete list of the different types, we are interested only in a count of the number of different appliances. As noted, the COUNT function will include duplicates in its result. However, we may specify that we want only *unique* values to be considered in evaluating the function. In this case, the system will only use a given value a single time. We do this by again applying the UNQ. operator.

APPLIANCES	INVENTORY ID	DESCRIPTION	VENDOR	COST	PRICE
		_DESC			
P.	CNT.UNQ._DESC				

Result: <u>COL 1</u>

2

The built-in functions (except COUNT) may also include calculated expressions. For example, suppose we want to know the maximum difference between price and cost. In processing the query below, QBE will go through every row of the appliances table and calculate the indicated expression (which gives the difference between price and cost). It will then choose the largest of these and place that value in Col 1 of the report. For our example database, $125.00 is the maximum difference.

APPLIANCES	INVENTORY ID	DESCRIPTION	VENDOR	COST	PRICE
				_C	_P
P.	MAX.(_P - _C)				

Result: <u>COL 1</u>

125.00

Built-in functions can also be used in condition boxes in combination with the grouping operator. Examples are given below.

Grouping

Suppose we wish to see the average prices of all the different appliance types. The "grouping" facility of QBE, in combination with the AVERAGE function, will generate such a list. The example below illustrates how the grouping facility is used. The G. operator in the description column indicates that rows from the appliances table which have the same value in the description column should be grouped together.

APPLIANCES	INVENTORY ID	DESCRIPTION	VENDOR	COST	PRICE
		G. _DESC			_PRICE
P.	_DESC	AVG._PRICE			

Result:

DESCRIPTION	COL 1
Refrigerator	275.00
Television	340.00

Conceptually we may think of the appliances table as being sorted into different groups corresponding to the different appliance descriptions. Thus, there may be one group of rows corresponding to the refrigerators, one group for the televisions, one group for the washers, etc. The number and types of groups depend on the specific make-up of the database. In our example, there would be two groups, refrigerators and televisions.

The example element, _DESC, represents those different groups. Thus, the target table is set up to indicate that a line on the report should be printed out for each _DESC group. This line should give the identifying value of the group and the average price of all the appliances in the group.

The G. operator may be used in more than one column of an example table. When it is used in more than one column, the groups are made up of those rows having common values in all of the columns containing the G. operator. In the example below we see the G. operator being used to group rows by the combined value of description and vendor. Thus, one group consists of refrigerators supplied by vendor 22, another group consists of refrigerators supplied by vendor 20, etc. This example also illustrates the use of the AO. operator in combination with the G. operator to sort the output.

APPLIANCES	INVENTORY ID	DESCRIPTION	VENDOR	COST	PRICE
		G. _D	G. _V		_P
P.	_D AO.	_V	AVG. _P		

Result:

DESCRIPTION	VENDOR	COL 1
Refrigerator	22	250.00
Refrigerator	20	300.00
Television	27	340.00

Suppose we want to see the average cost of appliances supplied by each vendor, but we specifically want to exclude those appliances whose price is less than or equal to $100. Clearly, we need to be able to place conditions on the rows included in our groups. The following query restricts the rows to be included in each group to those having a price over $100.

APPLIANCES	INVENTORY ID	DESCRIPTION	VENDOR	COST	PRICE
			_V G.	_C	>100
P.	_V	AVG._C			

It is also possible to place conditions on the groups. Suppose we want to repeat the above query, but we want to impose the additional condition that no group will be displayed unless it includes at least 3 rows. The condition in the condition box in the modified query below states that the number of inventory id's in any given group (in other words, the number of rows in the group) must be 3 or larger.

APPLIANCES	INVENTORY ID	DESCRIPTION	VENDOR	COST	PRICE
	_I		_V G.	_C	>100
P.	_V	AVG._C			

CONDITIONS
CNT. _I >= 3

Another example of using a condition with grouping is shown below. This query gives the average markup by appliance description (e.g., refrigerator or television), but it eliminates any groups which have an item marked up more than $500.

APPLIANCES	INVENTORY ID	DESCRIPTION	VENDOR	COST	PRICE
		_D G.		_C	_P
P.	_D	AVG.(_P-_C)			

CONDITIONS
MAX. (_P - _C) <= 500

Combining Data from Multiple Tables

Many problems require data from more than one table for their solution. By using example elements together with several example tables, we can obtain results that combine data. Suppose we want the locations of vendors who supply televisions. The two example tables below are tied together by the example element _V. QBE examines each row in the appliances table. Whenever it encounters a row with "Television" in the description column, it uses the value in the vendor column to find the corresponding row in the vendors table. The value in the vendor id column of the vendors table must match the value of vendor in the appliances table. The target table then indicates that the vendor id, city, and state should be printed.

APPLIANCES	INVENTORY ID	DESCRIPTION	VENDOR	COST	PRICE
		Television	_V		

VENDORS	VENDOR ID	CITY	STATE	RATING
	_V	_C	_S	

P.	_V	_C	_S		

The target table in the above example is not required. The same query without the target table is shown below.

APPLIANCES	INVENTORY ID	DESCRIPTION	VENDOR	COST	PRICE
		Television	_V		

VENDORS	VENDOR ID	CITY	STATE	RATING
	P. _V	P. _C	P. _S	

Several additional examples of queries and their solutions are shown to reinforce the concepts presented thus far.

QUERY. List salespeople who have sold appliances supplied by vendor 20.

APPLIANCES	INVENTORY ID	DESCRIPTION	VENDOR	COST	PRICE
	_ID		20		

SALES	DATE	TIME	SP NAME	INV ID	QTY	SALE AMT
UNQ.			P.	_ID		

QUERY: List salespeople who have sold appliances priced between $500 and $1000.

APPLIANCES	INVENTORY ID	DESCRIPTION	VENDOR	COST	PRICE
	_ID				_PR

SALES	DATE	TIME	SP NAME	INV ID	QTY	SALE AMT
UNQ.			P.	_ID		

CONDITIONS
_PR >= 500 AND _PR <= 1000

QUERY: List salespeople who have earned a commission exceeding $100 on a single sale.

SALESPEOPLE	NAME	ADDRESS	COMM RATE
	_SN		_CR

SALES	DATE	TIME	SP NAME	INV ID	QTY	SALE AMT
UNQ.			P. _SN			_SALEAMT

CONDITIONS
_CR * _SALEAMT > 100

QUERY: Give the names and addresses of salespeople who have made a sale with a gross profit (sale amount less cost of goods sold) of $500 or more.

APPLIANCES	INVENTORY ID	DESCRIPTION	VENDOR	COST	PRICE
	_ID			_COST	

SALESPEOPLE	NAME	ADDRESS	COMM RATE
UNQ.	P. _SN	P.	

SALES	DATE	TIME	SP NAME	INV ID	QTY	SALE AMT
			_SN	_ID	_QTY	_SALEAMT

CONDITIONS
_SALEAMT - (_QTY * _COST) >= 500

DATABASE MODIFICATION

In addition to the query facility, QBE provides operations for updating the contents of the tables in the database. Specifically, the operations supported which we will discuss here are insert, update, and delete.

Inserting Rows

To insert a single row into a table, the values desired for each column are entered into their columns in an example table. The first column, whose heading is the name of the table, will contain an "I." (for "insert").

APPLIANCES	INVENTORY ID	DESCRIPTION	VENDOR	COST	PRICE
I.	303	Freezer	24	300.00	375.00

Creating a Table

Suppose we wish to create a new table by selecting certain rows and columns from another table. This may be done by using the I. operator as shown in the example below. In this example we have selected rows for toasters, and have only included their inventory id's and prices.

APPLIANCES	INVENTORY ID	DESCRIPTION	VENDOR	COST	PRICE
	_ID	Toaster			_PR

TOASTLIST	INVENTORY ID	PRICE
I.	_ID	_PR

If we wanted to include only toasters whose price is between $50 and $100, we could use a condition box as shown below.

APPLIANCES	INVENTORY ID	DESCRIPTION	VENDOR	COST	PRICE
	_ID	Toaster			_PR

TOASTLIST	INVENTORY ID	PRICE
I.	_ID	_PR

CONDITIONS
_PR >= 50 AND _PR <= 100

Updating Rows

In contrast to the I. operator, the U. (update) operator is placed in the column to be updated. Thus, if we want to change the price of inventory item 505 to $210.00, we use the query below. This will change the price of every item with inventory id equal to 505 to $210. If only one appliances row has this value for inventory id, then only one row will be changed.

APPLIANCES	INVENTORY ID	DESCRIPTION	VENDOR	COST	PRICE
	505				U.210.00

Sets of rows can be changed using the U. operator. Suppose for example we wish to increase the price on every appliance by 5%.

APPLIANCES	INVENTORY ID	PRICE	PRICE
		_PR	U. 1.05 * _PR

Note that the price column appears twice in the example table. QBE provides facilities that allow the user to repeat columns in example tables. The first occurrence is used to define the example element _PR, and the second occurrence is used to define the update operation. Since the inventory id column is blank, there is no restriction on which rows are to be updated. Therefore, all rows have their prices changed by 5%.

Similarly, the following example shows how we may specify that all the appliances of vendor 23 should have their costs increased by 10%.

APPLIANCES	VENDOR	COST	COST
	23	_COST	U. 1.10 * _COST

Deleting Rows

The use of the D. (delete) operator is straightforward. "D." is entered in the first column of the example table, and the remaining columns are filled with appropriate qualifying information restricting the rows to be deleted. Suppose, for example, we want to delete inventory item 505.

APPLIANCES	INVENTORY ID	DESCRIPTION	VENDOR	COST	PRICE
D.	505				

If we wish to delete all appliances rows for vendor 24, we use the query below.

APPLIANCES	INVENTORY ID	DESCRIPTION	VENDOR	COST	PRICE
D.			24		

SUMMARY

As evidenced by the examples presented, QBE provides many of the same database access and modification capabilities as SQL. Its interface is much more visual, however, bringing those capabilities more in line with the needs of the end user, and fulfilling one of the key identifying criteria for a 4GL.

EXERCISES

Using the database definition below, write the QBE formats required to perform the stated queries.

APPMAST (invid, appname, vendor, cost, price)
SMAST (sname, saddress, commrate)
SALTX (saldate, saltime, sname, invid, salqty, saltot)

11. 1.   List all appliances (*appname*) and their vendors, without duplicate entries.

11. 2.   Put the above list in order by appliance name within vendor.

11. 3.   List the vendors of washers and dryers, without duplicate vendor names.

11. 4.   List the id's (*invid*) of televisions from vendor 20 having a cost over $100 and a price over $150.

11. 5.   List the vendors who supply items other than washers and dryers.

11. 6.   List the id's of items whose price is at least $100 greater than their cost.

11. 7.   Find the average cost and average price for dryers.

11. 8.   What is the total quantity sold of inventory items 101 and 105?

11. 9.   Give the average, maximum, and minimum sale quantity and sale total for each salesperson.

    a. Modify the above query to display only salespeople with a commission rate of 20% or more.

    b. Modify the above query to display only salespeople who have had at least 10 sales.

11.10.   What is the average cost for each type of appliance from vendor 22?

11.11.   What is the smallest commission rate for a salesperson who has sold a toaster?

11.12.   List the net profit (gross profit − commission) on all sales of refrigerators.

CHAPTER 12

QUERY-BY-FORMS

In Chapters 4 and 5 we discussed the SQL and QUEL relational languages. Both languages are supported by the INGRES relational database management system, a product of Relational Technology, Inc. (RTI). In support of INGRES, RTI provides a number of forms-oriented interfaces that give end users a variety of easily accessible applications capabilities. These interfaces go by the self-explanatory names of Applications-by-Forms, Report-by-Forms, Graph-by-Forms, and Query-by-Forms. The present chapter is devoted to a detailed discussion of Query-by-Forms (QBF). For additional information on the concepts of this chapter, refer to the reference under Relational Technology, Inc. (1982) in the bibliography.

QBF is a visual- and menu-oriented interface which allows end users to express queries without knowing the details of QUEL or SQL. Although its capabilities are limited in comparison to QUEL and SQL, QBF nevertheless provides a usable facility which emphasizes some important concepts which we have not previously investigated.

The QBF query process consists of two steps: Join Definition and Query Execution. If the query involves only one table in the database, then the Join Definition step may be omitted. However, if more than one table is involved, then Join Definition is needed to indicate how the tables are to be connected. We shall discuss Join Definition in the first section and Query Execution in the second.

Once again we use Halliday's retail database, as shown in Figure 12.1, this time with a few alterations from previous chapters. In particular, we have added a column to the customer master table indicating the customer's credit class. A customer's credit limit can be found by using the credit class as a key into the new credit rating table.

RETAIL MANAGEMENT DATABASE

INVENTORY MASTER (*invmast*)

invid	invcat	invname	qtystk	price
A53	Appliance	Television	5	75.00
A54	Appliance	Television	7	320.00
A61	Appliance	Washer	10	250.00
A62	Appliance	Washer	1	275.00
A63	Appliance	Washer	3	300.00
F30	Furniture	Chair	20	150.00
F33	Furniture	Chair	15	100.00
F84	Furniture	Sofa	6	450.00
F88	Furniture	Sofa	3	750.00

SALESPERSON MASTER (*spmast*)

spid	spname	commrate
101	Smith	.10
105	Jones	.15

CUSTOMER MASTER (*custmast*)

custid	custname	custaddr	custbal	credclas
200	C. Brown	111 Any St.	250.00	A
202	C. Green	4091 Main	100.00	B
205	C. White	255 B St.	400.00	A

SALES TRANSACTIONS (*saltx*)

saldate	saltime	spid	custid	cashchg	invid	salqty	salprice
6/02/--	14:00	101	202	A	A53	1	75.00
6/10/--	9:30	101	200	H	F88	1	750.00
6/13/--	10:15	105	200	H	F30	1	150.00
6/15/--	15:27	105	205	A	A61	1	250.00
6/23/--	9:45	101	202	H	F84	1	450.00

CREDIT RATING (*credrate*)

crclass	crlim
A	2000
B	5000

FIGURE 12.1   Database for Halliday's Retail Management System

JOIN DEFINITIONS

Suppose we wish to perform queries on the salesperson master *(spmast)* and sales transactions *(saltx)* tables. Since more than one table is involved, we must create a Join Definition (or "JoinDef") to define the two tables and their relationship. We initiate Join Definition by displaying the QBF Table Entry Form.

```
JoinDef Name:

Enter the table names and corresponding optional range
    variables in the tables below:

Master Tables:                        Detail Tables:
+----------------------------+        +----------------------------+
|  Table Name| Range Variable|        |  Table Name| Range Variable|
|===========+===============|         |===========+===============|
|           |               |        |           |               |
|           |               |        |           |               |
|           |               |        |           |               |
|           |               |        |           |               |
+-----------+---------------+         +-----------+---------------+

                 Table Field Format?   (y/n):

    Select the "Go" menu item to run the Join Definition.

Go   Blank  ChangeDisplay  Joins  Rules  Save    Help    End    Quit
```

The two boxes in the center of the display are used to define *Master* tables and *Detail* tables. Since the Master-Detail relationship is one of the most important concepts of QBF, we pause at this point for explanation.

Throughout this book we have used the concepts of the relational data model and its associated relational languages as the basis for our discussions of 4GLs. We have, however, omitted from our discussions an important aspect of the relational model: normalization. We have done this because the major thrust of this book is data manipulation rather than database design, and because the complexities of database normalization theory would take us too far astray from our theme. In the context of the present chapter, however, one aspect of normalization must be discussed in order for you to understand the full significance of QBF as a relational data manipulation language.

Consider the database of Figure 12.1. Each field in each table consists of "simple" elements. That is, each field is a single element rather than a set of elements. The employee table of Figure 12.2, on the other hand, contains a field (children) which is not simple. Since an employee could very well have more than one child, this field may contain multiple elements for a single employee record. The information contained in one table in Figure 12.2, however, could be expressed in two tables as we have done in Figure 12.3. This version of the database is similar to the database of Figure 12.1 in that all of the fields are simple. The database of Figure 12.3 is said to be in *first normal form,* since no field in the database has multiple entries. All of the databases which we have considered in this book are in first normal form.

EMPLOYEE

EMPNAME	ADDRESS	CHILDREN
Johnson	10 First St.	Anne, John, Elaine
Burgess	85 Third St.	Mary, Susan

FIGURE 12.2   Employee Database in Non-normalized Form

EMPLOYEE

EMPNAME	ADDRESS
Johnson	10 First St.
Burgess	85 Third St.

CHILDREN

EMPNAME	CHILDREN
Johnson	Anne
Johnson	John
Johnson	Elaine
Burgess	Mary
Burgess	Susan

FIGURE 12.3   Employee Database in First Normal Form

An important advantage of first normal form is that it allows the user flexibility in constructing logical relationships between tables. Some of the questions which users are likely to ask may be logically more difficult to formulate if the database tables are not in first normal form. We shall illustrate this in an example at the end of the chapter.

Although first normal form provides the most general and flexible format for a large variety of database queries, users frequently wish to see information in a non-normalized output format. Thus, for general usage we may wish to define an employee database as in Figure 12.3, but if the user were to state the specific query, "Show me a list of employees with their children," the query output would more naturally resemble Figure 12.2. The result of this query provides an example of what QBF calls the "Master-Detail" output format. For each master record there may be multiple detail records. In this example, for each employee record there may be multiple children records. In a Master-Detail output format, a single master record is displayed with multiple detail records.

Master-Detail Join Definitions

Now we return to our original problem of developing a Join Definition for doing queries on both the salesperson master and the sales transaction tables. Recall that on the Table Entry Form, previously shown, we indicate which tables are to form the JoinDef. If the tables can be combined most naturally in a Master-Detail format, then we indicate the Master table by entering its name in the "Master Tables" box, and we indicate the Detail table by entering its name in the "Detail Tables" box. In this case we wish to combine the two tables by showing each salesperson record together with all sales transactions for that salesperson. Thus, *spmast* is the Master and *saltx* is the Detail table.

```
JoinDef Name: spsales

Enter the table names and corresponding optional range
    variables in the tables below:

Master Tables:                        Detail Tables:
+-------------------------------+     +-------------------------------+
|  Table Name| Range Variable   |     |  Table Name| Range Variable   |
|==========+================     |     |==========+================    |
|  spmast    |                   |     |  saltx     |                  |
|            |                   |     |            |                  |
|            |                   |     |            |                  |
|            |                   |     |            |                  |
+----------+----------------+     +----------+----------------+

               Table Field Format?   (y/n): y
```

The range variable column in each table may be used to define a range variable (in the sense of QUEL—see Chapter 5) for each of the tables. These columns may be left blank, since the system will automatically use the table name as a range variable. However, if we were to join a table to itself, it would be necessary to define two different range variables for the table. The range variable stands for a particular (though unspecified) row in the table. If we have two range variables for the same table, the system views them as if there were two copies of the table, and each variable stands for a row in one of the copies.

Notice the question below the boxes, "Table Field Format? (y/n)," to which we have answered "yes". QBF uses the JoinDef to generate a form for displaying data on the screen. By requesting a table field format, we are asking QBF to design the form so that multiple records from the detail table will be placed in a "table field" box as shown at the bottom of the sample screen below.

```
                    Query Target Name is spsales

TABLE IS spmast

spid:   XXXXX

spname:   XXXXXXXXX

commrate:   XXXXXXX

TABLE(S):   saltx

+------------------------------------------------------------------------+
|  saldate| saltime| custid| cashchg| invid| salqty| salprice|
|  =======+========+=======+========+======+=======+=========+
|         |        |       |        |      |       |         |
|         |        |       |        |      |       |         |
|         |        |       |        |      |       |         |
|         |        |       |        |      |       |         |
+---------+--------+-------+--------+------+-------+---------+
```

As a result of our formulation of this JoinDef, QBF would generate a form similar to that shown above. In response to a query, the field names from *spmast* are displayed at the top of the form, with field values of a single *spmast* record in the areas marked by "X" immediately next to their respective field names. *Multiple saltx* records which correspond to the *spmast* record are displayed in the table field box at the bottom of the form. The example on the next page shows the display of Smith's *spmast* record together with its corresponding *saltx* records. Table fields are always used to display multiple records on the screen at one time.

This example shows records taken from the natural join of *spmast* and *saltx*. The join field in this case is *spid*. Since all of Smith's *spmast* and *saltx* records have the same value for *spid*, which is shown at the top of the form,

```
                    Query Target Name is spsales

TABLE IS spmast

spid:  101

spname:  Smith

commrate:  .10

TABLE(S):  saltx

+-------------------------------------------------------------------+
| saldate| saltime| custid| cashchg| invid| salqty| salprice|
|========+========+========+========+======+========+==========|
|  6/02/--| 14:00  |  202  |   A    |  A53 |   1   |    75.00 |
|  6/10/--|  9:30  |  200  |   H    |  F88 |   1   |   750.00 |
|  6/23/--|  9:45  |  202  |   H    |  F84 |   1   |   450.00 |
|        |        |        |        |      |        |          |
+--------+--------+--------+--------+------+--------+----------+
```

spid is not repeated in the table field. Thus, the table field shows the values of all *saltx* fields except *spid*.

Tables in a JoinDef are joined based on equality of values in columns from each table. We use the Join Specification Form (not shown here) to indicate the two columns. In this example we would specify that *spid* from *spmast* must equal *spid* from *saltx*. In this case the two columns have the same name in both tables, but this is not required.

We could have specified that a table field not be used on the form for this JoinDef. In that case the table field at the bottom of the form would be eliminated, and the fields from *saltx* would be displayed in the same manner as the fields from *spmast*. On a form without a table field, only one record from the join of the two tables could be displayed at a time.

Master-Master Join Definitions

We are not always interested in displaying data in a Master-Detail format. For example, we may merely be interested in knowing each customer's credit limit. Since there is only one credit rating record for each customer record, it does not make sense to set up a JoinDef in the Master-Detail format. Instead we use the Master-Master format.

The Table Entry Form for this JoinDef is shown below. Note that both tables have been entered into the Master Tables box. By entering them in this box, we indicate that the Master-Detail relationship is not desired for this JoinDef. We could have also listed both tables in the Detail Tables box.

For this kind of format it does not matter into which box the tables are entered as long as they are entered in the *same* box.

```
JoinDef Name: custcred

Enter the table names and corresponding optional range
    variables in the tables below:

Master Tables:                       Detail Tables:
+-----------------------------+      +-----------------------------+
|  Table Name| Range Variable|      |  Table Name| Range Variable|
|============+===============||      |============+===============||
|  custmast  |               |      |            |               |
|  credrate  |               |      |            |               |
|            |               |      |            |               |
|            |               |      |            |               |
|            |               |      |            |               |
+-----------+-----------------+      +-----------+-----------------+

            Table Field Format?   (y/n):


Select the "Go" menu item to run the Join Definition.

Go  Blank  ChangeDisplay  Joins  Rules  Save  Help  End  Quit
```

Using the Join Specification Form (not shown) we indicate that rows from the two tables are to be joined if the value in *credclas* of *custmast* is equal to the value of *crclass* in *credrate*. Even though the two columns have different names, we can specify that they are to be used in determining which records are to be joined.

If we specify that a table field should be built, then the entire form will be a table field as shown below. If we do not specify a table field, then the fields from the two tables will be shown separately, and only one join record at a time may be displayed on the screen.

```
            Query Target Name is custcred

TABLE(S):  custmast  credrate

+-------------------------------------------------------------------------+
|  custid| custname| custaddr          | custbal| credclas| credlim|
|=======+=========+===================+========+=========+========|
|   200  | C. Brown| 111 Any St.       | 250.00 |    A    |   2000 |
|   202  | C. Green| 4091 Main         | 100.00 |    B    |   5000 |
|   205  | C. White| 255  B St.        | 400.00 |    A    |   2000 |
|        |         |                   |        |         |        |
+-------+---------+-------------------+--------+---------+--------+
```

Menu Options

The Table Entry Form, on which we created JoinDefs, contains a horizontal menu at the bottom. The user may select any of these menu options to perform other functions. For example, the Join Specification Form can be displayed on the screen by selecting "Joins" from this menu. Also, if you desire to proceed immediately to query execution, the "Go" option may be selected. Other options may be selected to reset the form to blanks (Blank), to delete unneeded columns from the automatically generated form (ChangeDisplay), to set rules which apply to changing field values and deleting table records (Rules), to save the JoinDef for later use (Save), to obtain explanatory information (Help), to terminate work on the Table Entry Form (End), and to exit the QBF program (Quit).

QUERY EXECUTION

QBF supports the functions of retrieving, adding, and updating database records. The update function covers both changing and deleting records. We shall discuss all of these functions in this section.

Retrieve

Retrieval of data in QBF is similar to retrieval in Query-by-Example. Most of the major differences between retrieval in QBF and in QBE are directly related to the form on which queries are formulated and displayed. QBE generates a sample table form for each table in the query, whereas QBF generates a single form for an entire Join Definition. QBE uses a different form to display the retrieved data from the form used to state the query. QBF uses the same form for each. Finally, QBF can display data in a Master-Detail format, and QBE cannot. On the other hand, QBF does not support the built-in statistical functions (COUNT, SUM, AVERAGE, etc.) that QBE supports.

To formulate a query on the tables *spmast* and *saltx*, we first display the Query Target Form created for the JoinDef *spsales*, as shown earlier. Suppose we are interested in sales transactions of salespeople named Smith. We state the condition that the salesperson be named Smith by simply entering "Smith" on the blank form next to the label "spname", as shown at the top of page 274. Of course, the result of this query will be Smith's *spmast* record together with Smith's sales, and this information will be displayed in the table, as shown previously on page 271.

```
                    Query Target Name is spsales

TABLE IS spmast

spid:

spname:  Smith

commrate:

TABLE(S):  saltx

  +--------------------------------------------------------------+
  | saldate| saltime| custid| cashchg| invid| salqty| salprice|
  |========+========+=======+========+======+=======+=========|
  |        |        |       |        |      |       |         |
  |        |        |       |        |      |       |         |
  |        |        |       |        |      |       |         |
  |        |        |       |        |      |       |         |
  +--------+--------+-------+--------+------+-------+---------+
```

We may also use wildcard characters. For example, an asterisk (∗) stands for any number of unspecified characters and a question mark (?) stands for a single character. The next query requests all salespeople whose names start with "S".

```
                    Query Target Name is spsales

TABLE IS spmast

spid:

spname:  S*

commrate:

TABLE(S):  saltx

  +--------------------------------------------------------------+
  | saldate| saltime| custid| cashchg| invid| salqty| salprice|
  |========+========+=======+========+======+=======+=========|
  |        |        |       |        |      |       |         |
  |        |        |       |        |      |       |         |
  |        |        |       |        |      |       |         |
  |        |        |       |        |      |       |         |
  +--------+--------+-------+--------+------+-------+---------+
```

Comparison need not be based on equality of values. If we are interested in salespeople whose commission rate exceeds 10%, we use the query shown below. We may use any of the standard five relational operators for inequality ($<, >, <=, >=, !=$ [not equal]). We may use "$=$" as well, although if no relational operator is entered, equality is assumed.

```
            Query Target Name is spsales

TABLE IS spmast

spid:

spname:

commrate:  > .10

TABLE(S):  saltx

+--------------------------------------------------------------+     +
| saldate| saltime| custid| cashchg| invid| salqty| salprice|
|========+========+=======+========+======+=======+==========+
|        |        |       |        |      |       |          |
|        |        |       |        |      |       |          |
|        |        |       |        |      |       |          |
+--------+--------+-------+--------+------+-------+----------+
```

Suppose we are interested in salespeople whose names begin with "S" and whose commission rates exceed 10%. Then we simply combine both queries by entering the conditions in both fields. Entries in two separate fields imply, as in QBE, that *both* conditions must hold. Thus, entering the conditions in both fields is equivalent to the condition *spname = "S*" AND commrate > .10.*

Let us now extend the conditions in our example to the *saltx* table in addition to the *spmast* table. If we are interested only in the cash sales over $100 for the salespeople we have previously identified, we extend this query by placing entries in the *cashchg* and *salprice* columns of the table field as shown at the top of page 276.

The following QUEL condition, using range variables to qualify field names, is equivalent to the query condition above:

```
spmast.spname = "S*" AND spmast.commrate > .10 AND
     saltx.cashchg = "A" AND saltx.salprice > 100
```

```
                    Query Target Name is spsales

TABLE IS spmast

spid:

spname:  S*

commrate:  > .10

TABLE(S):  saltx

+--------------------------------------------------------------------+
|  saldate| saltime| custid| cashchg| invid| salqty| salprice|
|=========+========+=======+========+======+=======+==========+
|         |        |       |   A    |      |       |  > 100   |
|         |        |       |        |      |       |          |
|         |        |       |        |      |       |          |
|         |        |       |        |      |       |          |
+---------+--------+-------+--------+------+-------+----------+
```

Suppose that, in addition to the *saltx* records with cash sales over $100, we are also interested in charged sales transactions with a sale quantity greater than 1. This query requires the addition of an OR condition as follows:

```
spmast.spname = "S*" AND spmast.commrate > .10 AND
    ((saltx.cashchg = "A" AND saltx.salprice > 100)
    OR (saltx.cashchg = "H" AND saltx.salqty > 1))
```

All of this logic is captured in the form shown at the top of page 277. Thus, as in QBE, entries on the same line of a table field are connected by an implied AND, while entries on different lines are connected by an implied OR.

It is also possible to state multiple conditions on a single field. The condition = *"S*" OR = "B*"* entered in the *spname* field, and the condition > *5 AND < 10* entered in the *salqty* field, are permissible. Parentheses may also be used. If the condition is larger than the field's window on the form, then the condition scrolls within the field window.

```
                    Query Target Name is spsales

TABLE IS spmast

spid:

spname:  S*

commrate:  > .10

TABLE(S):   saltx

+-------------------------------------------------------------------+
|  saldate| saltime| custid| cashchg| invid| salqty| salprice|
|========+========+=======+========+======+=======+========|
|         |        |       |   A    |      |       |  > 100  |
|         |        |       |   H    |      |  > 1  |         |
|         |        |       |        |      |       |         |
|         |        |       |        |      |       |         |
+--------+--------+-------+--------+------+-------+--------+
```

Sorting Query Output

As in QBE, it is possible to specify that the results be ordered in QBF. Suppose we wish to order our results as follows:

- Salespeople should be placed in ascending order by commission rate.
- Salespeople with the same commission rate should be listed in alphabetical order.
- For any salesperson, sales should be listed in descending order by sale price.

To specify this, we select "Order" from the menu at the bottom of the display. This causes the system to display a fresh *spsales* form without data. We specify the desired ordering by entering values as shown on page 278. The "1" in the *commrate* field indicates that that field is to be the primary key and that records are to be placed in ascending order by the value of that field. The "2" in the *spname* field indicates that *spname* is the secondary key. The "3d" in the *salprice* field indicates that detail *(saltx)* records for each salesperson are to be placed in descending order by value of sale price. Since detail records are always secondary to master records, the sort sequence numbers placed in detail fields must always be higher than the numbers placed in master fields (indicating they are less significant).

```
                    Query Target Name is spsales

TABLE IS spmast

spid:

spname:   2

commrate:   1

TABLE(S):   saltx

  +---------------------------------------------------------------+
  | saldate| saltime| custid| cashchg| invid| salqty| salprice|
  |========+========+========+========+======+=======+==========+
  |        |        |        |        |      |       |    3d    |
  |        |        |        |        |      |       |          |
  |        |        |        |        |      |       |          |
  |        |        |        |        |      |       |          |
  +--------+--------+--------+--------+------+-------+---------+
```

Query results are displayed on the same form on which the query is formulated. Since more than one master record may satisfy the query criteria, QBF provides a means for the user to sequentially display each master record with its corresponding detail records. If there are more detail records than can fit at one time in the table field, then the user can scroll through the detail records while keeping the master record fixed.

Append

The form used to state queries and to display query results may also be used to add data to the database. At the user's request a copy of the form without data values is displayed, and data values can be entered as desired. The form is then transmitted to the system, one or more records are added to the tables, and a new copy of the blank form is displayed. If the form contains a table field, then multiple records can be added to the table. Otherwise, only one record for each table on the form can be added. If the form is for a Master-Detail JoinDef, then on a single screen the user can enter multiple detail records for each master record. The system will add these records to their respective tables.

Update

Updates are performed in QBF by first retrieving a set of records and then making changes to the set. Retrieval of records while in the update function follows exactly the same procedures as retrieval of records for query purposes. Thus, we shall be concerned here only with the process of making changes to a retrieved set of records.

Updates are of three types:

■ Addition of detail records for existing master records in a Master-Detail JoinDef.
■ Changes to existing master or detail records.
■ Deletion of existing master or detail records.

In the first case, detail records can be added for existing master records in a Master-Detail JoinDef. This is in contrast to the Append operation which is used to add *both* master and detail records. For example, if Smith has additional sales transactions, we can add these transactions to *saltx* by retrieving the master and detail records for Smith using the *spsales* JoinDef. We then place the cursor on the line in the table field immediately below the last detail sales record for Smith. We add records by entering values. We may add as many *saltx* records as we wish (providing, of course, that they belong to Smith). If the Master-Detail JoinDef does not contain a table field, then only one detail record will appear with Smith's master record. We select the QBF update menu function "AddDetail", and QBF blanks out the detail portion of the JoinDef form. We may then add a detail record.

Changes to existing detail and master records are made by simply displaying the record, moving the cursor to the field needing change, and entering the changes.

Deletions are of four types, depending on the form of the JoinDef. In a Master-Detail JoinDef *with a table field*, the user may delete the currently displayed master record together with all of its detail records, or may delete a single detail record or all of the detail records for this master record. In a Master-Detail JoinDef *without a table field*, the user may delete either the master record or the detail record currently being displayed. If the master record is deleted, then so are all associated detail records.

In a Master-Master JoinDef *with a table field*, the user may delete all displayed rows, or may delete only a single row. Deleting a row implies deleting both master records which make up the row. In a Master-Master JoinDef *without a table field* the user deletes the currently displayed row. Again, this implies deleting both master records. Single master records or detail records in a table field are deleted by placing the cursor on the selected row and indicating that the row should be deleted.

A FINAL EXAMPLE

In the first section of this chapter we noted that the Master-Detail format is often the most natural format for displaying data from two tables. As an illustration of this, throughout the chapter we have been using the *spsales* JoinDef, which combines data from the *spmast* and *saltx* tables in a Master-

Detail format. We also noted in the first section, however, that the normalized database design structure, which keeps master and detail information in separate tables, is a more flexible structure for general usage. We further illustrate this flexibility with a second example.

Suppose we wish to see a display of customer purchases. Customer information is contained in the *custmast* table, and purchase information is contained in the *saltx* table. Therefore, we need a JoinDef which specifies *custmast* as the Master table and *saltx* as the Detail table. The join field in this case is *custid*. If we also wish to see the customer's credit limit, we specify *credrate* as a second Master table, and specify that it is to be joined with *custmast* on the join fields *crclass* and *credclas*. QBF allows only one join between a Master table and a Detail table, but it allows multiple joins between Master tables or between Detail tables. In this case we are making only one Master-Master join and one Master-Detail join. The generated form with the data for C. Brown is shown below.

```
              Query Target Name is custbuys
TABLE IS custmast

custid:  200            custname:  C. Brown

custaddr:  111 Any St.

custbal:  250.00        credclas:  A

TABLE IS credrate

crlim:  2000


TABLE(S):  saltx

+---------+---------+---------+---------+---------+---------+---------+
|  saldate|  saltime|   spid  |  cashchg|  invid|  salqty|  salprice|
|=========+=========+=========+=========+=======+========+=========|
|  6/10/--|   9:30  |   101   |    H    |   F88 |    1   |   750.00 |
|  6/13/--|  10:15  |   105   |    H    |   F30 |    1   |   150.00 |
|         |         |         |         |       |        |          |
|         |         |         |         |       |        |          |
+---------+---------+---------+---------+-------+--------+----------+
```

This example illustrates the increased flexibility that the normalized approach provides. By normalizing data tables it is relatively easy to combine data in a variety of ways. If, on the other hand, the detail sales records had been placed in the salesperson master table, it might be logically difficult to extract them and then to combine them with the customer records. In the normalized format we can also easily combine sales records with inventory records. Finally, by maintaining a separate sales transaction table we can also easily perform manipulations on the sales transactions themselves.

REVIEW QUESTIONS

12.1.   What is the basic purpose of Join Definition in QBF?

12.2.   What is the meaning of first normal form in the relational data model? Why is it sometimes desirable to view data in a non-normalized format? What kind of Join Definition is used to display data in a non-normalized format?

12.3.   In which situations would we choose a Master-Detail format, and in which situations would we choose a Master-Master format?

12.4.   In a Master-Detail format, what is the difference between having a table field and not having a table field?

12.5.   Discuss the differences between data retrieval in QBF and data retrieval in Query-by-Example. What advantages do you see in having the query input form and the data output form be identical? Also, how do Join Definitions improve the formulation of queries?

12.6.   Compare and contrast the Append and Update operations of QBF with the Insert, Update, and Delete operations of Query-by-Example.

12.7.   How does the use of first normal form in a database with a large number of tables increase the flexibility of a large variety of users in making database queries?

EXERCISES

Using the database definition below, write the QBF formats required to perform the stated queries.

APPMAST (invid, appname, vendor, cost, price)
SMAST (sname, saddress, commrate)
SALTX (saldate, saltime, sname, invid, salqty, saltot)

12.1. List the names of salespeople who have a commission rate over 10%.

12.2. Put the above list in descending order by commission rate, and within commission rate in alphabetical order by salesperson name.

12.3. List the salespeople who have made single sales of more than $500.

12.4. List information about televisions from vendor 20 having a cost over $100 and a price over $150.

12.5. List the salespeople who live in Orem.

12.6. List the appliances other than washers and dryers.

12.7. List salespeople who have sold items having a unit price of at least $500.

12.8. List appliances of which more than one is sold on a single sale.

CHAPTER 13

CLOUT

CLOUT (Conversational Language Option) is a "natural language" product which provides a means of querying a database in English. The user enters queries in normal, conversational (though restricted) language, and the system responds with information extracted from the database.

A product of Microrim, Inc., CLOUT works in conjunction with R:BASE 5000 databases. It includes FileGateway software which converts databases originally created for use with other systems into a CLOUT-compatible format. CLOUT can be used even if R:BASE 5000 is not available. Thus, for example, a dBASE III user could convert dBASE III files via File-Gateway and use CLOUT to direct queries to this converted database.

Although the notion of communicating with computers in natural language has been attractive for many years, the difficulty associated with constructing natural language systems has prevented the realization of this goal. Natural language is imprecise and ambiguous, and fraught with many subtle nuances that make the construction of a natural language computer system extremely difficult (Harris 1985). In recent years, several natural language systems have attained a degree of commercial success, suggesting that the concept has some viability. Nevertheless, there remain a number of difficult problems to overcome. Natural language will undoubtedly be an area of intense research for many years.

This chapter illustrates both the advantages and the problems associated with a specific natural language product. It demonstrates the implementation of relational database language principles and more general principles of communication in a single software system. It will also examine the value of a natural language system as an end-user interface.

BASIC STRUCTURE

CLOUT provides the means for users to interact directly with a database via English. To determine the meanings of queries, CLOUT uses three sources of information:

- CLOUT's internal dictionary
- The structure of the specified database
- The user-generated, database-specific dictionary

Three Information Sources

CLOUT's internal dictionary consists of approximately 300 words, symbols, abbreviations, and phrases that are generally used in database queries. This dictionary is available regardless of the database being used. A sampling of the internal dictionary entries is given in Figure 13.1. The use of internal dictionary entries will be illustrated throughout this chapter.

a	about	all about	and	any	anybody
anyone	anything	approximately	ave	average	avg
between	but	contains	count	december	display
duplicate	each	equal	every	from	group by
had	has	have	he	her	him
his	how many	if	in	into	is
last	list	maximum	month	neither	now
obtain	of	omit	or	please	print
rank	same as	she	since	that	the
their	them	there any	today	top	under
what	when	where	which	who	whose

<	<=	⟨ ⟩	=	>
*	x	+	−	/

FIGURE 13.1   Sample Entries in CLOUT'S Internal Dictionary

When the database is specified, all of its table names, field names, and data values become available to CLOUT as the second source for interpreting queries. Throughout this chapter we shall use the database of Figure 13.2, the familiar Halliday's retail database. Thus, CLOUT has immediate access to such table names as *invmast* and *saltx*, field names such as *invid*, *invname*, and *salprice*, and data values such as Television, Smith, and C. Brown. These names will be important in stating queries and in defining the user-generated dictionary.

The user-generated dictionary contains definitions of terms which are entered by the user and which are generally alternative expressions for database terms. The terms in this dictionary may take a variety of forms, many of which we shall illustrate during the course of this chapter.

RETAIL MANAGEMENT DATABASE

INVENTORY MASTER (invmast)

invid	invcat	invname	qtystk	price
A53	Appliance	Television	5	75.00
A54	Appliance	Television	7	320.00
A61	Appliance	Washer	10	250.00
A62	Appliance	Washer	1	275.00
A63	Appliance	Washer	3	300.00
F30	Furniture	Chair	20	150.00
F33	Furniture	Chair	15	100.00
F84	Furniture	Sofa	6	450.00
F88	Furniture	Sofa	3	750.00

SALESPERSON MASTER (spmast)

spid	spname	commrate
101	Smith	.10
105	Jones	.15

CUSTOMER MASTER (custmast)

custid	custname	custaddr	custbal
200	C. Brown	111 Any St.	250.00
202	C. Green	4091 Main	100.00
205	C. White	255 B St.	400.00

SALES TRANSACTIONS (saltx)

saldate	saltime	spid	custid	cash	invid	salqty	salprice
6/02/--	14:00	101	202	A	A53	1	75.00
6/10/--	9:30	101	200	H	F88	1	750.00
6/13/--	10:15	105	200	H	F30	1	150.00
6/15/--	15:27	105	205	A	A61	1	250.00
6/23/--	9:45	101	202	H	F84	1	450.00

PAYMENT TRANSACTIONS (pmttx)

pmdate	custid	pmtamt
6/12/--	200	100.00
6/14/--	205	300.00
6/20/--	200	110.00

FIGURE 13.2   Database for Halliday's Retail Management System

Getting Started

At the beginning of a query session, CLOUT prompts the user for the name of the database before displaying its Main menu. If the database has never been used with CLOUT before, the screen shown below is displayed.

```
┌─────────────────New Dictionary───────────────────────────────┐
│ A new dictionary has been created for this database.  It is recommended
│ that you add synonyms for your fields.
│ Choose item #4 on the main menu:
│
│         4) Fine-tune the request process
│
│ and then choose item #1 on that menu:
│
│         1) Update a dictionary with database synonyms
└───────────────────────────────────────────────────────────────┘
Press any key to continue.................................................
```

This screen indicates that entries need to be placed in the newly created database dictionary. We begin by defining terms which are the English language equivalents of the field names in the retail database. Some of these terms and their equivalents are shown in Figure 13.3.

FIELD NAME	ENGLISH EQUIVALENT
invid	Inventory id
invcat	Inventory category
invname	Inventory name
qtystk	Quantity in stock
custname	Customer name
custaddr	Customer address
pmtdate	Payment date

FIGURE 13.3   English Equivalents of Database Field Names

After the initial screen, CLOUT displays its Main menu, shown at the top of page 287. CLOUT contains a number of submenus which are accessed via this Main menu. It provides considerable assistance to the user via these menus and associated help facilities. We shall limit our consideration, however, to the conversational request capability of Main menu selection 1.

```
┌─────────────────────────Main Menu──────────────────────────┐
│   1) Examine the data using conversational requests...........(1) │
│   2) Examine the structure of the database....................(2) │
│   3) Examine or modify dictionary entries (definitions).......(3) │
│   4) Fine-tune the request process...........................(4) │
│   5) Open a different database................................(5) │
│   6) Exit CLOUT...............................................(6) │
└──────────────────────────────────────────────────────────────┘

┌──────────────────────────────────────────────────────────────┐
│     Enter number corresponding to selection or ? for help........( ) │
└──────────────────────────────────────────────────────────────┘
```

RELATIONAL OPERATIONS

It is relatively easy to state queries that imply the relational operations of project, select, and join. The queries we examine in this section demonstrate the straightforward application of these relational operations. As we proceed, we shall discuss those aspects of natural language processing that arise in the queries we consider as examples.

Project

Suppose we want a list of inventory categories. The query *list the categories* will do the job, if we make one addition to the dictionary. At present, CLOUT knows that "inventory category" is equivalent to *invcat*. We make an additional entry which states that "category" is equivalent to "inventory category." CLOUT is able to interpret standard verb and noun endings, so it knows that "categories" refers to the same data item as "category." "List" is always in CLOUT's internal dictionary and means "display on the screen." Consequently, our query produces the result below.

```
┌═══════════════════════Current Series of Requests═══════════════════┐
│ list the categories                                                │
└════════════════════════════════════════════════════════════════════┘

Categories
----------
Appliance
Appliance
Appliance
Appliance
Appliance
Furniture
Furniture
Furniture
Furniture
```

We notice immediately that CLOUT has given us too much information by listing the same value more than once. Therefore, we revise the query to *list the categories, omitting duplicates* and obtain the desired output. We have developed a query corresponding to a genuine relational algebra project operation.

```
============Current Series of Requests============
| list the categories, omitting duplicates        |
==================================================

Categories
----------
Appliance
Furniture
```

Note the system's rather mechanical response to our first query. We asked for a list of categories, and it gave a list of categories. How was it to know we wanted duplicates omitted? Of course, it is obvious to us that any category on the list is needed only one time, so we assume the system will respond with the result we desire. Our English queries often do not explicitly reflect the many assumptions we make when we speak. Even in a "natural language" system, we must be careful to make our wishes explicit.

Select

The query *select items where price > 100* is expressed in a manner very close to the syntax of the relational algebra select operation. A more natural way of expressing this query is, *which items are priced over $100?*

The terms "items" and "over" require definition to CLOUT. We define "item" as *invid*, and "over" as "greater than." CLOUT can now process the query and give the result.

You should note two points. First, CLOUT correctly interprets the verb "priced" as equivalent to the noun "price" in the inventory master table.

```
============Current Series of Requests============
| which items are priced over $100?               |
==================================================

Items   Priced
-----   ------------
A54        $320.00
A61        $250.00
A62        $275.00
A63        $300.00
F30        $150.00
F84        $450.00
F88        $750.00
```

Second, the previous display shows only the two columns implied by the query—*invid* and *price*. If we desire more information, we must explicitly request it or redefine one of our terms so that the additional information is implicit in the definition of the term (e.g., redefine "items" to include *invname* as well as *invid*.)

Each time CLOUT executes a query, it remembers the context of the query. It then examines the next query to determine whether it implies that the user is referring to the context created by the previous query, and that therefore the new query should be carried out in light of the previous result. For example, we have executed the query, *which items are priced over $100?* Suppose the next query is, *which of these are furniture?*

The phrase "of these" refers to the result of the previous query, and CLOUT recognizes this. Therefore, it uses the previous query's result as the basis for a select operation and produces a new result.

```
══════════════════════════Current Series of Requests══════════════════════════
 which items are priced over $100?
 which of these are furniture?

Items   Priced         Invcat
-----   -------------  ----------
F30        $150.00     Furniture
F84        $450.00     Furniture
F88        $750.00     Furniture
```

Notice that three columns of information are now displayed instead of two. The reason that CLOUT displayed *invcat* as well as the other fields is as follows. When CLOUT encountered "furniture," which is a data value, it scanned the data values of the *invmast* records; finding "furniture" in *invcat*, CLOUT assumed that the query referred to the value in the *invcat* column. If it had found "furniture" in more than one column, CLOUT would have asked for clarification as to which column was intended in the query.

We continue illustrating CLOUT's use of context with an additional query: *what are their inventory names?* CLOUT recognizes "their" as referring to the previous query and responds with the appropriate result.

```
══════════════════════════Current Series of Requests══════════════════════════
 which items are priced over $100?
 which of these are furniture?
 what are their inventory names?

Items   Inventory Names  Priced         Invcat
-----   ---------------  -------------  ----------
F30     Chair               $150.00     Furniture
F84     Sofa                $450.00     Furniture
F88     Sofa                $750.00     Furniture
```

Note that all three queries in the series are listed at the top of the screen. If CLOUT determines that a query is related to a previous query, it lists both queries. If a fourth query is entered in a series, CLOUT scrolls the first query off the top of the screen and retains only the three most recent queries.

Suppose we are interested only in those items with fewer than 10 in stock. We enter *just the ones with fewer than 10 in stock*. CLOUT responds that it does not understand "fewer than."

```
=========================Current Series of Requests=========================
which of these are furniture?
what are their inventory names?
just the ones with fewer than 10 in stock

=================================Unknowns===================================

While interpreting your request, CLOUT did not recognize the indicated word
or phrase.  You can make a synonym for the phrase, correct the typing, or
delete the word (by pressing the [ENTER] key).  If a multi-word phrase is
a data item, then it needs to be quoted (for example, 'San Jose').  If a
single word is a data item, then it was not found in the database.  Enter ?
for further information, or press [ESC] to cancel this request.


Did not understand: fewer than
Please enter a synonym or change spelling
R>
```

The program requests a synonym, and we enter "less than". CLOUT also does not understand "stock," so we enter "quantity in stock" as a synonym, and CLOUT executes the query, with the following result.

```
=========================Current Series of Requests=========================
which of these are furniture?
what are their inventory names?
just the ones with fewer than 10 in stock
```

Items	Inventory Names	Priced	Invcat	Stock
F30	Chair	$150.00	Furniture	20
F84	Sofa	$450.00	Furniture	6
F88	Sofa	$750.00	Furniture	3

Unfortunately, this result is incorrect. What went wrong? Apparently, the phrase "fewer than 10 in stock" was not properly translated. If we revise the query to *just the ones with stock fewer than 10*, the word order of the query corresponds to the more formal query *select rows where stock < 10*. This revision produces the correct result.

```
==========================Current Series of Requests========================
| which of these are furniture?                                             |
| what are their inventory names?                                           |
| just the ones with stock fewer than 10                                    |
============================================================================
```

Items	Inventory Names	Priced	Invcat	Stock
F84	Sofa	$450.00	Furniture	6
F88	Sofa	$750.00	Furniture	3

This query compares "stock" with "10." If these two values are placed on the same side of the comparison operator ("fewer than"), the system produces an incorrect result. If they are placed on opposite sides of the comparison operator, the system performs correctly. Notice how casually we say "fewer than 10 in stock" in our everyday language. This term, which is so simple for us, is obviously not so simple for the system.

For our next example, consider the query *list sales charged*. What are "sales," and what does "charged" mean? We define "sale" as *saltx*, a table name. Thus, "sale" corresponds to an entire record, not just a single field. We define "charged" as *cashchg* = '*H*'.

```
==========================Current Series of Requests========================
| list sales charged                                                        |
============================================================================
```

Saldate	Saltime	Spid	Custid	Invid	Salqty	Salprice	Cashchg
06/10/--	09:30:00	101	200	F88	1	$750.00	H
06/13/--	10:15:00	105	200	F30	1	$150.00	H
06/23/--	09:45:00	101	202	F84	1	$450.00	H

We can also make queries involving partial strings, for instance *list customers living on Main*. "Living on" is defined as "custaddr contains the string". CLOUT must identify those customers who have "Main" somewhere in their address column.

```
==========================Current Series of Requests========================
| list customers living on Main                                             |
============================================================================
```

Customers	Custaddr
202	4091 Main

This result is somewhat unsatisfactory, since it does not give the customer's name. Therefore, we revise the definition of "customer" from *custid* to *custid* plus *custname*. With this new definition, the query yields the result shown at the top of page 292.

```
╔══════════════════Current Series of Requests══════════════════╗
║ list customers living on Main                                 ║
╚═══════════════════════════════════════════════════════════════╝

Customers   Custname      Custaddr
─────────   ───────────   ────────────────────────────────
202         C. Green      4091 Main
```

Let's try a query involving a date: *list sales before June 15*. CLOUT is not sure which field "June 15" refers to, as can be seen by its response.

```
╔══════════════════Current Series of Requests══════════════════╗
║ list sales before June 15                                     ║
╚═══════════════════════════════════════════════════════════════╝
┌──────────────────────Data/Field Ambiguity────────────────────┐
│                                                               │
│ The indicated item was recognised as a data value, but the    │
│ field with which it should be associated could not be          │
│ determined.  Enter the name of the field that corresponds to   │
│ this data item.                                                │
│                                                               │
│ To get a list of the fields in your database, select: 'View   │
│ the database structure' from the 'Help Options' menu.  If     │
│ this is not a data item, press [ESC] to cancel this request.   │
│                                                               │
└───────────────────────────────────────────────────────────────┘

The field for the following data item is not clear: June 15

Enter the field name for this data item (or [ESC]):
```

We enter *saldate* in response. Note that CLOUT is able to understand that "June" is the same as "6" in the month area of a date field.

```
╔══════════════════Current Series of Requests══════════════════╗
║ list sales before June 15                                     ║
╚═══════════════════════════════════════════════════════════════╝

Saldate
─────────
06/02/--
06/10/--
06/13/--
```

CLOUT is also able to help us correct spelling errors. If we enter the query *list salespeope with commission rates over .13*, CLOUT responds "By 'salespeope' did you mean 'salespeople'?" When we reply "yes," CLOUT corrects and processes our query.

```
                        ══Current Series of Requests═══════════════
   │ list salespeople with commission rates over .13                │

   Salespeople  Commission Rates
   -----------  ----------------
   Jones                 0.15000
```

Frequently, we are interested in items that are only approximately close to a given value. We can make a value "fuzzy," so that items close to the value will be selected, by using the term "about": *list sales that are about $100*. Since *saltx* contains two numeric fields (*salqty* and *salprice*), CLOUT is unsure as to which field to search. We first indicate that $100 refers to *salprice*, and CLOUT then proceeds with the query, displaying the result.

```
                        ══Current Series of Requests═══════════════
   │ list sales that are about $100                                  │

   Saldate   Saltime    Spid   Custid  Cashchg  Invid  Salqty      Salprice
   --------  --------   ----   ------  -------  -----  ----------  ------------
   06/02/--  14:00:00   101    202     A        A53         1        $75.00
   06/13/--  10:15:00   105    200     H        F30         1       $150.00
```

Note that CLOUT interprets "about" as meaning "round up to or truncate down to" the amount given. Thus, $75.00 rounds up to $100, and $150.00 truncates down to $100, so both of these sales are selected and displayed.

Join

A join is needed whenever the information required to answer a query resides in more than one file. Thus, the query *which salespeople have sold televisions* requires a join. In fact, two joins are required since we will want to define "salespeople" to include their names from the *spmast* file and since "television" is contained in the *invmast* file. This query requires the joining of the *spmast*, *saltx*, and the *invmast* files. CLOUT handles these two joins without a hitch. We should mention, however, that the word "sold" was first defined as equivalent to "sale". Although CLOUT can handle standard verb and noun endings, we must define irregular verb forms.

```
                        ══Current Series of Requests═══════════════
   │ which salespeople have sold televisions?                        │

   Salespeople  Invname
   -----------  ----------
   Smith        Television
```

Our next example illustrates that, in general, CLOUT cannot answer queries that require the comparison of one row in a table with another in the same table. Suppose we are interested in identifying customers who have purchased furniture *and* appliances. This query requires joining three tables, as in the previous query. Customers must then be extracted whose names appear in a row with "furniture" as the category *and* in a row with "appliance" as the category. Two versions of this query fail to produce the correct result.

```
════════════════════════Current Series of Requests════════════════════════
 list customers who bought furniture and appliances.


Custid  Custname          Invcat
------  ----------------  ----------
202     C. Green          Appliance
205     C. White          Appliance
200     C. Brown          Furniture
202     C. Green          Furniture
200     C. Brown          Furniture
```

```
════════════════════════Current Series of Requests════════════════════════
 who bought furniture?


Who Bought          Invcat
----------------    ----------
C. Brown            Furniture
C. Green            Furniture
C. Brown            Furniture
```

```
════════════════════════Current Series of Requests════════════════════════
 who bought furniture?
 just those who bought appliances


Who Bought          Invcat
----------------    ----------
C. Green            Appliance
C. White            Appliance
```

We should note that this query provides an illustration of a frequently occurring ambiguity in the English language. When we say, "List customers who bought furniture and appliances," do we mean "List customers who bought furniture and customers who bought appliances" or do we mean "List customers who bought both furniture and appliances?"

The first interpretation of this query presumes the "and" is intended to be a logical "or," whereas the second interpretation presumes the "and" is intended to be a logical "and". When we formulated the query, we intended the second interpretation. Quite possibly CLOUT assumed the first interpretation.

ORDERING RESULTS

We can order results by using words such as "sort", "rank", and "group". The query *sort sales by sale price* produces the result shown below. Note that ascending order is assumed in the absence of other instruction.

```
==============================Current Series of Requests==============================
  sort sales by sale price

Saldate    Saltime    Spid   Custid   Cashchg   Invid   Salqty        Salprice
--------   --------   ----   ------   -------   -----   ----------   ------------
06/02/--   14:00:00   101    202      A         A53     1               $75.00
06/13/--   10:15:00   105    200      H         F30     1              $150.00
06/15/--   15:27:00   105    205      A         A61     1              $250.00
06/23/--   09:45:00   101    202      H         F84     1              $450.00
06/10/--   09:30:00   101    200      H         F88     1              $750.00
```

If we wish descending order, we enter *sort sales by sale price in descending order*. However, the result this time gives us less information than desired.

```
==============================Current Series of Requests==============================
  sort sales by sale price in descending order

Sale Price
-----------
    $750.00
    $450.00
    $250.00
    $150.00
     $75.00
```

The reasons for this are not clear. Possibly CLOUT focused only on the verb "sort," in combination with the last part of the query "sale price in descending order," to produce a list of sale prices in descending order.

We remedy this problem by using "list all about" in an appropriate manner: *list all about sales sorted by sale price in descending order*. The result shows that "list all about" causes CLOUT to list the entire record.

```
==============================Current Series of Requests==============================
  list all about sales sorted by sale price in descending order.

Saldate    Saltime    Spid   Custid   Cashchg   Invid   Salqty        Salprice
--------   --------   ----   ------   -------   -----   ----------   ------------
06/10/--   09:30:00   101    200      H         F88     1              $750.00
06/23/--   09:45:00   101    202      H         F84     1              $450.00
06/15/--   15:27:00   105    205      A         A61     1              $250.00
06/13/--   10:15:00   105    200      H         F30     1              $150.00
06/02/--   14:00:00   101    202      A         A53     1               $75.00
```

We can also designate a different field on which to sort. This example shows that CLOUT continues to assume descending order once we have requested it for a sort in the same context.

```
══════════════════Current Series of Requests══════════════════
│ list all about sales sorted by sale price in descending order. │
│ sort them by customer id                                       │

Saldate     Saltime    Spid   Custid   Cashchg   Invid   Salqty        Salprice
--------    --------    ----   ------   -------   -----   ------   ------------
06/15/--    15:27:00    105    205      A         A61         1         $250.00
06/23/--    09:45:00    101    202      H         F84         1         $450.00
06/02/--    14:00:00    101    202      A         A53         1          $75.00
06/10/--    09:30:00    101    200      H         F88         1         $750.00
06/13/--    10:15:00    105    200      H         F30         1         $150.00
```

Items can also be grouped by a common value of a designated field. The next example shows the grouping of *invmast* records by category.

```
═══════════════════════Current Series of Requests═══════════════════════
│ list inventory item, names, quantity in stock, and price, grouped by category │

Start of Category: Appliance
Item   Names         Quantity In Stock    Price
----   ----------    -----------------    ------------
A53    Television                    5         $75.00
A54    Television                    7        $320.00
A61    Washer                       10        $250.00
A62    Washer                        1        $275.00
A63    Washer                        3        $300.00
End of Category: Appliance

Start of Category: Furniture
Item   Names         Quantity In Stock    Price
----   ----------    -----------------    ------------
F30    Chair                        20        $150.00
F33    Chair                        15        $100.00
F84    Sofa                          6        $450.00
F88    Sofa                          3        $750.00
End of Category: Furniture
```

CALCULATIONS

As we have seen throughout this book, the solutions to many queries require that calculations be performed on table data. CLOUT's internal dictionary supplies words that imply certain aggregate functions (sum, total, average, etc.). Additionally, we can define words and phrases in terms of arithmetic formulas.

For our first example, suppose we define the phrase: *dollar value of inventory = qtystk * price*. Recall, moreover, that we have defined "items" as the inventory id. If we enter the query *list dollar value of inventory items*, CLOUT automatically performs the calculation and lists the result.

```
════════════════════════Current Series of Requests═══════════════════
  list dollar value of inventory items


Dollar Value of Inventory   Items
-------------------------   -----
              $375.00       A53
            $2,240.00       A54
            $2,500.00       A61
              $275.00       A62
              $900.00       A63
            $3,000.00       F30
            $1,500.00       F33
            $2,700.00       F84
            $2,250.00       F88
```

CLOUT supports the aggregate functions of count, total, maximum, minimum, average, standard deviation, and correlation, which operate on sets of table rows. Thus, if we enter the query *what is the total of sale price for all sales*, CLOUT uses the total function to produce the result. Note that CLOUT prints only the summary result and omits the printing of detail.

```
════════════════════════Current Series of Requests═══════════════════
  what is the total of sale price for all sales?


Total of Sale Price: $1,675.00
```

If we are interested in sales with above average price, we enter the query *show me all about sales with a sale price above average*. Notice that CLOUT prints the average amount as well as the detail information called for. This makes it easy to check the validity of the result.

```
════════════════════════Current Series of Requests═══════════════════
  show me all about sales with a sale price above average
```

Saldate	Saltime	Spid	Custid	Cashchg	Invid	Salqty	Sale Price
06/10/--	09:30:00	101	200	H	F88	1	$750.00
06/23/--	09:45:00	101	202	H	F84	1	$450.00

Average: $335.00

The next example is a rather lengthy query statement which uses the max and min functions, keying on the words "highest" and "lowest".

```
╔══════════════════Current Series of Requests══════════════════╗
║ show me all about the sales with the highest sale price and the lowest sale ║
║ price.                                                        ║
╚═══════════════════════════════════════════════════════════════╝

Saldate     Saltime    Spid   Custid   Cashchg   Invid   Salqty        Salprice
--------    --------    ----   ------   -------   -----   ----------    ------------
06/02/--    14:00:00    101    202      A         A53     1                 $75.00
06/10/--    09:30:00    101    200      H         F88     1                $750.00

Highest Sale Price: $750.00
Lowest Sale Price:  $75.00
```

Implied conditions can be combined with these functions, as illustrated in the next query.

```
╔══════════════════Current Series of Requests══════════════════╗
║ what is the total sale price of all furniture?                ║
╚═══════════════════════════════════════════════════════════════╝

Total Sale Price: $1,350.00
```

The above query requires a join (*saltx* with *invmast*) and requires that CLOUT identify the column to which "furniture" belongs. CLOUT handles both of these, and then selects those rows in *saltx* which identify furniture sales and totals the sale price.

Grouping can also be added. Assume we define commission as *salprice * commrate*. The execution of the query *list total commission by salesperson* requires three steps:

■ A join to perform the commission calculation.
■ The calculation of commission for each row in *saltx*.
■ Totaling of the commission calculation result by salesperson.

```
╔══════════════════Current Series of Requests══════════════════╗
║ list total commission by salesperson                          ║
╚═══════════════════════════════════════════════════════════════╝

Total Commission   Salesperson
----------------   -----------
         $60.00    Jones
        $127.50    Smith
```

QUERIES INVOLVING COMMON LINGUISTIC CONCEPTS

In this section we give examples of CLOUT's handling of queries involving three common linguistic concepts: top and bottom members of a set; yes/no questions; and who, when, and where questions.

Top/Bottom

A common type of query requests identification of the "top so-many" members of some set. For example, we might be interested in the top 3 salespeople or the top 10 selling products. Similarly, we may be interested in the "bottom so-many" of some category. Note, for instance the following query and result:

```
════════════════Current Series of Requests═══════════════
  list the name and category of the top 2 items by price

Name          Category    Items   Price
----------    ----------  -----   ------------
Sofa          Furniture   F88        $750.00
Sofa          Furniture   F84        $450.00
```

"Items" has been previously identified to CLOUT as *invid*. When we specify "price," we are indicating which field to use for comparison in determining the "top 2". This is necessary since *invmast* also includes *qtystk* as a numeric field. In a similar manner, we could request the bottom two items. Note also that the order of the fields corresponds to the order in which they were identified in the text of the query.

Yes/No Questions

Questions which can be answered "Yes" or "No" are also common, and CLOUT will detect this kind of question and answer it appropriately.

```
════════════════Current Series of Requests═══════════════
  Are any televisions priced under $100?


Yes!
```

In this case, the answer gives somewhat less information than would be desirable. So we ask CLOUT to list them.

```
┌─────────────────────Current Series of Requests═══════════════════┐
│ Are any televisions priced under $100?                            │
│ list them                                                         │
└───────────────────────────────────────────────────────────────────┘

Priced          Invname
-----------     ----------
    $75.00      Television
```

Again, the information is inadequate, so we make the request more explicit:

```
┌─────────────────────Current Series of Requests═══════════════════┐
│ Are any televisions priced under $100?                            │
│ list them                                                         │
│ list them with their inventory id and quantity in stock           │
└───────────────────────────────────────────────────────────────────┘

Inventory Id   Quantity In Stock   Priced         Invname
-----------    -----------------   -----------    ----------
A53                            5       $75.00      Television
```

Who, When, and Where

As part of the dictionary definition process, we can specify the meanings of such terms as "who," "when," and "where." Suppose, for example, that we associate these terms with the fields as shown:

- Who: Salesperson name
- When: Sale date, Sale time
- Where: Customer address

```
┌─────────────────────Current Series of Requests═══════════════════┐
│ who has a commission rate over .11                                │
└───────────────────────────────────────────────────────────────────┘

Spname     Commission Rate
--------   ---------------
Jones            0.15000
```

In the above query, CLOUT identifies two fields, *spname* and *commrate*, to be displayed in the query. It also knows that it must compare *commrate* with .11 to determine whether the contents of a given *spmast* record should be displayed.

The next query requires two joins. CLOUT keys on three words—who, sold, television—to identify *spmast*, *saltx*, and *invmast*, respectively, as the tables to be joined.

```
════════════════════════Current Series of Requests═══════════════════════════
│ who has sold a television                                                    │
└──────────────────────────────────────────────────────────────────────────────┘

Spname     Invname
--------   ----------
Smith      Television
```

"Who" identifies a person. In this case, it identifies a salesperson. But there are other people in our database, most notably customers. We can distinguish salespeople from customers by defining the phrase "who bought" or "who buys" to mean customer name.

```
════════════════════════Current Series of Requests═══════════════════════════
│ who bought sofas?                                                            │
└──────────────────────────────────────────────────────────────────────────────┘

Who Bought         Invname
----------------   ----------
C. Green           Sofa
C. Brown           Sofa
```

The next query uses the result of an earlier query to ask for additional information. "When" means sale date and sale time, so CLOUT adds that information.

```
════════════════════════Current Series of Requests═══════════════════════════
│ when did Smith sell a television                                             │
└──────────────────────────────────────────────────────────────────────────────┘

Saldate    Saltime    Spname     Invname
--------   --------   --------   ----------
06/02/--   14:00:00   Smith      Television
```

The following "where" query requires the joining of *custmast*, *saltx*, and *invmast*. However, only two of these tables are identified in the query itself. Consider the following list of query terms and definitions:

- where: Customer address
- people: Customer name
- who bought: Customer name
- furniture: Inventory category

These terms relate to the *custmast* and *invmast* tables. However, CLOUT is able to link them to *saltx,* because it keeps track of all table links based on common column names. Using concepts of the relational model, CLOUT knows that *invid* in *invmast* is the same as *invid* in *saltx,* and that *custid* in *custmast* is the same as *custid* in *saltx.* Thus, CLOUT can successfully carry out the query. Note that we again have to eliminate duplicates.

```
═══════════════════════Current Series of Requests═══════════════════
  where are the people who bought furniture, omitting duplicates?

Custaddr                           People        Invcat
----------------------------       ------------  ----------
111 Any St.                        C. Brown      Furniture
4091 Main                          C. Green      Furniture
```

SUMMARY

We have seen in this chapter how a natural language system can be used to extract information from a relational database. We have also seen some of the problems which the ambiguity inherent in natural language presents to the developer of a system such as CLOUT. CLOUT deals with this ambiguity in several ways. In some cases, CLOUT gives a "simple-minded" answer, such as when it lists all inventory categories, with numerous duplicates, thus requiring the user to enter "omitting duplicates." In some other cases, CLOUT asks for clarification of a specific word or phrase in order to continue. However, in yet other cases, for example "List buyers of furniture *and* appliances", CLOUT assumes a particular interpretation of a query when another interpretation is intended.

In estimating the value of CLOUT as a system, we consider both its strengths and its weaknesses. On one hand, CLOUT provides at least partial solutions to such problems as context and misspelling. It remembers our previous queries and responds to a new query in light of the results previously obtained. It also attempts and sometimes succeeds in finding the word we had in mind when we misspell a word in a query. Moreover, it is particularly adept at handling queries involving statistical functions and multiple joins.

On the other hand, CLOUT seems unable to compare rows within a table (or possibly, it sometimes makes unjustified assumptions about query interpretation); it has trouble with a phrase like "fewer than 10 in stock"; and it does not handle ascending and descending sort order in the same way.

On balance, we may conclude that despite its shortcomings, CLOUT provides an excellent illustration of the utility of natural language for making database queries. It is clear that some of its failings are due to the difficulty of interpreting natural language, whereas some may simply be due to its weaknesses as a database handler. Since improvement in both of these areas can be anticipated in current and future natural language systems, it seems likely that natural language interfaces will play an increasingly important role in data processing systems in the years to come.

DISCUSSION QUESTIONS

13. 1.   Develop several English language sentences which are ambiguous. What would be required to clarify them?

13. 2.   Consider the sentence: "The boy told his brother he had received some money." Which words are ambiguous in this sentence? What additional information is needed to remove the ambiguities?

13. 3.   What are the three parts of CLOUT's dictionary? What are the differences between them? In what ways are they used differently by CLOUT?

13. 4.   Using the chapter's database, develop English language queries that would result in the relational language operations of project, select, and join. See how many different ways each of these queries can be phrased.

13. 5.   Why does CLOUT require us to include the phrase "omitting duplicates?" Can you think of a situation for which we would not want duplicates omitted? Why doesn't CLOUT always omit duplicates, unless instructed otherwise?

13. 6.   Develop a series of queries illustrating the principle of context saving. That is, develop a series of queries such that each query depends on all of the previous queries. See how many queries you can develop in such a series.

13. 7.   Why is the phrase "fewer than 10 in stock" difficult for CLOUT to handle? What additional capability does CLOUT need in order to handle such a phrase? Are there additional ways of expressing the same phrase which may also present difficulties?

13. 8.   CLOUT translates English language nouns into database items (fields, tables, etc.) which are also nouns. What are the different ways that verbs can be translated?

13. 9.   Words that CLOUT ignores are called "noise words." List some noise words.

13.10.   What is required to detect spelling errors and help the user correct them? Suppose the first letter in a word is incorrect. Does that make the correction process more difficult for the system?

13.11.   What is meant by a "fuzzy value?" Do you agree with CLOUT's interpretation of "about?" Should the system allow the user to specify his own interpretation of "about?"

13.12. Why are queries that require multi-row comparisons difficult for the system to handle?

13.13. Discuss CLOUT's strength in handling grouping and statistical functions.

13.14. What must the system do in order to handle Top/Bottom questions and Yes/No questions?

13.15. How many different tables in the sample database could properly define the term "who?" How many different columns in different tables could properly define the term "where?" Does CLOUT appear to be limited in the number of different meanings it can provide for these terms?

BIBLIOGRAPHY

Applied Data Research, Inc. 1983. *ADR/IDEAL Application Development Reference Manual.* Princeton.

Ashton-Tate. 1985. *Learning and Using dBASE III PLUS.* Torrance.

———. 1985–2. *Programming with dBASE III PLUS.* Torrance.

Boar, B.H. 1984. *Application Prototyping: A Requirements Definition Strategy for the 80s.* John Wiley & Sons.

Brooks, F.P. 1975. *The Mythical Man-Month.* Addison-Wesley.

Brown, Carl. 1986. *Essential dBASE III.* Brooks/Cole.

Chamberlin, D.D. 1980. A summary of user experience with the SQL data sublanguage. *Proceedings of the International Conference on Data Bases, Aberdeen, Scotland, July 1980.* 181–203.

Codd, E.F. 1970. A relational model of data for large shared data banks. *Communications of the ACM* 13(6).

———. 1972. Relational completeness of data base sublanguages. *Data Base Systems,* ed. Randall Rustin. Prentice-Hall.

———.1982. Relational database: A practical foundation for productivity. *Communications of the ACM.* 25(2).

———. 1983. Foreword to *Relational Database Systems.* Ed. Joachim Schmidt and Michael Brodie. Springer-Verlag.

Date, C. J. 1984. *A Guide to DB2.* Addison-Wesley.

———. 1986. *An Introduction to Database Systems.* Vol. 1. Addison-Wesley.

———. 1987. *A Guide to the SQL Standard.* Addison-Wesley.

Ehrenreich, S.L. 1981. Query languages: Design recommendations derived from the human factors literature. *Human Factors* 23(6): 709–725.

Gray, Peter. 1984. *Logic, Algebra and Databases.* Ellis Horwood Limited.

Harris, M.D. 1985. *Introduction to Natural Language Processing.* Reston.

IBM. 1983. *IBM Database 2 SQL Usage Guide,* by Per Groth. GG24–1583–00.

————. 1984. *Query Management Facility: User's Guide and Reference.* SC26–4096–1.

Martin, James. 1982. *Application Development Without Programmers.* Prentice-Hall.

Martin, James, and Carma McClure. 1985. *Diagramming Techniques for Analysts and Programmers.* Prentice-Hall.

Merrett, T.H. 1984. *Relational Information Systems.* Reston.

Prague, C.N., and J.E. Hammitt. 1986. *Programming with R:base 5000.* TAB BOOKS, Inc.

Relational Technology, Inc. 1982. *INGRES Database and Application Systems.* Vols. 1–3, (VAX/VMS Version 1.4). September 1981.

Schmidt, Joachim W., and Michael L. Brodie, eds. 1983. *Relational Database Systems.* Springer-Verlag.

Simpson, Alan. 1985. *Understanding R:base 5000.* SYBEX.

————. 1986. *Understanding dBASE III PLUS.* SYBEX.

Stonebraker, M.R., E. Wong, P. Kreps, and G. Held. 1976. The design and implementation of INGRES. *ACM Transactions on Database Systems* 1(3).

Suppes, Patrick. 1957. *Introduction to Logic.* Van Nostrand.

Ullman, Jeffrey D. 1982. *Principles of Database Systems.* Computer Science Press.

Zloof, Mosche M. 1975. Query by example. *AFIPS Conference Proceedings, NCC.* 431–438.

————. 1981. QBE/OBE: A language for office and business automation. *IEEE Computer* (May).

INDEX